EAP now! preliminary

English for Academic Purposes

Teacher's Book

KATHY COX · DAVID HILL

PEARSON Education Australia

Copyright © Kathy K Cox and David Hill 2007

Pearson Education Australia
Unit 4, Level 3
14 Aquatic Drive
Frenchs Forest NSW 2086

www.pearsoned.com.au

The Copyright Act 1968 of Australia allows a maximum of one chapter or 10% of this book, whichever is the greater, to be copied by any educational institution for its educational purposes provided that that educational institution (or the body that administers it) has given a remuneration notice to Copyright Agency Limited (CAL) under the Act. For details of the CAL licence for educational institutions contact: Copyright Agency Limited, telephone: (02) 9394 7600, email: info@copyright.com.au

All rights reserved. Except under the conditions described in the Copyright Act 1968 of Australia and subsequent amendments, no part of this publication may be reproduced, stored in a retrieval system or transmitted in any form or by any means, electronic, mechanical, photocopying, recording or otherwise, without the prior permission of the copyright owner.

Senior Acquisitions Editor: Andrew Brock
Senior Project Editor: Rebecca Pomponio
Copy Editor and Proofreader: Jane Tyrrell of Editing Solutions
Cover and internal design by Peta Nugent
Cover photographs supplied by the authors and publisher with permission
Typeset by Midland Typesetters, Australia

Digitally printed in Australia by Ligare Pty Ltd

1 2 3 4 5 11 10 09 08 07

National Library of Australia
Cataloguing-in-Publication Data

Cox, Kathy, 1945– .
 EAP now! : English for academic purposes : preliminary.

 Includes index.
 ISBN 9780733978081 (teachers bk.).

 1. English language – Study and teaching – Australia –
 Foreign speakers. 2. English language – Problems,
 exercises, etc. I. Hill, David, 1969– . II. Title.

428.2407094

Every effort has been made to trace and acknowledge copyright. However, should any infringement have occurred, the publishers tender their apologies and invite copyright owners to contact them.

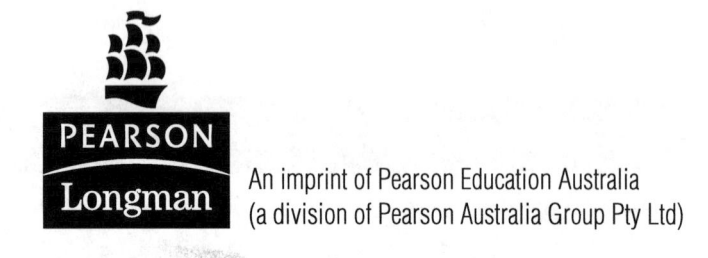

PEARSON
Longman   An imprint of Pearson Education Australia
(a division of Pearson Australia Group Pty Ltd)

PREFACE

EAP Now! Preliminary has been designed for students who have academic aims and need to learn English at Intermediate level. It serves as an *introduction* to English for Academic Purposes (EAP). It extends the topics, themes and types of language to include those that students will encounter at university and college, presented at an appropriate English language proficiency level, and takes students from Intermediate level up to a level at which they may embark on *EAP Now!* (Upper Intermediate).

The book is organised around topics, chosen to cover a wide range of human experience, and which are approached in a way that bridges everyday conversational language and academic expression.

The areas of grammar usually included within General English Intermediate level text/course books are covered in the Language Spotlight sections in each unit. The grammar is contextualised as is vocabulary learning. The book also incorporates recent theories of English language teaching: genre; a systemic functional approach to grammar and texts; and developments within lexical and task-based approaches. Critical Thinking is integrated with Reading, Listening, Writing and Speaking activities as well as learning technologies.

Information technology and the world wide web are utilised for research tasks and for additional readings for students. Teachers may choose from varied activities and suggestions for extension. There are appendices which include an academic word list and parts of speech, a self-correction memory bank and a self checking guide for writing paragraphs. Also included at the back of the book are references and the text for an information gap activity.

Listening from the audio CDs is contextualised within each unit's theme. A variety of accents are introduced to students so they understand what the 'real world' of lectures could be like.

By comparison with other Intermediate General English course books, all explications are contextualised and linked with themes. There is more written output together with a variety of oral literacy tasks which are both guided and open-ended. More out-of-class tasks are suggested and there are longer reading texts using controlled intermediate level language. Academic themes and introductions to the kinds of tasks that students will encounter in further and higher education better reflect the aims of students heading for these areas of study.

TO THE TEACHER

AIMS AND FOCUS OF *EAP NOW! PRELIMINARY*

The aim of the *Teacher's Book* is to assist you in implementing courses that are designed for students at a broadly Intermediate level who wish to follow academic conventions. They may have goals leading to university or other further or higher education conducted through the medium of English, while still requiring instruction in the language.

The aims of the series are:
- to provide a single Preliminary EAP course book which combines skills using a thematic approach, which will motivate students as they consider a wide range of human experience, and which enables the activities in each unit to keep to a consistent context with a coherent flow.
- to provide a Preliminary EAP course book which is interesting and enjoyable to students of varying ages from older teenagers upwards.
- to enable students to become familiar with, and to practise applying, English-medium academic conventions while learning English at an Intermediate level.
- to provide listening and speaking skills through introductory academic themes and genres.
- to introduce students to critical thinking around issues and provide them with tools for expressing opinions around that thinking.
- to encourage students to work independently and consider out-of-class study with discussion questions, films, extra reading and essays.
- to provide model essays and grammar in context for teachers to share with students.
- to encourage students to work in teams and to actively engage in one another's efforts, in addition to individual task-based learning.
- to broaden students' general knowledge and introduce a wide range of vocabulary.
- to provide experience in listening to other accents in a variety of contexts.
- to provide a Teacher's Book that assists teachers in the process of teaching EAP at a Preliminary level, and one which goes further than an 'answer' book.

Each unit contains seven skills which are thematically linked. Critical Thinking is often integrated with critical reading as well as listening. Students are asked to consider and form their own opinions about issues. English for the Internet Age is used primarily for research and is located at the end of each unit. The seven skills are:
- Speaking
- Reading
- Writing
- Listening
- Language Spotlight (grammar and vocabulary)
- Critical Thinking
- English for the Internet Age

There are also suggestions for further practice at the end of each unit – see the last item below.

Speaking
Each unit begins with speaking activities. They introduce the unit and often the work done there facilitates speaking later in the units. Further speaking activities also occur either as part of Listening, Reading, Writing or Language Spotlight sections or as an extra speaking section. Some pronunciation work is included and students are provided with many signposts and phrases to get them speaking. Issues-based questions appear with informative readings for background information and students are encouraged to agree or disagree in order to express their own opinions. They are provided with the grammar that allows for asking questions with tags, asking for clarification, expressing opinions, recounting experiences, and open discussion amongst other points.

Reading
The texts are as authentic as possible and students are asked to consider them globally. Therefore, during each reading, teachers should request students to examine the text, using the five questions below.
- What is the type of text (genre)?
- What is the source of the text?
- Who wrote it?
- What possible slant or purpose might it have?
- Who is the audience it is written for?

These five questions are included in most units to remind students to consider what they are reading before they begin. A good deal of information may be gleaned prior to diving into a text.

The Reading sections are intended to go some way towards helping students cope independently with the more lengthy and complex texts that they will have to deal with in their college or university courses.

Writing
At this level of proficiency writing tasks are generally kept shorter than for students at higher proficiency levels. The emphasis is upon the genres that make up writing within academic contexts, and the schema (or map) and grammar that construct them. Thus, the writing tasks examine and reproduce reports, explanations, arguments, reviews, correspondence and discussions. Particular attention is paid to linking the Language Spotlight or grammar section to each genre, and students are taught to discover how the grammar creates meaning within each text or discourse.

Listening
EAP Now! Preliminary sets a new standard for audio CDs. Transcripts are lively and interesting, and sound effects have been included to increase the sense of reality. Students hear an introduction to each listening which 'sets the scene' by introducing and activating their own field of knowledge around the topic. There are pre-listening activities which further enhance the student's ability to approach each listening with a specific purpose in mind. There are different accents to reflect real life contexts within a multi-cultural society.

Language Spotlight

We named this section Language Spotlight because in it we turn the spotlight onto the language that is important for carrying out the tasks at hand; in other words we shine the spotlight on elements of grammar and vocabulary that appear in texts that students have recently considered. In that way, language is introduced and explicated in context. Most units have two Language Spotlights – one considering language arising out of the written texts in the unit, and the other dealing with spoken language from the listening. The terminology used should be familiar to students and teachers who have some traditional background in English. The section also introduces new terms for describing specific language functions.

Critical Thinking

Critical Thinking is a natural part of Western education. Students are encouraged to consider issues in order to learn how to make and then express opinions both in writing and speaking. To consider something critically is to have an open mind about an issue and to listen to arguments with which they may not agree. Students are treated as cultural informants in that there is inquiry concerning their own ways of being. Students expressing what happens in their own cultures and comparing and contrasting that to what they experience or read about is encouraged throughout *EAP Now! Preliminary*.

English for the Internet Age

The world wide web is an important tool in education today. University lecturers now place substantial amounts of work on computer for students to access independently. Readings, lectures and references and sometimes even exams are computer based. Computer-based learning is a reality and students need practice in accessing information by research. Each unit in *EAP Now! Preliminary* offers suggestions for further work using websites previously researched by the authors. Students are encouraged to visit these websites or to carry out independent research around proposed topics that link to the theme of the unit.

Further practice

This section, at the end of each unit, not only encourages further reading and research as mentioned above, but also encourages students to watch films that link with the theme of the unit, in order to help them gain further experience of the language practised in the units in an enjoyable way. There are also questions that can be used for discussion or essay writing practice by the students, either following teacher direction or through independent study.

We wish your students success with their studies, and hope they and you both enjoy using this book.

Kathy K Cox
David Hill

ABOUT THE AUTHORS

KATHY K COX

was born in California and settled in Australia in 1970. Educated in Florida when shocking racial segregation was the norm, she became a committed exponent of equality. Attending the Universities of Hawaii and Wollongong, Australia, deepened and widened that commitment. After teaching in Pago Pago, American Samoa, she travelled throughout Asia and the Pacific. She was Director of Studies at APC, Sydney, for a decade and has enjoyed a life long career in TESOL and in the writing of English learning materials.

DAVID HILL

grew up in the north west of England. After studying at the University of Durham, his fascination for other cultures took him around the world and eventually inspired him to become a teacher of English. David has previously taught in the UK, Turkey and Japan. He now lives in Australia, where he has worked in various teaching and management positions, including Director of Studies.

ACKNOWLEDGEMENTS

Kathy would like to thank the students and colleagues from around the world who throughout many years have provided the impetus for creating English language books. Thank you to Diane Larsen-Freeman and Mary Kalantzis for their inspiration as researchers and writers who justify and illuminate a true student based approach.

Kathy also extends personal thanks to her good friends Peter and Rosemary for their patient work-shopping of ideas and interest in her projects; to David & Susan from APC; to teachers and administrators who have trialled materials and provided useful feedback; to Murray, for his ongoing support and encouragement; and to her mother, K.C., loving thanks for being a life long linguistic and personal mentor.

• • •

David would like to thank the numerous students, friends and colleagues he has worked with and learned so much from over the years, and in particular those who have assisted with the review process for this book – you know who you are! He would also like to thank the editorial and production team for their valuable contributions to the project. David also extends his special thanks to Chie, whose help, encouragement and support has been immensely valuable.

CONTENTS

Preface – Teacher's Book	iii
To the Teacher	iv
About the Authors	vii
Acknowledgements	viii
Contents Map	xiv

UNIT 1 CUSTOMS — 1

SPEAKING 1: BUILDING THE FIELD	**2**
Vocabulary about customs	2
Talking about customs	2
READING: INTRODUCTION TO A GLOBAL APPROACH TO READING (PREDICTING, SKIMMING, PURPOSE AND CRITICAL READING) – A TRAVEL BROCHURE	**2**
Introduction to prediction	3
Introduction to skimming	3
Texts and their purpose	3
Introduction to critical reading – The five questions for any reading	4
LANGUAGE SPOTLIGHT 1: CLAUSE AND SENTENCE STRUCTURE	**5**
Clause structure	5
Sentence structure	6
WRITING: GENRE	**7**
Putting ideas in order	7
Writing to follow a genre	7
LISTENING: MAIN IDEAS AND SPECIFIC INFORMATION – LECTURE ON WEDDING CUSTOMS; CONVERSATION BETWEEN TWO STUDENTS	**7**
Vocabulary around romance and marriage	7
Discussion and prediction	8
Listening for main ideas	8
Listening for specific information	10
Do you need to understand every word?	11
Listening to compare	11
Discussion	13
LANGUAGE SPOTLIGHT 2: PHRASAL VERBS	**13**
About phrasal verbs	13
Practice	15
SPEAKING 2: SPECIFIC AND GENERAL QUESTIONS; LEARNING STYLES QUIZ	**15**
Specific questions	15
General questions	16
How do you like to learn languages?	16
FURTHER PRACTICE: READING, FILMS AND FUN	**16**

UNIT 2 TRADE — 17

SPEAKING 1: BUILDING THE FIELD	**18**
Asking questions about trade	18
READING 1: MAKING GENERALISATIONS – CASE STUDY	**18**
Making generalisations from a case study	18
READING 2: SCANNING, FINDING MEANING FROM CONTEXT, TRACKING PARTICIPANTS – INFORMATION REPORT	**19**
Introduction to the Silk Road	19
Introduction to scanning	19
Introduction to finding meaning from context	20
Tracking participants	21
The five questions for any reading	22
LANGUAGE SPOTLIGHT 1: VOCABULARY DESCRIBING GRAPHS AND TABLES	**22**
Further vocabulary for describing graphs and tables	22
Noun forms of the verbs	23
Practice – describing graphs and tables	23
Have a go!	23
WRITING: INFORMATION REPORT	**24**
Generic features of an information report	24
Write an information report	25
LISTENING 1: NUMBERS – PROPERTY AUCTION	**25**
Numbers	25
LISTENING 2: IDENTIFYING STAGES – SPOKEN EXPLANATION	**27**
A spoken explanation signalling new stages	27
LANGUAGE SPOTLIGHT 2: PAST SIMPLE, USED TO AND PAST PERFECT	**28**
Explanations	28
SPEAKING 2: SENTENCE STRESS, COLLOQUIALISMS AND EXPRESSING OPINIONS	**29**
Practising conversations	29
What do you think? Expressing personal opinions	29
FURTHER PRACTICE: READING, FILMS AND FUN	**29**

UNIT 3 — DEMOGRAPHICS — 31

Introduction for teachers	32
SPEAKING 1: BUILDING THE FIELD: INTRODUCTION TO DEMOGRAPHY AND SOCIETY	**32**
Discussion	32
Vocabulary	32
READING: PREDICTING; MEANING FROM CONTEXT – AN EXPLANATION ESSAY	**32**
Pre-reading discussion	32
Predicting from the introduction	33
Finding meaning from context	34
Pronunciation – Word stress and shifting stress	34
Discussion	35
LANGUAGE SPOTLIGHT 1: PASSIVE VOICE	**35**
Identifying passive voice	35
When is passive voice used?	36
Practice	37
WRITING: STRUCTURE OF AN EXPLANATION ESSAY	**39**
Generic features of an explanation essay	39
Write your own explanation essay	40
LISTENING: PREDICTING, NOTE-TAKING AND DIFFERENT ACCENTS – EXPLANATIONS	**40**
Prediction	40
Listening and note-taking (different accents)	40
Discussion	41
LANGUAGE SPOTLIGHT 2: PRESENT CONTINUOUS, PRESENT SIMPLE AND ZERO CONDITIONAL	**42**
Identifying use	42
Practice	43
Personalised practice	43
SPEAKING 2: CLARIFICATION	**43**
Expressions for requesting clarification	43
Practice	43
FURTHER PRACTICE: READING, FILMS AND FUN	**44**

UNIT 4 — ENERGY — 45

SPEAKING: BUILDING THE FIELD: INTRODUCTION TO THE TOPIC OF ENERGY	**46**
Understanding energy	46
Recognising an issue	46
For or against	46
Definitions in context	46
Signposting in speaking/talking about an issue	47
READING: STAGES IN ARGUMENT, DEFINITIONS IN CONTEXT, TOPIC SENTENCES AND LOCATING POINTS IN ARGUMENT	**47**
Staging – The outline, the schema, the map	47
WRITING: AN ARGUMENT	**49**
Staging in an argument	49
LANGUAGE SPOTLIGHT: VERB FORMS AND FUNCTIONS	**51**
Gerunds and infinitives	51
LISTENING: ENERGY TO BURN	**52**
Listening for meaning and content	52
FURTHER PRACTICE: READING, FILMS AND FUN	**54**

UNIT 5 — COMMUNICATION — 55

SPEAKING 1: BUILDING THE FIELD	**56**
Types of communication	56
READING: MAIN IDEAS & SPECIFIC INFORMATION – EXPLANATION ESSAY	**56**
Discussion – Communication and miscommunication	56
Reading for main ideas	56
The five questions for reading any text	57
Reading for detail	57
Discussion	59
WRITING: FORMAL AND INFORMAL EMAILS; FORMAL LETTERS	**59**
Reasons for writing emails and letters	59
Conventions for emails and letters	59
Write your own correspondence	61
LISTENING: SPECIFIC INFORMATION – TELEPHONE CONVERSATIONS	**61**
Listening for specific information	61
Scanning and finding meaning from context	62
Listening for specific information	63
Roleplays	64
LANGUAGE SPOTLIGHT: WILL (INSTANT DECISIONS); FIRST CONDITIONALS	**65**
Uses of *will*	65
Instant decisions	65
Real conditionals – Form and use	65
Real conditionals – Practice	66
SPEAKING 2: MAKING REQUESTS	**66**
Requests	66
FURTHER PRACTICE: READING, FILMS AND FUN	**67**

UNIT 6 POLITICS — 69

LANGUAGE SPOTLIGHT 1: PREFIXES AND SUFFIXES — 70
Greek and Latin into English! — 70

SPEAKING 1: BUILDING THE FIELD — 70
Thinking for yourself and talking about it — 70
What is politics? — 70

READING: DISCUSSION ESSAY — 70
Form and comprehension – Features of individual paragraphs — 70
Understanding — 71

WRITING: DISCUSSION GENRE — 71
Map or schema of discussion essay — 71

LANGUAGE SPOTLIGHT 2: TALKING ABOUT FUTURE PREDICTIONS (*GOING TO*), MODALITY (PROBABILITY), PRESENT SIMPLE TENSE — 73
Future predictions – *Going to* — 73
Modality – *Probably* or *possibly* — 73
Present simple tense — 74

SPEAKING 2: AGREEING OR DISAGREEING — 74
Discussion – Future of government — 74

LISTENING: MINI-LECTURE, GOVERNMENT AND POLITICS, NOTE-TAKING FROM LISTENING — 75
Importance markers – Intonation, stress, emphasis — 75

FURTHER PRACTICE: READING, FILMS AND FUN — 78

UNIT 7 MEDIA — 79

SPEAKING 1: BUILDING THE FIELD — 80
The range of media — 80

READING: IDENTIFYING TEXT TYPE; COHESION – ADVICE AND INSTRUCTIONAL TEXTS — 80
Identifying text type — 80
Meaning behind the words — 80
The five questions for any text — 80
Cohesion — 81

LANGUAGE SPOTLIGHT: LONGER NOUN GROUPS — 81
What is nominalisation? — 81
Understanding nominalisations — 82
Giving instructions — 82
Practising giving instructions — 83

WRITING: PROCEDURAL GENRE — 83
Stages in an advice article — 83
Write an a advice article — 85

LISTENING 1: NOTE-TAKING – LECTURE ABOUT MEDIA REPORTS — 85
Opinions in the media — 85
Listening and note-taking — 86
Discussion — 89

LISTENING 2: LISTENING TO AND FOLLOWING INSTRUCTIONS – MAKING A FILM — 90
Making a film — 90
Order of stages — 90
Listening for specific information — 91

SPEAKING 2: SURVEY – PREFERENCES AROUND MEDIA CHOICES — 91
Discussion — 91
Survey — 91

FURTHER PRACTICE: READING, FILMS AND FUN — 91

UNIT 8 ART — 93

SPEAKING: BUILDING THE FIELD — 94
Discussion and vocabulary — 94
More vocabulary fun — 94

READING 1: A REVIEW — 95
The five questions for reading any text — 95

LANGUAGE SPOTLIGHT 1: REPORTED SPEECH — 96
Reporting direct speech — 96
Verb tense changes when reporting speech — 96

READING 2: AN ARTICLE — 97
Another view of art – *Art as technology* — 97
Scanning — 97

PRE-LISTENING: OPINIONS — 98
Thinking about opinions — 98

LISTENING: REVIEW, OPINIONS, TAG QUESTIONS — 98
Locating opinions, summarising — 98

LANGUAGE SPOTLIGHT 2: TAG QUESTIONS — 100
Practise speaking — 100
Voice down tag questions — 100
Voice up tag questions — 100

WRITING: YOUR OWN REVIEW — 100
Writing a review — 100

FURTHER PRACTICE: READING, FILMS AND FUN — 101

UNIT 9 ARCHITECTURE — 103

SPEAKING: BUILDING THE FIELD — 104
Compare and contrast — 104
Function (What's it for?) — 104
Comparisons — 104

READING: BROADENING GENERAL KNOWLEDGE — 104
Classical and ancient architecture around the world — 104

WRITING 1: SHORT ANSWERS — 107
Comprehension — 107
Finding the main ideas — 107

LANGUAGE SPOTLIGHT & WRITING 2: NOMINALS AND NOMINALISATION (NOUNS) — 107
Writing – Refer to *Architecture around the world* — 107

LISTENING: DIFFERENTIATING BETWEEN HYPOTHESIS AND FACT — 108
Pre-listening — 108
Listening for certainty versus speculation — 108
Thinking about the listening; value judgment — 110

FURTHER PRACTICE: READING, FILMS AND FUN — 110

UNIT 10 INDIGENOUS PEOPLE — 111

SPEAKING 1: BUILDING THE FIELD — 112
Discussion – What do you know about Aboriginal people? — 112

READING: FACTUAL INFORMATION — 112
The five questions for reading any text — 112
Reading a report — 112
Recognising definitions in context — 114
Factual information in reports — 115
Comparing texts for bias — 115
Locating language choices which create intention — 116
Rewrite — 118

LANGUAGE SPOTLIGHT 1: PRESENT PERFECT TENSE — 118
When do we use present perfect tense? — 118
Which tense? — 120
Personalised practice – Changes and experiences — 121

WRITING: AN INFORMATION REPORT — 121
Write a report — 121

LISTENING: INTERVIEW WITH AN AUSTRALIAN ABORIGINAL ARTIST — 121
Introduction to Aboriginal art — 121

Listening for main points and details — 122
Listening for specific points – Shapes and forms — 123

LANGUAGE SPOTLIGHT 2: PRESENT PERFECT CONTINUOUS TENSE — 124
When do we use present perfect continuous tense? — 124
Which tense? — 125
Personalised practice — 126

SPEAKING 2: CONTEXTS FOR PRESENT PERFECT TENSE AND PRESENT PERFECT CONTINUOUS TENSE — 126
Talking about recent experiences — 126
Guess what I've been doing? — 126
Whom do you admire? — 126

LANGUAGE SPOTLIGHT 3: WHERE DID THIS COME FROM? — 126
Matching texts to their sources — 126

FURTHER PRACTICE: READING, FILMS AND FUN — 127

UNIT 11 LANDSCAPES — 129

SPEAKING 1: BUILDING THE FIELD — 130
Discussion — 130
Vocabulary — 130

READING 1: COMPREHENSION — 131
Applying knowledge — 131

LANGUAGE SPOTLIGHT 1: MAKING COMPARISONS — 131
Similar and different — 131
Compare and contrast — 132

LISTENING: INTERVIEW WITH AN AUSTRALIAN FARMER — 133
Pre-listening — 133
Explanations, definitions, examples, solutions — 133

SPEAKING 2: SOLUTIONS — 135
Discussion – Proposing solutions — 135

WRITING: SOLUTIONS — 135
Writing a solution — 135

READING 2: COMPREHENSION — 135
Meaning in context and recognising facts — 135

LANGUAGE SPOTLIGHT 2: HOW TO ADD EXTRA INFORMATION — 135
Adjectival relative clauses — 135

FURTHER PRACTICE: READING, FILMS AND FUN — 136

UNIT 12 WORLD — 137

SPEAKING 1: BUILDING THE FIELD — 138
Quiz – Making guesses — 138

READING: SKIMMING, SCANNING AND NOTE-TAKING; FINDING MEANING FROM CONTEXT — 138
Cities – Your experiences — 138
Skimming, scanning and note-taking — 138
The five questions for any text — 139
Finding meaning from context — 139
Discussion — 139

LANGUAGE SPOTLIGHT 1: UNPACKING NOMINALS — 140
Written style — 140

WRITING: REVIEW OF GENRES; MATCHING GENRES TO TASK — 140
Review of genres — 140
Matching genres to task — 141
Writing — 142

LISTENING: SPECIFIC INFORMATION – TUTORIAL — 142
What do you do at college or university? — 142
Listening for specific information — 143

LANGUAGE SPOTLIGHT 2: REVIEW OF FUTURE TENSES — 145
Intentions — 145
Decision, intentions and arrangements — 145
Practice — 145

SPEAKING 2: PROJECT: ROLE-PLAY — 146
Role-play — 146

FURTHER PRACTICE: READING, FILMS AND FUN — 146

REFERENCES — 147

APPENDIX 1 ACADEMIC WORD LIST AND PARTS OF SPEECH — 148

APPENDIX 2 SELF-CORRECTION MEMORY BANK — 155

APPENDIX 3 SELF-CHECKING GUIDE – WRITING A PARAGRAPH — 156

INDEX — 159

CONTENTS MAP

Critical Thinking and English for the Internet Age are incorporated into the Reading, Writing, Listening and Speaking activities throughout. Extra speaking practice is included in the Reading, Writing, Listening and Language Spotlight activities.

UNIT NUMBER AND THEME	READING (SKILLS, TEXTS)	WRITING GENRES
1 Customs	*introduction to a global approach to reading:* prediction 3 skimming 3 purpose 3 critical reading 4	*introduction to text structure & purpose:* staging in texts 7 following a genre 7
2 Trade	*reading a case study and an information report:* making generalisations 18 scanning 19 finding meaning from context 20 tracking participants 21	information report 24
3 Demography	*reading using inference:* predicting 32 meaning in context 32	explanation 39
4 Energy	*reading an argument:* stages 47 definitions in context 47 topic sentences 47 points in arguments 47	argument 49
5 Communication	*reading to summarise:* for main ideas 56 for detail 57	correspondence 59
6 Politics	*reading a discussion:* paragraphs 70 language features 70	discussion 71
7 Media	*reading different text types:* identifying text type (instructional, advice) 80 identifying style (formal, humourous etc) 80 cohesion 81	procedure 83

LISTENING	SPEAKING	LANGUAGE SPOTLIGHT
listening in order to: predict 8 find main ideas 8 find specific information 10 **CD 1 – T2 Lecture on wedding customs 9** **CD 1 – T3 Conversation between two students 12**	building the field: customs 2 discussions about customs and traditions 2 speaking generally and specifically 15	clause structure 5 sentence structure 6 phrasal verbs 13
listening: for numbers 25 to identify stages 27 **CD 1 – T4 Property auction 26** **CD 1 – T5 Information and summary report 28**	building the field: trade 18 discussions about global trade 18 sentence stress 29 colloquialisms 29 expressing personal opinions 29	vocabulary for graphs and tables 22 parts of speech 23 past simple 28 used to 28 past perfect 28
listening in order to: predict 40 take notes 40 **CD 1 – T6 Students report on social change 41**	building the field: demography 32 asking for clarification 43	passive voice 31 present simple 42 present continuous 42 zero conditionals 42
listening for: interrogative 'what' 52 **CD 1 – T7 Dialogue between three friends 53**	building the field: energy 46 signposting in speaking: giving reasons 47	longer verb groups 51 gerunds 51 infinitives 51
listening for: specific information 61, 63 expressions for phone calls 62 **CD 1 – T8 Leaving a phone message 61** **CD 1 – T9 Returning a phone call 64**	building the field: communication 56 making requests 66	reacting/instant decisions (*will*) 65 1st conditionals (real conditionals) 65
listening in order to: take notes 75 **CD 1 – T10 Lecture about politics & government 75**	building the field: politics 70 agreeing and disagreeing 74	prefixes and suffixes 70 talking about future predictions 73 *going to* 73 modality 73 probability 73 present simple tense 74
listening to and following instructions: taking notes 85, 86 identifying stages 90 obtaining specific details 91 **CD 1 – T11 Lecture about media reports 88** **CD 1 – T12 How to make a film 90**	building the field: media 80 discussion about use of the media 80 conducting a survey: preferences around media choices 91	introduction to nominalisation 81 imperatives 82 advice/instruction structures 82

UNIT NUMBER AND THEME	READING (SKILLS, TEXTS)	WRITING GENRES
8 Art	*reading a review:* description 95 scanning 97 comprehension 97	review 100
9 Architecture	*reading historical information:* definitions 104 comprehension 104 main ideas 104	historical information 107
10 Indigenous/Aboriginal people	*reading for facts vs opinion:* identifying fact 112 sarcasm 115 bias 115 point of view 115	information report 121
11 Landscapes	*reading factual information:* vocabulary extension 131 applying knowledge 131 meaning from context 135 recognising facts 135	problems and solutions 135
12 The World	skimming 138 scanning 138 note-taking 138 meaning in context 138	review of genres 140 matching genre to task 141

Bonus CD Tracks from *EAP Now!*
CD 2 – T4 The new student
CD 2 – T5 Going down fighting (a play)

LISTENING	SPEAKING	LANGUAGE SPOTLIGHT
listening to: expressing opinions 96 identify opinions 98 tag questions 98, 100 voice intonation 98, 100 **CD 1 – T13 Reality TV show review 98**	building the field: art 94 expressing opinions 2 94	modality 96 reported speech 96 tense changes 96 tag questions 100
listening to: differentiating between hypothesis and fact 108 locating certainty 108 critically weigh up an issue 110 **CD 1 – T14 Workmen on a building site 109**	building the field: architecture 104 offering value judgments 104	nominalisation 107
listening for: main points 122 spoken information that links to visual information 123 **CD 2 – T1 Television interview with an Aboriginal artist 122**	building the field: indigenous people 112 general knowledge: indigenous people 112 talking about experiences 126	linking the past to now 118 present perfect 118 present perfect continuous 124
listening for: solutions 133 explanations 133 examples 133 **CD 2 – T2 Radio interview with an Australian farmer 133**	building the field: landscapes 130 discussion: proposing solutions 135	making comparisons 131 adding extra information 135 adjectival relative clauses 135
listening for: specific information 142 **CD 2 – T3 Tutorial: planning a new suburb 143**	building the field: the world 138 speculation: general knowledge quiz 138 tutorial project: role-play 146	unpacking nominals 140 review of future tenses 145

1 CUSTOMS

'when in Rome, do as Rome does'

BY THE END OF THIS UNIT, STUDENTS SHOULD:

- know more vocabulary for talking about customs, culture, romance and marriage .... Speaking 1: Task A **2**; Listening: Task A **7**
- be more fluent and confident when talking about customs, culture, romance and marriage .... Speaking 1: Task B **2**; Listening: Task G **13**
- be able to predict when reading and listening, and be aware of the usefulness of this skill .... Reading: Task A **2**; Listening: Task B **8**
- be able to skim (read quickly to get the main ideas)... Reading: Task B **3**
- be more aware of different written genres and their purpose .... Reading: Task C **3**
- be prepared to think about five standard questions every time they read .... Reading: Task D **4**
- be able to correct and avoid mistakes in sentence structure and clause structure .... Language Spotlight 1: Tasks A and B **5–6**
- be aware of staging in written texts and how this relates to genre..................................... Writing: Task A **7**
- have practised writing to follow a particular genre .... Writing: Task B **7**
- have improved their ability to predict and listen for main ideas and specific information .... Listening: Tasks B, C, D and F **8–11**
- be aware of the reasons why you don't always have to understand every word when listening .... Listening: Task E **11**
- be able to use phrasal verbs correctly, and be aware of their informality .... Language Spotlight 2: Tasks A and B **13–15**
- be able to discuss ideas on specific topics and understand how you like to learn a language .... Speaking 2: Tasks A, B and C **15–16**
- have a better understanding of their learning style, and know some different ways to improve their English ... Speaking 2: Task C **16**

CUSTOM n. pl., CUSTOMS [UNCOUNTABLE AND COUNTABLE]: something that is done by people in a particular society because people have been doing it the same way for a long time.

This unit introduces some of the concepts of academic English, while following a theme that is particularly relevant to students wanting to study cross-culturally: culture and customs.

SPEAKING 1 — BUILDING THE FIELD

Task A | Vocabulary about customs ▶▶ SB P. 2

1. Students, in pairs, look at the pictures in the book and talk about them as much as possible. The pictures show festivals and ceremonies from around the world. This may activate some vocabulary in readiness for Question 2.
2. Students help each other, in pairs, to match some vocabulary with its meanings. You may have to explain to students that (n) after a word indicates that it is a noun, (adj) indicates an adjective, and (vb) indicates a verb.

ANSWERS

WORDS	MEANINGS
ceremony	an important event in which traditional actions are performed in a formal way
celebration	an event or party when many people show they are very happy about something (eg winning a sporting event, a birthday)
festival	an occasion when there are performances of dancing, music, films, plays, parades, etc, usually happening in the same place every year
parade	an event where musical bands, decorated trucks, dancers, etc pass down the street.
religion (n) / religious (adj)	a belief in one or more gods
society (n) / social (adj)	all the people in a country, sharing the same customs, laws, etc
tradition (n) / traditional (adj)	a way of doing things that has been the same for a very long time.

After this, students can return to the pictures and see if they can add anything to what they said in Question 1, using the new vocabulary.

Task B | Talking about customs ▶▶ SB P. 2

1. Students tell their partners (in pairs) about a time they saw or participated in:
   - a ceremony
   - a festival
   - a parade
   - a religious event.
2. In small groups, students talk about what people in their cultures do around various traditions listed in the Students' Book. They then look at whether there is a difference between generations, by comparing how their grandparents' generation followed the tradition, and how they follow it today.

The traditions they talk about are:
- Sending cards for birthdays, New Year or other special days
- Having parties for birthdays
- Greeting people the first time you meet them (eg bowing)
- Going outside the house to meet friends (eg to restaurants, pubs).

You could also add to the list, or ask students to think of other traditions to talk about.

READING — INTRODUCTION TO A GLOBAL APPROACH TO READING (PREDICTING, SKIMMING, PURPOSE AND CRITICAL READING) – A TRAVEL BROCHURE

This section shows students how to deal with texts in a holistic way in preparation for coping with the much longer texts that they will encounter in their further studies. As throughout the book, non-academic texts are used to: (a) add variety, (b) ensure that there is breadth to students' English language development, ie to ensure they learn outside of academic contexts as well as within, and (c) to introduce concepts useful for academic English with text types that allow interest to be maintained.

Here, students are introduced to the idea that texts come in various types, that each type has a different purpose, and that the purpose influences the features of the text type. One approach to critical thinking is also demonstrated. This involves thinking about five questions that can be asked about almost any text (and which are asked consistently throughout the book), focusing on the text's author, the intended audience and purpose.

Task A | Introduction to prediction ▶▶ SB P. 2

Depending on how often the students have come across this concept before, this task introduces or consolidates the concept of prediction to help them to quickly orientate to the text and to activate any prior knowledge of the topic.

① Students are asked to look quickly at the first page of a text (part of a brochure) and to answer some questions which direct them to use pictures, the title and headings to make predictions. It is reproduced in their books with all text apart from the title and headings too small to read, to force them to use the title, headings and pictures to predict.

> **ANSWERS**
>
> a. Look at the pictures. What is the topic?
>   *Japan / travel / tourism / …*
>   *(any of these, or anything similar, are OK).*
> b. Look at the title. Who is the brochure for:
>   (i) students?
>   (ii) tourists? ← *Correct*
>   (iii) religious people?
> c. Use the headings. Which from the following list does the brochure NOT tell you about?
>   (i) where the festivals are
>   (ii) the cheapest supermarket
>   (iii) why the places are interesting
>   (iv) information about local schools ← *Correct, as this would not usually be included in tourism brochures, and does not correspond to any of the headings.*
>   (v) information about the festivals
>   (vi) the kind of transport to be used.

② Students say whether they think certain statements are most likely to be true or false. (The Students' Book points out that we call these guesses 'predictions', and that making predictions can help in quickly understanding a text.)

> **ANSWERS**
>
> a. The tour will visit a very modern shrine: *Likely to be false – the title talks about traditions.*
> b. In one of the festivals on this tour, you will see people walking on fire: *Likely to be true – a picture shows this.*
> c. The festivals on the tour are very boring to watch: *Likely to be false – it's highly unlikely that a tour company would take people to see boring events, and the picture would, to most people, look interesting.*
> d. The tour will use only public transport: *Likely to be false – the title mentions a luxury tour, and it's unlikely that public transport would be considered luxury.*
> e. The tour operates every weekend of the year: *Likely to be false – festivals are not usually that regular.*
> f. The tour visits more than one festival: *Likely to be true – the title mentions festivals in the plural.*

Task B | Introduction to skimming ▶▶ SB P. 3

① Students read the following explanation:

> When reading, it isn't always helpful to read every word. Sometimes you only need to find the main ideas – reading only for main ideas is called **skimming**. At other times, skimming helps to find the right part of the text quickly, ie, the part that might have the information you're looking for.
>
> **Note:** Skimming is reading quickly (without reading every word) to find the main ideas.

② Next, students are referred to the brochure they made predictions from in Task A, but this time it is shown full sized, with text large enough to read. Students answer the questions in their books by skimming.

> **ANSWERS**
>
> 1. Headings help find the main ideas.
> 2. a. The Itinerary section
>   b. The section headed 'Your tour – The history and magic of the festivals'
>   c. The section headed 'What the price includes'
>   d. The 'Itinerary' section
>   e. The section headed 'Your tour – The history and magic of the festivals'.

Task C | Texts and their purpose ▶▶ SB P. 3

The Students' Book gives a brief explanation of genre/text type, and mentions that each genre/text type has a purpose. The rest of the activity allows students to work with this concept. Show the students texts of various types that they might have some familiarity with, eg an advertisement, a magazine article and a text book, and ask them why they

Unit 1 Customs | 3

think each was written. Then, ask them, in pairs or small groups, to list as many different features of each text as they can. Examples to help them include the following:
- advertisements have lots of text but few pictures
- magazine articles usually have more exciting writing than text books.
- text books usually have more difficult/longer words than magazine articles

❶ Students match text types from a list to the most appropriate purpose from another list.

Depending on the students' backgrounds, the words *orientation booklet* and *encyclopaedia article* might have to be explained.

The lists haven't been numbered. This is to discourage students from simply writing numbers next to each word, which would mean less engagement with the meaning.

ANSWERS

TEXT TYPE	PURPOSE
advertisement	to sell something
information leaflet about a library	to give information about how to use the services
information leaflet about a tourist attraction	to make something sound interesting
map	to help you know where to go
bus timetable	to give information about times and routes
newspaper article	to give information about recent events
this course book	to help people use English in their future study
orientation booklet for your language school	to help students understand what they have to do and why
shopping list	to help you remember what to buy
dictionary	to help people find the pronunciation of words, see examples of how they are used and find out their meaning
encyclopaedia article	to give information

> **Variation:** With an imaginative class, instead of the task as given in the book, task types could be written on the board and students asked to work in groups to suggest their own purposes.

❷ For homework, students are asked to find as many texts as they can, for example, in newspapers and on signs (they can bring them to college or, in the case of signs and notices, copy them into a notebook). They then write the purpose for each.

This can be made into a competition – who in the class, or which pair in the class, can make the biggest list?

Task D | Introduction to critical reading – The five questions for any reading ▶▶ SB P. 5

❶ Students are introduced to some of the ideas that will assist in critical thinking by examining a small advertisement for the kind of tour that appeared previously in this section. Five questions are given – these are used with many of the texts in this book, to get students into the habit of thinking about text type, source, author, purpose and audience every time they read.

ANSWERS

a. **What is it?** (What type of text is it?)
   (i) a sign
   (ii) an advertisement ← *Correct*
   (iii) an information leaflet

b. **What is the source?** (Where is it from?)
   (i) a writer
   (ii) an encyclopaedia
   (iii) a travel company ← *Correct*

c. **Who is the writer?**
   (i) a government employee
   (ii) someone working for a travel company ← *Correct*
   (iii) a famous writer

d. **What purpose does the writer have for writing it?**
   (i) to give information
   (ii) to make you want to buy the tour ← *Correct*
   (iii) to make you interested in Japanese culture

e. **Who is the intended audience?** (Who was it written for? Who should read it?)
   (i) ordinary people who like travelling ← *Correct*
   (ii) children
   (iii) ordinary people who don't have much money.

2 Students attempt the same questions but using the brochure they looked at earlier in this unit.

> **ANSWERS**
>
> The first answer is given as an example in the Students' Book.
> [a] **What is it?**
> Part of a travel brochure
> [b] **What is the source?**
> A travel company
> [c] **Who is the writer?**
> An advertiser, marketer or salesperson (perhaps a travel company employee or someone working in a travel agency)
> [d] **What purpose does the writer have for writing it?**
> To make people want to purchase the tour
> [e] **Who is the intended audience?**
> Customers of the travel company

LANGUAGE SPOTLIGHT 1 — CLAUSE AND SENTENCE STRUCTURE

Task A | Clause structure ▶▶ SB P. 5

This section aims to ensure that students are all using the same terminology and have the same basic understanding of sentence structure, to facilitate quick explanations and assistance, especially with writing.

The activity in the book assumes that students already know the names of the different parts of speech and can identify them.

1 Students draw boxes around each clause in the paragraph they are given, and underline the verb group, as a means of finding out how good they are at this, or to give practice, depending on the skills of your class.

The Students' Book briefly explains that a clause must have a subject and a verb, and for simplicity the exceptions (eg imperatives and cases of ellipsis) have been missed out.

> **ANSWER**
>
> Vertical bars indicate clause breaks, Underlining indicates verbs.
> There are many famous views in Japan. ||| In one of them, there is an orange gate in the sea. ||| It is at a place called Miyajima, near the city of Hiroshima. This kind of gate is called a torii, ||| and there is one of these at the entrance to most Shinto shrines. ||| Shinto is one of the main religions in Japan, ||| and the places of worship in Shinto are called shrines. When people go through the torii, ||| they are entering the shrine. The one at Miyajima is unusual ||| because you have to go through it by boat. ||| In fact, most people walk into the temple through other torii.

2 This question introduces the idea of *circumstance*, which covers most parts of the sentence apart from the subject, verb group and object. The term has been borrowed from systemic functional linguistics (eg Halliday & Matthiessen, 2004) due to its power in covering a category of language which traditionally has a whole range of labels, including prepositional phrases, adverbial phrases and sentence adverbials. Circumstances give information about where, when, why or how something happens, etc.

Students mark the subjects and objects in one way, and the circumstances in another way, in a paragraph they are given (for example, double underlining for subject and object, and dotted underlining for circumstances).

> **ANSWERS**
>
> Double underline indicates a subject or an object (for the purposes of simplification, a complement is considered an object here). Dotted underline indicates a circumstance.
>
> There are many famous views in Japan. In one of them, there is an orange gate in the sea. It is at a place called Miyajima, near the city of Hiroshima. This kind of gate is called a torii, and there is one of these at the entrance to most Shinto shrines. Shinto is one of the main religions in Japan, and the places of worship in Shinto are called shrines. When people go through the torii, they are entering the shrine. The one at Miyajima is unusual because you have to go through it by boat. In fact, most people walk into the temple through other torii.

3 To deal with the common mistakes of missing out the subject of some clauses, or including more than one subject, students are asked to find and correct the mistakes in some sentences they are given. (This is a common problem for Spanish and many eastern Asian students, as it links in with how their languages deal with cohesion.)

> **ANSWERS**
>
> Added or changed words are underlined. Removed words are crossed out.
> a. When I go to another country, I want to travel to many places, because I like learning about other cultures.
> *(The final clause has no subject.)*
>
> b. However, my friend he likes beaches, and he just stays in one place.
> *(Only one subject is possible in each clause.)*
>
> c. One of the most interesting cultures in the world, it is Japanese culture.
> *(Again, only one subject is possible in a clause.)*

Unit 1 Customs | 5

d. In Japan there are many shrines / ~~In~~ Japan has many shrines.
(Either the 'dummy subject' there has to be introduced, or the preposition In has to be removed to turn the circumstance In Japan into a subject.)

e. If you go to Japan you should visit Miyajima.
(Because there are two finite verbs/verb groups, there are two clauses, so there must be two subjects.)

f. Some people ~~they~~ don't like travelling. / They don't like travelling.
(Again, two subjects aren't possible. Which one is removed depends on the cohesion with any previous sentence.)

Task B | Sentence structure ▶▶ SB P. 6

1 This can be an awareness-building activity or a task to activate prior knowledge, depending on your students. They are shown an example of a simple sentence, a compound sentence and a complex sentence, and asked to count the clauses in each and try to notice the difference.

a. We will take you on a tour to the island of Miyajima.

b. We will take you on a tour to the island of Miyajima, and you'll see some wonderful views.

c. We think you will enjoy your tour of Miyajima because there are some wonderful views.

> The Discussion section in the Students' Book briefly tells students about the different kinds of clause, with advice that using complex sentences give a more sophisticated feel to their writing, and may help them achieve higher marks in exams. Subordinators allow a wider range of relationships between ideas to be expressed.

2 Students mark some sentences according to whether they are simple, compound or complex.
The paragraphs from the Students' Book are reproduced below for your convenience.

> [a] Fire walking ceremonies are held in many cultures around the world, in countries such as India, Africa, South Eastern Europe, North America and Japan. [b] These ceremonies are usually connected with religion, and have many purposes including healing sick people and making people spiritually clean. [c] It looks dangerous but usually no-one gets hurt. [d] However, if you walk too slowly or stand still, your feet might get burnt!

> [e] Taking part in a fire-walking ceremony is not dangerous for several reasons. [f] Firstly, because you walk quickly, your feet don't spend much time on the hot wood. [g] Also, the wood has usually cooled a little before the fire walk starts.

ANSWERS

a. simple **c.** compound **e.** simple **g.** complex
b. compound **d.** complex **f.** complex

3 Students now find a list of conjunctions used in texts in this unit, and place them in a table to show whether they are coordinators or subordinators. Refer students back to the texts if necessary. There are more subordinators than shown here – the ones in the table are just examples.

ANSWERS

COORDINATORS	SUBORDINATORS
(used in compound sentences)	*(used in complex sentences – they begin subordinating clauses)*
and	because
but	if
or	before
	after
	until
	when
	whenever
	while
	even if

4 Students now use the knowledge they have gained or reviewed in this section to correct the punctuation and capitalisation in the following paragraphs. The text in the Students' Book is reproduced below for your convenience *(Note: Students should find a total of nine corrections.)*

> When you visit London. You will find people of many different cultures. It is one of the most culturally diverse cities in the world. And the people living there speak over 300 languages between them.
> Because of this variety of cultures. You will easily be able to find food from many different countries. Different cultural groups often live in specific areas. For example. If you feel like having Chinese food. Just go to Chinatown, near Leicester Square. Where there are many Chinese restaurants. There are also many festivals in London, the biggest one of the year is the Notting Hill Carnival. Which includes Caribbean music and dancing. If you like variety. London is a very good place to live.

> **ANSWER**
>
> Punctuation and capitalisation that has changed is marked by **bold** type and <u>underlining</u>.
>
> When you visit Londo**n**<u>, y</u>ou will find people of many different cultures. It is one of the most culturally diverse cities in the worl**d**<u>, a</u>nd the people living there speak over 300 languages between them.
>
> Because of this variety of culture**s**<u>, y</u>ou will easily be able to find food from many different countries. Different cultural groups often live in specific areas. For exampl**e**<u>, i</u>f you feel like having Chinese foo**d**<u>,</u> <u>j</u>ust go to Chinatown, near Leicester Squar**e**<u>, w</u>here there are many Chinese restaurants. There are also many festivals in Londo**n**<u>. T</u>he biggest one of the year is the Notting Hill Carniva**l**<u>, w</u>hich includes Caribbean music and dancing from many different cultures. If you like variet**y**<u>, L</u>ondon is a very good place to live.

WRITING — GENRE

This section introduces students to the idea that different text types have different features such as staging (the idea of text types and their purpose was introduced in the reading section of this unit).

Task A | Putting ideas in order ▶▶ SB P. 8

This task guides students through an example of how texts in English progress from general ideas to the more specific, and that in each paragraph of a text there is usually a pattern of ideas, for example they might be in chronological order.

① Students look back at the brochure in the reading section of this unit and answer questions about the progression of ideas.

> **ANSWERS**
>
> a. Which section of the brochure gives the most general information? *The first*
> b. Which sections give the most detailed information? *Itinerary, What the price includes, and What to bring – in other words, those sections nearer the end*
> c. What patterns do you notice? *The text starts with more general information and moves on to more detail.*

② Students are now asked to look within two of the sections (the *Introduction* on the first brochure page, and the *Your tour* section), and to look at the progression of ideas within each section.

> **ANSWERS**
>
> (i) Paragraph on first page: [a] Starts with general information and becomes more detailed
> (ii) 'Your tour' section: [c] follows a time order
> (iii) 'Itinerary' section: [c] follows a time order

Task B | Writing to follow a genre ▶▶ SB P. 8

Here, students are asked to produce their own tour information leaflet, based on the model in the reading section, giving them the chance to practise writing to follow a genre (though the only language features they have come across so far are the progression of ideas).

This task starts with some speaking while students talk through their ideas. At this stage they should be encouraged to ask for, or look up, any vocabulary they need. They should be strongly encouraged to ask each other questions about their plans, as this will help them find out what other people may be interested in if they were to go on the trip being planned.

This is best done in mixed nationality pairs. If this is not possible, then try to pair people from different parts of the country.

The steps, as they appear in the Students' Book, are:
1. Choose a place to write about.
2. Make a rough itinerary
3. Tell your partner about your tour. Your partner will ask questions.
4. Write the brochure, checking that the paragraphs and ideas follow the patterns you found earlier in this unit.
5. Swap your brochure with someone else. Check that – (a) the paragraphs move in time order (chronological order), and (b) each section has the same purpose as the example.

LISTENING — MAIN IDEAS AND SPECIFIC INFORMATION – LECTURE ON WEDDING CUSTOMS; CONVERSATION BETWEEN TWO STUDENTS

Task A | Vocabulary around romance and marriage ▶▶ SB P. 8

① Students help each other to put a list of words about romance and marriage in time (chronological) order (some may happen at the same time). Students should be encouraged to find out the meanings of unfamiliar words from other students or, if necessary, from a dictionary.

Unit 1 Customs | 7

> **ANSWERS**
> - start going out with each other/start dating
> - get engaged
> - choose the best man and the bridesmaids
> - have the stag night/have the hen's party
> - have a wedding/a wedding ceremony }
> - get married
> - have a wedding reception
> - go on a honeymoon

Through doing this activity, students should find out (if they don't know already) the difference between a stag night and a hen's party.

② Students help each other to work out together the difference between sets of words with similar meanings.

> **ANSWERS**
> a. A marriage is for the whole time the couple are married, but a wedding is just on the first day of the marriage, the wedding day.
> b. A bride is female and a groom (also bridegroom) is male
> c. *Groom* is a word only used around the time of the wedding. After the wedding, during the marriage, he is a husband. Similar for *bride* and *wife*.
> d. *Partner* is a modern word used for both males and females; for people who are married or who are living together as if married; and also for members of same-sex couples.

③ In small groups, students guess the meaning of the following items of vocabulary, checking the meaning in a dictionary if no one in the group knows.
  a. a registry office wedding
  b. to elope
  c. to get a divorce/to get divorced/to divorce.

They then give their opinions of when each might be allowed, in order to use the vocabulary as much as possible.

Task B | Discussion and prediction ▶▶ SB P. 8

① Students talk with a partner or small group about wedding ceremonies in their own cultures. They are asked to think especially about:
- what events happen during the ceremony and at the party afterwards
- any symbols and their meanings (eg wedding rings)
- any people who have a special role (eg to look after the wedding ring)
- the people who come to the wedding ceremony and the reception.

The meaning of *symbol*, together with its adjectival and general noun forms *symbolic* and *symbolism* may have to be pre-taught.

If students are from different cultures, they can look for similarities and differences between weddings in each others' countries. If they are all from the same culture, each pair can try to find regional differences, or role-play explaining weddings in their country to a foreigner.

At the end of this task, ask students to mention any new vocabulary they heard from their partner(s) or elsewhere during this activity. This hopefully will not only emphasise the usefulness of learning vocabulary from each other, but will also allow further opportunity for recycling.

② Students are now shown a short note about the lecture they will hear in the next task. This note is of the kind found in university subject handbooks – it is included in the Students' Book not just to make students aware that such notes exist (a point that should be emphasised), but also to use as the basis for making predictions, thereby helping the students understand how such notes in subject handbooks can help them.

Task C | Listening for main ideas ▶▶ SB P. 9

One aim of this book is to help students deal with the expression of abstract ideas that they will have to deal with in their further studies courses. This listening takes a topic that many students will find interesting and have some prior knowledge of, and deals with it in a slightly academic, abstract way. The careful scaffolding provided in previous and subsequent tasks should help the students. The lecture has been broken down into sections that are dealt with one-by-one, again to make it easier.

If your students are lacking in confidence with listening, the tasks could be spread over a series of lessons.

Some lower frequency vocabulary is included – without it, the lecture would sound decidedly less authentic. The words *symbol/symbolism/symbolic* have already been introduced, and suggestions for vocabulary to pre-teach include: *bachelor degree, kilt, broom*.

This listening has been broken down into different sections. First students listen to the introduction, for the main ideas of the lecture. Remind students about what they discovered in the reading section of this unit – that ideas usually proceed from general to specific – and mention that this pattern applies to lectures too.

Students tick the ideas as they hear them. One is an odd one out, not mentioned, which the students have to identify.

Give students time to read the list of topics in their books before starting the recording. Depending on the level of the class, it may be a good idea to stop after each paragraph in the recording script. Stop anyway after 2 minutes, 53 seconds (the end of the second paragraph in the recording script).

> **ANSWERS**
>
> *Main topic of the lecture:*
> a. Wedding customs in different cultures
>
> *To be mentioned later:*
> b. Religious and spiritual beliefs
> c. Differences in wedding customs within a country
> d. Recent changes in wedding customs

> *To be mentioned in the next part of the lecture:*
> e. Wedding clothes
> f. Rituals – bride leaves family or joins another
> g. How to stop bad luck ← *Not mentioned*
> h. Symbol of promises
> I. Religious part of the ceremony
> j. Wedding reception.

Recording script

> **Note 1:** Braces are used to indicate intended forms where conversational slips occur. For example, if the script says *They goes {go} to the party*, the correct form is *They go to the party*.
>
> **Note 2:** In this recording, timings are given at the end of each paragraph, to make it easier to find the right place if listening to only a section.

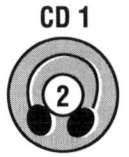

CD 1

CD 1, track 2: Customs Unit 1
(9 minutes, 27 seconds)

Listening 1: Lecture on wedding customs

Narrator: This listening is part of a university lecture, the kind of lecture that might be in the first year of a bachelor degree. It is from a module about customs in different cultures. It takes an interesting topic and introduces it in an academic way.
(Lecture hall noises, scraping chairs, general crowd/student muddle.)

(0 minutes, 35 seconds)

Lecturer: Well, good morning everyone. Now, as I mentioned last week, today's lecture is going to be about wedding ceremonies in different cultures. Now, these ceremonies mark one of the most important of life events, and even in cultures that have largely left their traditions behind, weddings are full of actions that have a great deal of symbolic meaning. Later on we'll look at how we can find out a lot about the religions and spiritual beliefs of cultures by studying wedding ceremonies. Also, we'll look at some examples of differences in marriage customs within a country, you know, to see how much the culture tolerates diversity. And similarly, recent changes in customs will show us something about the social changes in the country – you know, how much the culture is OK with change, and what modern influences are changing that culture. But before that, we'll go briefly through some of the symbolism in wedding ceremonies.

Now, for example, the couple getting married, especially the bride, wear costumes special to the event. Wedding ceremonies usually also include a ritual that symbolises, well, the transfer of either the bride or the groom from one family to the other, or alternatively a joining together of the two families. There is also often a symbol, you know, such as a ring or a necklace, which represent the promises, you know, the long-term commitment the bride and groom make to each other. And, also, traditionally, there is almost always a religious element to this ceremony ... so that everyone gets involved, everyone, sorry, I'll breath ... so that everyone involved gets the idea the marriage is something the relevant god or gods are happy with. Now to put that in other words, to get divine approval for the union. And, the best bit for many people, there is usually a feast and a party after the ceremony, to add a celebratory, happy atmosphere for the couple.

(2 minutes, 53 seconds)

Now, we'll start with the most obvious visual elements – the costumes, and especially the choice of clothes. It's usually the bride who's the centre of attention here, although the groom often does wear especially smart or traditional clothes for the ceremony. For example, yeah, at Scottish weddings he usually wears a kilt. Unlike the groom, though, the bride often wears clothes that are bought especially for the occasion. The colour of her dress usually has a special symbolic meaning. In many Western cultures, and more and more often in Eastern cultures, elaborate white dresses are worn. In the past, white used to mean purity and childhood innocence. Chinese brides traditionally wore red, a colour that in Chinese culture represents good luck – now that's very important in a marriage, wouldn't you say? Now, nowadays, a Chinese bride may wear several different dresses during the wedding ceremony, usually a traditional red dress near the beginning and a Western-style white one later.

(4 minutes, 7 seconds)

Different cultures also look on marriage in different ways. In countries such as, let's say, China, Korea, Turkey, at the wedding the bride literally changes family – What does that mean? Well, she leaves her parents' family and joins her new husband's family. Now, sometimes, she might never see her parents again, so complete is the change. Now, as many of you realise, there is something similar in Western weddings. At the beginning of the ceremony, after everyone has arrived at the church, the bride usually walks down the middle of the church with her father, while everyone watches. During the ceremony, her father 'gives her away', and at the end she leaves with the groom.

(5 minutes, 3 seconds)

And also, at some part of the ceremony, it usually involves {there is usually} a symbolic action to represent the act of marriage, and {this} may involve well, some object that's worn, usually by the bride from the time of the ceremony until she dies, yeah, hm, or until the end of the marriage. Now, it's used as a symbol that the person is in a committed relationship and therefore is not available to other people. For example, in Indian weddings there is often a kind of necklace, now, this is called a mangalsutra … now, I'll just write that up on the board … now, it's tied around the bride's neck during the ceremony. Oh, yeah, I should also mention that in some parts of India it might be called a mangalya, or a thaalli, which can be spelt in two different ways, I'll write that on the board as well, t-h-a-a-l-l-i, or simply t-a-l-l-i … got that? OK. A more familiar example to Western people, and indeed to people from many cultures, is the wedding ring. Now, traditionally, the man gives it to the woman, and nowadays, it's also common for the woman to do the same for the man. What does the ring symbolise? It symbolises eternal commitment and love … ah – the circle of the relationship and love for each other will continue forever. This tradition is spreading to many other cultures around the world, although each often has their own, well, older tradition. In traditional Thai weddings, for example, the relatives tie the hands of the bride and groom together. And in Black American weddings, the couple might jump over a broom together, although they often exchange rings as well.

(7 minutes, 3 seconds)

Usually there is also some symbolic wish for fertility. The example from Western wedding is the throwing of confetti over the bride and groom as they leave the church. These days, the confetti is paper or sometimes rice … however, that tradition came from a ritual from before Christian times, when, would you believe it, nuts were thrown over the happy couple. Now, I think the connection between the nuts and new life and hence fertility, is, umm, as you can appreciate, much clearer than with paper confetti! The wheat used to make the wedding cake is also a symbol of fertility, as are the grains thrown on the ground in front of the bride as she travelled into the place of the wedding in China. Flowers can also serve the same purpose.

(7 minutes, 58 seconds)

After the ceremony itself, well, there is almost certainly a party, which can go on all evening, or in cultures such as in India for several days, and sometimes even weeks. Now, in Western societies, people know this as a reception and {it} has certain fixed elements, well, for example, the seating arrangements for close family members of the newly married couple, and speeches made by particular people in a particular order. And there is usually a large, multi-tiered wedding cake, and this is cut by the bride and groom together at the end of the ceremony. And this cutting together is yet another symbol showing that from now on, they will do many things together. And it's also a symbol of their shared future life together. Another example of the wedding feast is with Islamic weddings – now in these, the feast may go on for one or two days, but never three – because that is considered, well, too much like showing off.

(9 minutes, 6 seconds)

And presents are usually given as well – now, in many cultures these are often household goods as the couple traditionally set up a new home …

Task D | Listening for specific information ▶▶ SB P. 9
Students read the questions in their books, then listen and answer them. A strong class may be able to go straight through to the end of the recording, but the CD can be stopped at the end of each section, and the section repeated as necessary. (Questions are grouped according to the paragraphs in the transcript, and timings for each section are given in amongst the answers.) This section starts at 2 minutes, 53 seconds into the recording.

ANSWERS

1. Who is the centre of attention, the bride or the groom? *The bride*
2. What did the white colour of wedding dresses symbolise, in the past? *Purity and childhood innocence*
3. What colour do Chinese brides traditionally wear? What does this colour symbolise? *Red, to symbolise luck*

4. Do Chinese brides change clothes during the wedding day? *Yes, at least twice – usually a traditional red dress near the beginning and a white, Western-style one later*

(4 minutes, 7 seconds)

5. Name one country in which the bride 'changes family'? *Any one from: China, Turkey, Korea*
6. Who is with a Western bride when she enters the church? *Usually her father*
7. Who is with her when she leaves? *Her new husband, the groom.*

(5 minutes, 3 seconds)

8. What is worn to symbolise the marriage in India?
   a. a ring
   b. a necklace ← *Correct*
   c. a special colour of clothing
   d. a special hair style.
9. What is a spelling of this Indian symbol of marriage? *t-h-a-a-l-l-i , or t-a-l-i*
10. Traditionally, did the woman give the man a wedding ring (in Western weddings)? *No, the man gives it to the woman.*
11. In what country are the bride and groom's hands sometimes tied together? *Thailand*

(7 minutes, 3 seconds)

12. Throwing confetti is a wish for fertility (fertility: ability to have babies)
    a. true ← *Correct*
    b. false
    c. no information given.
13. Before confetti, people used to throw *rice or nuts* over the couple
14. Other symbols of fertility are _____ and _____ *Any two from: nuts, the wheat used to make the wedding cake, the grains thrown on the ground in front of the bride as she travelled into the place of the wedding in China, or flowers.*

(7 minutes, 58 seconds)

15. Which are longer, wedding parties in India or in Western countries? *In India*
16. Western weddings don't have which of the following:
    a. special seating arrangements
    b. people making speeches
    c. people giving money, not presents ← *This one. Presents are preferred!*
    d. the bride and groom cutting the cake together.

17. According to the lecturer, the longest weddings in Islamic cultures are *two* days long.

Task E | Do you need to understand every word? ▶▶ SB P. 10

① Students look at underlined words in two sentences (below) taken from the listening. These are words that students at this level are unlikely to understand – the point is to improve confidence in extracting meaning without understanding every word. Ask students if they needed to understand the underlined words while listening for the answers to the questions in Tasks C and D – in this way, students may realise they are already using context to assist with understanding meaning – and making this explicit to them should help to develop confidence in using inference to understand the meaning of words or expressions they might not know.

- … we'll start with the most obvious <u>visual elements</u> – the costumes, and especially the choice of clothes …
- In many Western cultures, and more and more often in Eastern cultures, <u>elaborate</u> white dresses are worn …

② Ask students how they know the main point of the sentences.

ANSWERS

- First sentence: the words after the hyphen list the visual elements, thus showing the meaning.
- Second sentence: as the underlined word is an adjective, it is less likely to carry meaning that is essential to the sentence than if it was a verb or the main noun of a subject or object.

③ Ask students if they always need to understand every word, to understand the main points?

ANSWER

Hopefully by now students will answer 'no'! If they persist in answering 'yes', you will probably have plenty of ammunition to explain why, as they gave answers to tasks C and D.

Task F | Listening to compare ▶▶ SB P. 10   CD 1

This task moves on to the next CD recording of the unit. Students listen to two students talking to each other after the lecture on the previous listening. They are talking about weddings in Japan. Ask the students to fill in the gaps which show some differences and similarities between a typical Japanese wedding and a typical Western wedding.

Unit 1 Customs | 11

ANSWERS

KAORI'S SISTER (JAPANESE STYLE WEDDING)	WHAT MICHAEL IS USED TO (WESTERN STYLE WEDDING)
ceremony in a ¹*hotel*	ceremony in a religious building, eg a church
traditional weddings usually follow *Shinto* style	traditional weddings are usually Christian
modern weddings are often ²*Christian* style	
the priest performed a ritual with a ³*tree branch* while chanting	
the ⁴*groom* made a promise to the ⁵*bride*	the bride and groom make promises to each other
the bride and groom exchange ⁶*rings*	the bride and groom exchange rings
the wedding party is in a ⁷*hotel*	
people give ⁸*money* as a wedding present	people give household goods as wedding presents
the bride wore ⁹*two* dresses	the bride wears the same dress all the time

Recording script

Note: Braces are used to intended forms where conversational slips occur. For example, if the script says *They goes {go} to the party*, the correct form is *They go to the party*.

CD 1 — CD 1, track 3: Customs, Unit 1
(6 minutes, 31 seconds)

Listening 2: Conversation between two students after the lecture on wedding customs (the previous listening)

Narrator: This listening is between two students as they walk out of the lecture that you heard in the previous unit. Michael is a local student, and is very interested in the culture of the overseas student he has just met, Kaori, from Japan.

(Sound of students talking as they leave a lecture theatre, fades down as the speakers start speaking.)

Michael: Hmm, that was interesting wasn't it?
Kaori: Yes, it was … good to hear about the weddings in different cultures. I found out all sorts of interesting things. But he didn't say much about Japanese weddings.
Michael: No, he didn't, and that's a pity. Are they similar to anything he mentioned?
Kaori: Well, I'll say that's … 'yes' and 'no'. I went to my sister's wedding a few months ago, not long before I came here, actually.
Michael: Oh, did you? I bet that was interesting!
Kaori: Well, I've been to a few so I know what they're like … interesting in a different way for me … er, seeing my sister go off and leave the family. It was kind of like, er, saying goodbye to her.
Michael: So … tell me what happens …
Kaori: Mmm, I guess there are two stages. The first was kind of the religious part, in a hotel.
Michael: Er, hang on, in a hotel? … you mean, the religion owns hotels?
Kaori: Oh, no, the hotel has a special hall for weddings, and there are {is} a kind of Shinto shrine there
Michael: A what, er, Shinto?
Kaori: Yeah, that's the native religion of Japan. People who want traditional weddings usually choose Shinto, and people wanting modern style usually go for Christian style – although not for religious reasons. There are sometimes Buddhist wedding ceremonies as well, but usually only for the people who follow Buddhism strongly.
Michael: Oh, I see, you mean so the people can choose a style of wedding, they don't just have to follow a religion! Eh, that's cool. Eh, want to sit down? … sounds like this'll take a few minutes .. want to pop in here for a coffee?
Kaori: Oh yes, that's {a} good idea.
Michael: Now, let's see, where were we? Oh yeah, you were telling me about your sister's ceremony.
Kaori: Oh, yes, the priest was doing all kinds of things to purify everyone. He waved a tree

	branch around while he was chanting ... it was a very traditional atmosphere. And then my sister's hus ... and then my sister's boyfriend ... oooh, sorry, her husband-to-be, made his promise to her ...
Michael:	Like to love, honour and obey?
Kaori:	Yeah, something similar – that's what people say at Western weddings, isn't it?
Michael:	Well, maybe they miss out the obey bit these days.
Kaori:	And then they performed a small ritual with sake, drinking from each other's sake cups ... and then they exchanged rings.
Michael:	Oh, is that bit traditional, I mean, the exchanging of rings, you know?
Kaori:	Oh no, that's like the lecturer said ... exchanging rings is being taken up by other cultures.
Michael:	Oh yeah, that's right. And then what happened?
Kaori:	Everyone moved to a big room in a {the} hotel. The bit before that was only for close family, like a private ceremony. The next bit was like the reception in Western weddings, with lots of friends and other people who knew the couple, as well as other {others} in the family. We all went to the big room, signed our names and handed over the present.
Michael:	Ohhhh, what do people usually give? I mean, is it like in Western countries where it's, you know, usually things for the house, and the poor couple get 27 toasters and nothing they really need?
Kaori:	Nope, we don't give presents, just money. We put about twenty or thirty thousand yen in an envelope and hand the envelope over. That's about 100 or 150 pounds.
Michael:	Wow, now that's a generous present! What about the wedding dress?
Kaori:	Yeah, she wore two different dresses.
Michael:	Not at the same time, I hope!
Kaori:	No, don't be silly! It's a bit like the Chinese wedding dress custom that the lecturer described. People usually change during the wedding – sometimes there are more than two dresses. My sister only wore two – she wore a traditional wedding kimono for the religious part, then changed to a Western dress during the reception. But it wasn't white, it was light blue.
Michael:	So what was the reception like?
Kaori:	Well, it's kind of {a} mixture of fun and formality – the older people make long speeches and the younger people sing together and entertain everyone! It ... you know, even my dad's boss gave a speech.
Michael:	Hang on a minute, your dad's boss! What was he doing at the wedding?
Kaori:	Well, actually, he was the most important person there to make a speech – there should be someone old and wise to make a {the} first speech, it makes it feel like it's dignified and has got a {the} approval of someone important. And we ate and ate lots of food ... I think there were 12 courses.
Michael:	12? Wow, at least no one went hungry! But it all sounds really expensive!
Kaori:	Yeah, I always reckon you have to be rich to get married in Japan nowadays ... sometimes, people travel to other countries to get married– that way, you know, not many people can come, so it's a lot cheaper!
Michael:	What, even with the cost of travel?
Kaori:	Yeah, well, they'd go on a honeymoon anyway. And, it's not just the expense. If there {are} fewer guests, the feeling is closer, and more personal – some people <u>like</u> that.
Michael:	Oh, I see ... sounds a bit like eloping!

Task G | Discussion ▶▶ SB P. 10

Various questions are provided for students to discuss in small groups.

PHRASAL VERBS

Task A | About phrasal verbs ▶▶ SB P. 11

❶ Students look at a short conversation in their books and circle each verb. They are also asked the questions on the next page, which lead to a definition of a phrasal verb.

> **ANSWERS**
>
> **a.** Circle each verb:
>   A: Hey, Libby, (have) you (heard)? Tom's (going out) with Rebecca!
>   B: Really! I (know) they (get on) well with each other, that ('s) good news!
>   A: Yeah, they (got together) at Rebecca's sister's wedding last week
>   B: I (was going) to (drop in) on Rebecca later … (can't wait) to (hear) the whole story
>
> **b.** Which verbs have more than one word (these are called phrasal verbs)?
>   - *going out*
>   - *get on*
>   - *got together*
>   - *drop in*
>
> **c.** What is the meaning of each phrasal verb?
>   *(students may be able to work out some of the meaning from context, or at least make guesses)*
>   - go out (with someone): *have a relationship with each other as boyfriend and girlfriend*
>   - get on (with someone): *like each other; have a friendly relationship with each other*
>   - get together: *usually means* meet *but in this context, start their relationship as boyfriend and girlfriend*
>   - drop in: *visit*
>
> **d.** For each phrasal verb, does each word in the verb help you find the meaning?
>   No. For example, take <u>get on</u>. Adding the meanings of <u>get</u> and <u>on</u> does not result in the meaning of the phrasal verb <u>get on</u>. This idiomatic nature of phrasal verbs is one of their defining features.

> **ANSWERS**
>
> | PHRASAL VERBS | REGULAR VERBS |
> |---|---|
> | bring up (eg children) | raise |
> | carry on (doing something) | continue |
> | carry out | do |
> | drop in (on someone) | visit |
> | die out | stop happening (eg a tradition) |
> | give up (something/doing something) | stop doing |
> | look up to (someone) | admire |
> | look down on (someone) | disrespect |
> | look into (something) | investigate |
> | put up with (something) | tolerate |
> | try out (something) | test |
> | wake up | awaken |

> **Note:** Phrasal verbs are *usually less formal and more conversational* than their regular verb equivalents.

Some writers (eg Kennedy, 2003) make a distinction between verbs combined with adverbs and verbs combined with prepositions, calling the former phrasal verbs and the latter prepositional verbs. However, this book stays with the terminology that's more likely to be familiar and useful to students, putting all varieties of multi-word verbs in the category of phrasal verbs. Besides, the distinction is so subtle that it is not likely to be of advantage to the students.

❷ Ask students, in pairs, to match the phrasal verbs listed in their books with the one-word verbs also listed. They will already know some of them. For other words, a class set of English-English dictionaries will be useful. Ask them, while doing this, to think about whether the phrasal verbs are more formal or informal than the other verbs – they will know some anyway, and the conversation in Question 1 will also give them clues.

❸ This question introduces the concept that some phrasal verbs are separable and others aren't. Ask students to look at the sentences in the Students' Book, noticing particularly where the particle of the phrasal verb comes in relation to the object of the sentence.

They should notice that, in the first group (with *give up*), the particle can come immediately after the verb or after the object, that is, the phrasal verb can separate unless the object is a pronoun, in which case, it *must* separate.

(Incidentally, constructions such as *Tom should give smoking up*, ie with the verb separated and with a non-pronoun object, are possible but can sound rather awkward.)

The second group (with *put up*) shows a phrasal verb with a different behaviour. This one cannot separate even with a pronoun.

Phrasal verbs generally fall into these two categories and students have to learn which is which.

Task B | Practice ▶▶ SB P. 11

① Ask students to re-write the sentences in their book with a phrasal verb in place of the regular verb. Point out that some of these sentences sound very formal, thus re-writing them with the phrasal verbs should make them sound more natural.

ANSWERS

a. Her father was well known for working for charities. She *looked up* to him.
b. His mother *wakes* him *up* early every morning.
c. The town's traditional festival has fewer and fewer people taking part each year. However, the mayor doesn't want the town to *give* it *up*.
d. People ask the surgeon to perform many operations every year. He still *carries* them *out*, even though he's seventy.
e. Japan has many interesting festivals. The university professor is *looking into* how they began.
f. Their children are very respectful. Their parents are *bringing* them *up* in traditional ways.
g. Before he buys a new computer, he wants to *try* it *out* at home.
h. Your snoring's terrible! I won't *put up* with it any more!
i. *Drop in* any time! You're very welcome!

The next two activities are fluency activities to practise using phrasal verbs, and they should be modified depending on your students' preferences and learning styles. Alternatively, these games could be used as warm-ups or review activities in subsequent lessons. For each activity, students should be encouraged to use phrasal verbs they already know as well as the ones in this unit. It may help to get students to brainstorm lists of phrasal verbs in groups, and then give feedback to the class, before commencing either of these activities.

The last person holding the ball loses the game.

② Get students into small groups. Give each group a ball (or make one by screwing up some scrap paper). Each group should choose a topic to tell a story about – you can give them some ideas (see below) if this helps. The student who starts should keep talking until they use a phrasal verb, at which point they pass the ball to the next student, who then continues the story from where the last person left off. So they continue, until you, after a time limit, stop the game. The person holding the ball at this point is 'out'. This can be repeated several times.

③ In pairs, students should tell a story for up to two minutes, using as many phrasal verbs as possible. Each time, the partner who is listening will count the number of phrasal verbs used. The winner of each round is the partner who used the most.

You will probably have to give students some topics to get them started – some ideas are given below.

Suggested topics for activities 2 and 3
- a famous actor or singer
- a cartoon character
- someone in your class
- a dog or cat

SPEAKING 2 | SPECIFIC AND GENERAL QUESTIONS; LEARNING STYLES QUIZ

The specific questions in Task A, which are around the topic of this unit, relate to students' personal experiences, and thus are the kinds of questions that are most common in General English classes that the students may have experienced before. Students will naturally use lots of personal pronouns (*I, you* etc). Task B on the other hand gives far more general questions, which shouldn't be answered with personal pronouns except to illustrate a general point with examples from the students' own experience. Students will get far more familiar with the general type of questions as they continue their EAP career, but if this is early in their EAP course, it may be necessary to push students quite hard to avoid too much personal anecdote in their answers. Task B may be good preparation for certain exams which reward an ability to move away from talking about the personal.

Task A | Specific questions ▶▶ SB P. 12

The questions in the Students' Book tell the students exactly what to do. It may help to introduce Question 1 (about things students found surprising when they visited another country) with personal anecdotes of your own.

For convenience, here are the students' questions.

① Tell your partner about some time when you visited another country (perhaps where you are studying, if it isn't your own country) and were surprised by a cultural difference. Also, what cultural similarities surprised you?

② Tell your partner about a festival that you went to in your country. Then your partner will ask you questions about the festival.

③ Imagine your speaking partner is a friend from another country, and will visit your family soon. Tell your friend about the customs they will need to know. Your friend will ask you what to do in certain situations.

Unit 1 Customs | 15

Task B | General questions ▶▶ SB P. 12

Ask students to think quietly about the questions in their Students' Books, making notes in their note books. Emphasise that these are only to help them with ideas for speaking – this is not a writing exercise.

Then students should tell their ideas to the group, who will then discuss them.

Again, here are the students' questions for your convenience:

a. Do you think it is important to continue the traditions of the past?
b. Do you think that traditions should change with the influence of other cultures? (Perhaps think about the effect of US culture on the rest of the world)
c. How much do you think movies and music from other cultures have changed your culture from when your grandparents were young?
d. Has the culture in your country changed a lot over the last 50 years?
e. Do you expect your country's culture will change a lot in the future?

Task C | How do you like to learn languages? ▶▶ SB P. 12

This is an extra fun activity similar to one in Unit 1 of *EAP Now!* It is designed to acquaint students with their own style of learning, especially if they have not considered it much before, and to assist them and encourage them to experiment with different methods of learning. It may also reassure them that there is not only one way to learn successfully.

Students answer the questions in the Students' Book. Then, they refer to a box on the next page to find a score based on their answers. This then refers them to a box that gives some features of their learning style (that hopefully they will identify with), together with some advice about how they can compensate for any bias that their natural learning style may introduce to their language learning, for example, being overly focused on accuracy to the detriment of fluency.

When they have completed this, ask them to form groups of three students with opposite learning styles (as closely as the learning style distribution in the class allows), and to discuss the strengths and weaknesses of each learning style. Then, ask them to list suggestions for their own study, possibly based on how their partner studies. Encourage them to experiment with these different learning styles.

FURTHER PRACTICE: READING, FILMS AND FUN

READING

Travel guides can give some good information about cultures. For example, try:

http://www.lonelyplanet.com/worldguide/ or
http://travel.roughguides.com/destinationshome.html.

For more specific information about countries, you can look at:

http://www.infoplease.com/countries.html and
http://www.cia.gov/cia/publications/factbook/

http://www.shaadi.com/wedding/rituals/wedding.php explains several different wedding traditions common in India.

http://weddings.lovetoknow.com/wiki/Main_Page has quite a lot of information on Western weddings.

http://www.central-mosque.com/fiqh/Wedding.htm lists and explains some of the rules of Islamic weddings.

FILMS

There are many films showing people dealing with living in different cultures. For example:

Bend it like Beckham, directed by Gurinder Chanda. A comedy about a girl who is a member of a family from India living in London. She wants to play soccer, but her family have other ideas.

Seven Years in Tibet, directed by Jean-Jacques Annaud. An Austrian is lost in Tibet.

Dances with Wolves, directed by Kevin Costner. An American soldier learns about Native American culture.

Weddings were the topic of part of this unit, and the following films show weddings in different cultures:

India: *Monsoon Wedding*, directed by Mira Nair.

Australia: *Muriel's Wedding*, directed by PJ Hogan.

USA: *Father of the Bride*, directed by Charles Shyer.

QUESTIONS

1. What happens on a child's birthday in your country?

2. Describe a typical baby naming ceremony in your culture. Are there sometimes variations (differences) from the traditional ceremonies? If so, describe the differences.

3. When some people get married, they choose to make the ceremony different from what is traditional in their culture. For example, they hold the ceremony on a beach at sunset, or the wedding dress is a different colour. What would happen at your ideal wedding, and why?

4. Many countries have national days on which people might dress in traditional costumes, eat special food, or take part in ceremonies and processions. Describe a day like this from your own culture.

5. Should marriage be for life? Or is it OK for people to be married more than once during their lifetime?

2 TRADE

'a thief passes for a gentleman when stealing has made him rich'

BY THE END OF THIS UNIT, STUDENTS SHOULD:

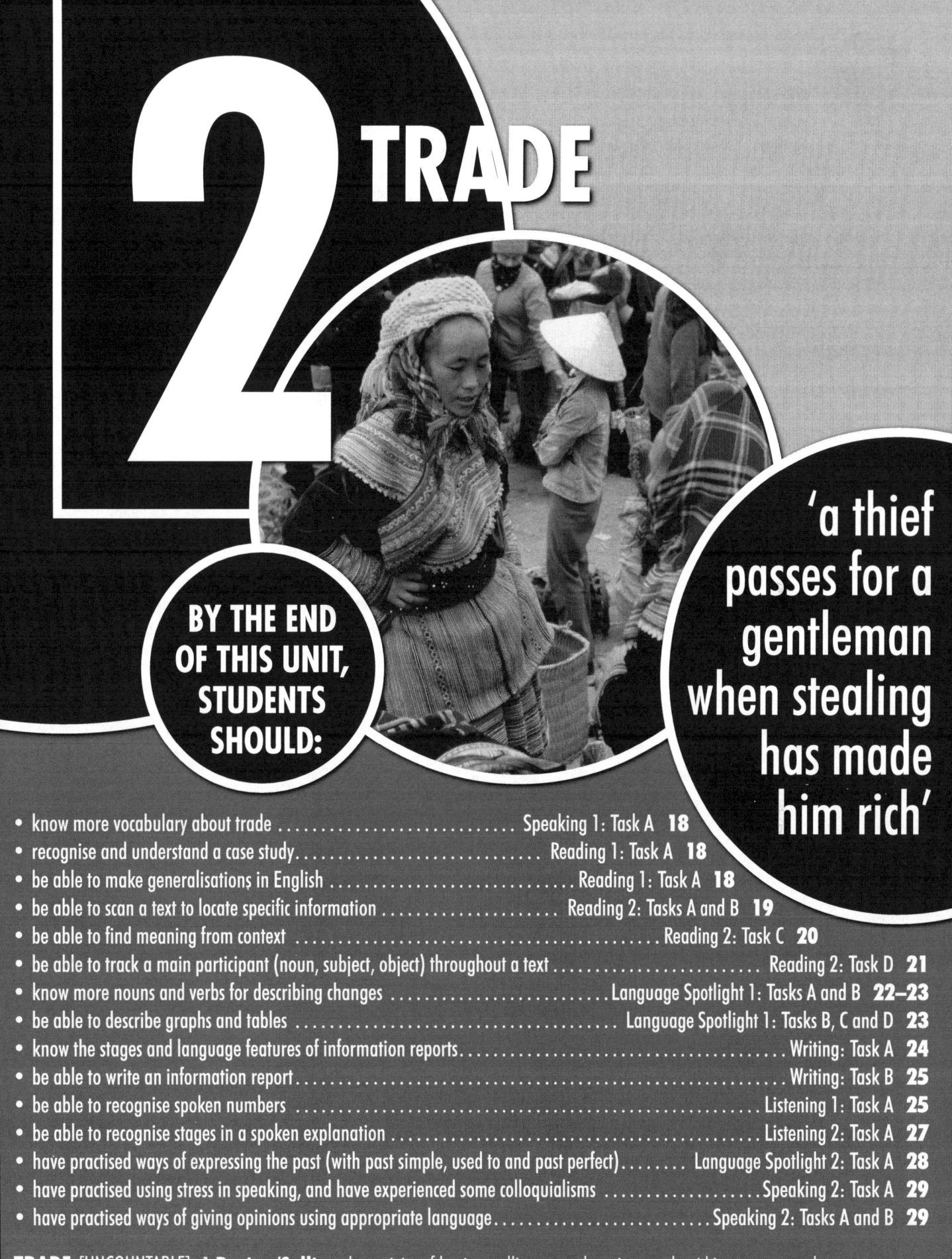

- know more vocabulary about trade .... Speaking 1: Task A **18**
- recognise and understand a case study .... Reading 1: Task A **18**
- be able to make generalisations in English .... Reading 1: Task A **18**
- be able to scan a text to locate specific information .... Reading 2: Tasks A and B **19**
- be able to find meaning from context .... Reading 2: Task C **20**
- be able to track a main participant (noun, subject, object) throughout a text ..... Reading 2: Task D **21**
- know more nouns and verbs for describing changes .... Language Spotlight 1: Tasks A and B **22–23**
- be able to describe graphs and tables .... Language Spotlight 1: Tasks B, C and D **23**
- know the stages and language features of information reports .... Writing: Task A **24**
- be able to write an information report .... Writing: Task B **25**
- be able to recognise spoken numbers .... Listening 1: Task A **25**
- be able to recognise stages in a spoken explanation .... Listening 2: Task A **27**
- have practised ways of expressing the past (with past simple, used to and past perfect) .... Language Spotlight 2: Task A **28**
- have practised using stress in speaking, and have experienced some colloquialisms .... Speaking 2: Task A **29**
- have practised ways of giving opinions using appropriate language .... Speaking 2: Tasks A and B **29**

TRADE [UNCOUNTABLE]: 1 **Buying/Selling** the activity of buying, selling, or exchanging goods within a country or between countries; = commerce; *There has been a marked increase in trade between East and West.* 2 **The hotel/tourist etc trade** the business done by companies, hotels etc; 3 **Amount of business** [U] *BrE* business activity, especially the amount of goods or products that are sold; = business: *A lot of pubs nowadays do most of their trade at lunchtimes.* 4 **An exchange of things** [sing.] *AmE* when you exchange something you have for something that someone else has: *Let's **make a trade**.*

SPEAKING 1 — BUILDING THE FIELD

Task A | Asking questions about trade ▶▶ SB P. 16

① Divide students into pairs. Student A asks Student B questions. The format for answering is provided for Student B in the Students' Book. They exchange places after Question [h] and repeat the conversation. The questions are:
- **a.** Student A: Do you know what trade means?
- **b.** Student A: Have you traded something in your life?
- **c.** Student A: What items did you trade and how old were you when you did this? *(answer truthfully)*
- **d.** Student A: Can you give me a definition – can you tell me what the word 'trade' means? *(tell in own words)*
- **e.** Student A: What country do you come from? *(answer truthfully)*
- **f.** Student A: What is your country famous for trading? *(Note: In this question students research the definitions of export and import.)*
- **g.** Student A: What does your country export?
- **h.** Student A: What does your country import?

ANSWERS

1. f. Definition of export and import from *Longman Dictionary of Contemporary English*, 2003 New Edition.

Export – Verb form 1. to sell goods to another country. Noun form 1. the business of selling and sending goods to other countries.

Import – Verb form 1. to bring a product from one country into another so that it can be sold there. Noun form 1. a product that is brought from one country into another so that it can be sold there, or the business of doing this. 2. something new or different that is brought to a place where it did not previously exist: *The beetle is thought to be a European import.* 3 formal importance or meaning: *a matter of no great import.*

2. Students write the question words that were used.
- a. Do you?
- b. Have you?
- c. What?
- d. Can you?
- e. What?
- f. What?
- g. What?
- h. What?

READING 1 — MAKING GENERALISATIONS – CASE STUDY

Task A | Making generalisations from a case study ▶▶ SB P. 16

This is a basic introduction to a case study and provides ways of drawing and expressing general conclusions (making inferences) from texts. The case study text is taken directly from a text book for business studies courses (Hartley, 2002).

① This question sets the scene.
② and ③ These questions direct students to respond to the text on a personal level.
④ Students now look at generalisations. You may have to explain "appropriate conclusion" by giving the answer to the first question (question a) as an example.
⑤ Students induce some of the grammatical and lexical choices involved in expressing generalisations.
⑥ This question provides some personalised practice in making generalisations. This may be relevant to the speaking section of various international English examinations.

For those students who are from educational cultures in which the drawing of conclusions is not emphasised, this task gives exposure to the expectations of a 'Western' educational system.

ANSWERS

Answers to Questions 1, 2 and 3 will vary.

4. (i) Students are asked to put a tick or a cross against the appropriate conclusion from the case study.

- **a.** *If a salesperson asks a customer as soon as they enter the shop 'May I help you?', they might make the customer feel uncomfortable.*
  Yes (✓): Kevin 'hated pushy sales people who …' Because this is true for Kevin, it might be true for other people as well. A key word here is *might*. Without this word, the conclusion is invalid.
- **b.** *In Kevin's culture, shop sales people don't try to help customers.*
  (X) No: this is unlikely to be generally true because Kevin felt irritated when people didn't help him.
- **c.** *Customers who don't ask for help don't get served.*
  (X) No: just because it happened once, in this case, doesn't mean it's generally true. In fact, Kevin's annoyance that no-one helped him indicates this point probably isn't generally true.
- **d.** *In Kevin's culture, customers don't ask for help.*
  (X) No: Kevin didn't ask for help, but this doesn't mean that other people don't ask for

18 | EAP Now! Preliminary English for Academic Purposes Teacher's Book

help. Again, it isn't safe to draw a conclusion from just one example.
  e. *In Kevin's culture, if people want to replace something that's broken, they always bring the broken thing to the shop.*
     (X) Again, one example proves nothing.
  f. *A shop might sell more things if the sales people speak to customers.*
     (✓) Yes – they would have sold a plate if they had asked Kevin if he wanted help.
  (ii) Students work out which of the statements in (i) is the main point of the case study and why.

  Point [f] is the main point (points to indicate this are: the title of the case study; that a theme throughout is that the shop assistants ignored Kevin; that Kevin couldn't get the help he wanted and left without buying anything.)
5. Generalisations
  a. Which tenses/verb forms are usually used for generalisations? (These are commonly used in other generalisations.) *Present simple or present modals.*
  b. Do generalisations use specific words for people (like me, he or the person's name), or do they use general words (eg customers, people)? *General words*
  c. Do generalisations use singulars or plurals? *Plurals (for the general words from [b])*
6. Personalised practice. Answers will vary.

The price paid for ignoring the customer

With a wallet in one hand and a broken plate in the other, Kevin entered the shop.

As he walked around the store, he noticed that it was empty; he was the only customer on both floors. The only other people in the building were three sales people standing around one of the sales counters.

At first, Kevin was quite happy to browse because he hated pushy sales people who approach every new customer as soon as they start looking at something and ask 'Can I help you?'. However, as time passed, Kevin started to become a little irritated, especially when he noticed that the three staff were all standing around the sales counter discussing the choice of music being played over the in-store PA system.

Kevin was confused. There was no-one else in the shop; people could see him easily and, for good measure, his wallet and broken plate made his purpose for being in the shop very clear. His intention to buy a new plate could not have been more clear.

All the tried and tested attempts to attract the staff's attention like coughing, picking up the merchandise and rattling the cutlery failed. So did walking directly past the front counter where the staff were still talking about themselves.

After 15 minutes of being ignored, what else could Kevin do? He left the shop.

READING 2 | SCANNING, FINDING MEANING FROM CONTEXT, TRACKING PARTICIPANTS – INFORMATION REPORT

Task A | Introduction to the Silk Road ▶▶ SB P. 18

This task provides an introduction to the field of the next text in this section, activating knowledge of this field. Students discuss some questions given in the Students' Book before proceeding to the reading.

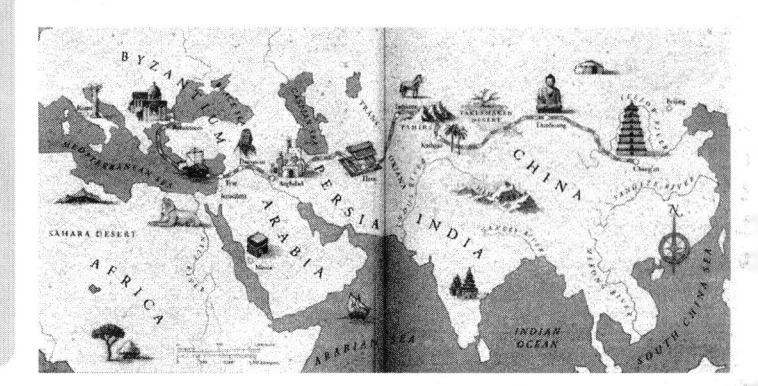

Source: The Oracle Education Foundation (ND), '*The Silk Road: Linking Europe and Asia by Trade*'. Available: http://library.thinkquest.org/13406/sr/, accessed 8 January 2007.

Task B | Introduction to scanning ▶▶ SB P. 18

This task introduces scanning, specifically in order to find the right place in the text to find answers to questions.

In Question 1, ask students to read the questions before they start reading the text. The words in bold appear in a later task about finding meaning from context, so don't explain their meaning here. The words have been carefully chosen such that, even if the students don't know all of them, the context should provide sufficient information for them to complete the task. By doing this, they should increase their confidence in dealing with unknown vocabulary.

It's important to give a time limit for scanning, after they have read the questions (1 minute).

Note: There are two stages to answering Questions [a] to [h]: in Question 1, they only locate where in the text they will find the answer, and in Question 2 they actually provide the answer. The reason is that they will not have time to write (or think about) the actual answers while scanning.

ANSWERS

1.

Line nos		
7	[a]	How were **goods** carried?
17	[b]	Why did Chan Ch'ien make **alliances** with the local tribes?
32	[c]	Was silk **lucrative**?
36	[d]	Which **commodities** were silk traded for?
39	[e]	What effect did high **duties** have on the cost of silk in the Roman Empire?
48	[f]	When did trade along the Silk Road first **decline**? Why?
53	[g]	When did trade **increase**?
56	[h]	Why did Silk Road trade finally **decrease**?

2. Suggested answers
   - [a] on animals/by caravan
   - [b] to expand the silk trade to the smaller tribes
   - [c] yes
   - [d] eg silk, gold and silver
   - [e] silk became even more expensive
   - [f] by 760AD, because thieves started to attack the caravans again
   - [g] 11th and 12th centuries and 1276–1368
   - [h] sea trade routes became safer

3 Some students resist strategies that don't involve reading every word, and will answer 'yes' to the question 'Did you read the whole text to find these answers?'. If they do, try to convince them that, when they are at university or in other further studies, they will have so much to read that they won't have time to read the whole text. You might show some real university/college reading material to students at this point.

4 Ask students whether they would scan, skim or read everything in detail in each of the situations given in their text books.

ANSWERS

QUESTION	ANSWER
[a] finding someone's number in a phone book	scanning
[b] finding out about a bank account by reading a small leaflet	reading in detail
[c] finding the interest rate of a bank account by reading a small leaflet	scanning
[d] finding a price in a leaflet	scanning
[e] understanding a complicated explanation	reading in detail
[f] looking for a date in a text	scanning
[g] finding all the reasons that the Silk Road trade declined	reading in detail (or skimming, depending on how much detail is given for each reason)
[h] finding the main points covered in a book chapter	skimming
[i] finding a paragraph in a book chapter about the first Silk Road traders	skimming and scanning

Task C | Introduction to finding meaning from context ▶▶ SB P. 19

Some of the words here relate to trade, while others are useful for describing rises and falls over time. Graphs and tables are often used to describe such rises and falls, which are the subject of the Language Spotlight 1 section, following.

ANSWERS

WORDS	MEANINGS
goods	things that are traded
alliances	countries or people that have decided to work together to help each other
lucrative	something that makes lots of money
commodities	things that are bought and sold – usually something natural, eg metal or food.
duties	taxes on things imported into a country
decline	to get lower, to go down
increase	to get higher, to go up
decrease	to get lower, to go down

Note: **Bold** words are to help with the answers to Task C, Question 1. Circled and *italicised* words are the answers to Task D, Question 1. Underlined words are the answers to Question 2 of the Language Spotlight 2 section on page 28 of this book and page 24 of the Students' Book.

The Silk Road: Linking Europe and Asia through *Trade*

1 The Silk Road is one of the best known ancient trading routes. It was a **major link** between East and West, and for this reason, it has been very important in history.

Origins

5 Originally, the Chinese traded silk within its own empire. Caravans, which were large groups of animals carrying **goods** for *trade*, would carry silk from the empire's interior to the western edges of the region. Often thieves would attack these caravans hoping to
10 capture the *traders'* valuable goods. As a result, the Han Dynasty extended its military defences further into Central Asia from 135 to 90 BC to protect these caravans.

Chan Ch'ien, the first known Chinese traveller
15 to make contact with the Central Asian tribes, later thought of expanding *the silk trade* to include these smaller tribes and therefore made **alliances** with them. Because of this idea, the Silk Road was born. The route grew with the rise of the Roman Empire, because *the*
20 *Chinese gave silk to the Roman and Asian governments as gifts.*

Spanning Two Continents

The 11,000 kilometre route spanned China, Central Asia, Northern India, and the Parthian and Roman
25 Empires. It connected the Yellow River Valley to the Mediterranean Sea and passed through the present-day countries of Iran, Iraq and Syria.

People who lived in the North West of India, near the Ganges River, played important roles as middlemen
30 in the *China-Mediterranean silk trade* because as early as the third century AD, they understood that silk was a **lucrative** product of the Chinese Empire. *The trading relationship between the Chinese and the Indians* grew stronger with increased Chinese expansion into Central
35 Asia. The Chinese would trade their silk with the Indians for **commodities** such as jade, gold, and silver, and the Indians would trade the silk with the Roman Empire. Silk proved to be an expensive import for the Roman Empire since heavy **duties** were collected across
40 India and Central Asia by the Parthian Empire.

Social Consequences of the Silk Road

Because of the number of people travelling along the Silk Road not only goods but also ideas were conveyed. One of the most important effects of *the trade route*
45 was that Buddhism spread from India to China.

The Silk Road's Decline

As table 1 shows, by 760 AD, *trade* along the Silk Road had **declined**. This was because robbers had started to attack the caravans again. Trade revived considerably
50 in the eleventh and twelfth centuries when China became largely dependent on *its silk trade*. In addition, *trade* to Central and Western Asia as well as Europe **increased** from 1276 to 1368 when the Mongols controlled China. However, after that, *overland trade*
55 became increasingly dangerous, and sea routes *became* more popular, so *trade* along the Silk Road **decreased**.

Period	Years	Trade activity
Warring States Period	before 206BC	none
Roman Empire/Han Dynasty	206BC – AD220	some
Early T'ang Dynasty	6th–7th century AD	the highest of all
Middle of T'ang Dynasty	AD760	less
Song Dynasty	11th – 12th century AD	higher again
Yuan Dynasty	AD1276–1368	even higher
Ming Dynasty	15th century AD	much lower

65 **TABLE 1:** Trade activity along the Silk Road
Source: adapted from The Oracle Education Foundation (ND), 'The Silk Road: Linking Europe and Asia by Trade'. Available: http://library.thinkquest.org/13406/sr/, accessed 8 January 2007.

Task D | Tracking participants ▶▶ SB P. 20

In English, readers (and writers) keep a main idea and sometimes many main ideas in their minds as they read. A main idea is usually a participant. In this example, students follow 'the Silk Road' through the text noting where it is mentioned using referencing and substitution. Writers reference and substitute in order to avoid repetition.

Once your students complete the tracking of the phrase 'the Silk Road' and its forms, you could also track the concept of 'trade'. That concept is italicised rather than circled in the text.

Both main participants are found in the title of the historical report and that is usually the case.

Example 1: Tracking participants 1

Track the word 'road'. Follow the word throughout the text. In English, we use substitution as well as repetition (repeating a word).

> The road is long. It was made by men. The road is famous around the world. The road is really a silk route. It is a trading route. It is the Silk Road.

Unit 2 Trade | 21

Another way to show the links is by displaying them in a linear manner. This could go on the board.

The road
It
The road
The road
silk route
It
trading route
It
Silk Road

Example 2: Tracking participants 2
Track the word 'history'. Follow the word throughout the text.

(History) repeats (itself). If we study (it), we are supposed to learn from (it). (The past) is supposed to be a guide for humans. Without (it) we lose our way. Without knowledge of (prior events), we can repeat our mistakes. We need to study (history) to have better societies.

As in Example 1 this can be shown by displaying them in a linear manner on the board.

History
Itself
it
it
The past
it
prior events
history

Students track the participant – 'the *Silk Road*' – throughout the reading, (a historical report – *The Silk Road: Linking Europe and Asia through Trade*), circling each reference to it. The first paragraph is done for them in the Students' Book.

ANSWER

Please see the text in Task C above – the answers to this question are circled. Where something is circled and italicised this is because a participant also refers both to 'the Silk Road' and to 'trade'.

Task E | The five questions for any reading ▶▶ SB P. 20
Here, the five questions refer to the text *The Silk Road: Linking Europe and Asia through Trade,* in the Students' Book.

ANSWERS

[a] **What are you reading? What is it?** (an article, poem, a review, an extract from somewhere, a definition, a short story, an essay?)
A historical text titled, 'The Silk Road: Linking Europe and Asia Through Trade'. It's an information report genre; a historical report.

[b] **What is the source?** In other words, where does the text come from? (Newspaper, journal, text book, novel, dictionary, thesaurus, magazine?).
Adapted from a website listed beneath the reading text, published by the Oracle Foundation.

[c] **Who is the writer?**
In this case, we don't know the original author (just their organisation). However, it has been adapted, so the writers of some small parts of it are the author/s of this book, ie the book we are studying from, K Cox & D Hill.

[d] **What purpose does the writer have for writing the text?**
It has more than one purpose. First, the purpose is to provide some history around the Silk Road – its origins, location, social consequences and decline. Secondly, since the authors of the book adapted it, it is meant to teach us grammar as well.

[e] **Who is the intended audience?**
Anyone interested in the Silk Road, maybe high school students, students using this book to get better at English.

VOCABULARY DESCRIBING GRAPHS AND TABLES

Task A | Further vocabulary for describing graphs and tables ▶▶ SB P. 20
This task adds to the vocabulary for describing changes with time introduced in the previous section, and assists students in their awareness of the different forms of these verbs.

ANSWERS

1. Match words with similar meanings:
One group of similar meaning: *decline, drop, fall, decrease, reduce*
Another group of similar meaning: *increase, rise, climb, grow*

2. Write the past simple form of each of the words and the past participle.

BARE INFINITIVE	PAST SIMPLE FORM	PAST PARTICIPLE
climb	climbed	climbed
decline	declined	declined
decrease	decreased	decreased
drop	dropped	dropped
fall	fell	fallen
grow	grew	grown
increase	increased	increased
reduce	reduced	reduced
rise	rose	risen

Task B | Noun forms of the verbs ▶▶ SB P. 21

Students now extend their ability to use the vocabulary further by looking at noun forms of the verbs. This also raises their awareness of parts of speech, and provides an opportunity to review *there is/are/was/were* – a structure that students often forget to use.

[f] and [g] of Question 1 show that this language point can be applied to other tenses.

ANSWERS

1. A sentence transformation activity, where students are asked to change the noun form of a word into a verb.
   a. There was an **increase** in the number of robberies on the Silk Road.
      → *The number of robberies on the Silk Road increased.*
   b. After this, there was a **decline** in trade on the Silk Road
      → *After this, trade on the Silk Road declined.*
   c. There was a **decline** in Silk Road trade to almost nothing when travel by ship became safer than the overland route.
      → *Silk Road trade declined to almost nothing when travel by ship became safer than the overland route.*
   d. There was significant **growth** in Australia's exports of iron during 2005.
      → *Australia's exports of iron grew significantly during 2005.*
   e. There was a rise in the number of overseas students in New Zealand between 1985 and 2005
      → *The number of overseas students in New Zealand rose between 1985 and 2005.*
   f. There has been a **growth** in my vocabulary since I started using this book
      → *My vocabulary has grown since I started using this book.*
   g. I'm hoping that my English level will **rise** quickly over the next year
      → *I'm hoping that there will be an increase in my English level over the next year.*

2. What pattern do you notice in the noun and verb forms of most of these words? *For many of these words, the noun form and the verb form are the same.*

3. Gap fill (answers may vary, as long as they represent the arrows and fit the context correctly):

   I started learning English in junior high school, but I wasn't very good and my level **went up** [↑] very slowly. I think this was because I couldn't see a good reason to learn English at that time. However, I became more interested in English later and my level **increased** [↑] more quickly. Then, when I studied for the university entrance exams, my English ability **rose** [↑] even faster. But, when I was at university, I didn't need to use English at all, so my level **fell** [↓]. After university, I worked with people from East Asia, and I had to use English with them. Therefore my English **got better** [↑] again. After a couple of years, I decided to study in the UK, so I had to study for an English exam. Therefore there was another **rise** [↑] in my English level, but not as fast as I wanted. When I went to the UK, though, there was a much faster **increase** [↑] in my English level, because I could practise outside class, and because when I learnt something in lessons, it wasn't long before I heard or saw examples in real life. Now, I'm studying hard – I think my reading ability is **getting better** [↑] because I have to read many journal articles every day, but my speaking level is **dropping** [↓]!

Task C | Practice – Describing graphs and tables ▶▶ SB P. 22

This is an information gap activity: students will have to refer to information in Appendix 4 at the back of their text books. Each student describes a graph to a partner who draws it according to what they understand.

Task D | Have a go! ▶▶ SB P. 22

By completing Question 1, students have the information and support to produce extended answers in Question 2. Encourage plenty of questions in Question 2 to ensure interactivity and that the language becomes real to the students.

WRITING

INFORMATION REPORT

Task A | Generic features of an information report ▶▶ SB P. 22

The Students' Book explains that the *Silk Road* text in the previous section is an information report, and that the main purpose of an information report is to give facts (rather than opinions) and to say what happened, or what exists.

❶ Students see the following table, showing the stages of an information report.

STAGE	SUB-STAGE	PURPOSE
Introduction	General statement	To introduce the topic of the information report, and to define it.
	Justification (optional)	To show why the topic is important
Points (in logical order)	*for each point:*	
	Theme	To introduce the point
	Elaboration	To give further information about the point

Note: This book uses the term *theme* instead of the more common *topic sentence* because the theme is not always a single sentence – it may be a clause within the sentence, or might be longer than a sentence.

❷ Students draw boxes around (or colour) the stages in the *Silk Road* text on page 19 of their books. The introduction is shown for them as an example on page 22 of their books. If this is the first time they have done an activity like this, be prepared to give them plenty of help.

❸ and **❹** These questions focus on the ordering of ideas within an information report, questions **❺** and **❻** direct students to some of the language features of this genre.

ANSWERS

1. Students read the table above only.
2. Students draw boxes or colour the stages in the Silk Road text.

General statement: The Silk Road is one of the best known ancient trading routes.

Justification: It was a major link between East and West, and for this reason, it has been very important in history.

Origins ← *Theme of 1st point*

Elaboration of 1st point: Originally, the Chinese traded silk within its own empire. Caravans, which were large groups of animals carrying goods for trade, would carry silk from the empire's interior to the western edges of the region. Often thieves would attack these caravans hoping to capture the traders' valuable goods. As a result, the Han Dynasty extended its military defences further into Central Asia from 135 to 90 BC to protect these caravans.

Theme of 2nd point: Chan Ch'ien, the first known Chinese traveller to make contact with the Central Asian tribes, later thought of expanding the silk trade to include these smaller tribes and therefore made alliances with them.

Elaboration of 2nd point: Because of this idea, the Silk Road was born. The route grew with the rise of the Roman Empire, because the Chinese gave silk to the Roman and Asian governments as gifts.

Spanning Two Continents ← *Theme of 3rd point*

Elaboration of 3rd point: The 11,000 kilometre route spanned China, Central Asia, Northern India, and the Parthian and Roman Empires. It connected the Yellow River Valley to the Mediterranean Sea and passed through the present-day countries of Iran, Iraq and Syria.

Theme of 4th point: People who lived in the North West of India, near the Ganges River, played important roles as middlemen in the China-Mediterranean silk trade because as early as the third century AD, they understood that silk was a lucrative product of the Chinese Empire. The trading relationship between the Chinese and the Indians grew stronger with increased Chinese expansion into Central Asia. The Chinese would trade their silk with the Indians for commodities such as jade, gold, and silver, and the Indians would trade the silk with the Roman

Empire. Silk proved to be an expensive import for the Roman Empire since heavy duties were collected across India and Central Asia by the Parthian Empire.

Elaboration of 4th point

Theme of fifth point

Social Consequences of the Silk Road

Because of the number of people travelling along the Silk Road not only goods but also ideas were conveyed. One of the most important effects of the trade route was that Buddhism spread from India to China.

Elaboration of fifth point

Theme of sixth point

The Silk Road's Decline

As table 1 shows, by 760 AD, trade along the Silk Road had declined. This was because robbers had started to attack the caravans again. Trade revived considerably in the eleventh and twelfth centuries when China became largely dependent on its silk trade. In addition, trade to Central and Western Asia as well as Europe increased from 1276–1368 when the Mongols controlled China. However, after that, overland trade became increasingly dangerous, and sea routes became more popular, so trade along the Silk Road decreased.

Elaboration of sixth point

3. Which of the following best describes the kind of logical order in this text?
   a. *time order (chronological)* ← *Correct*
   b. order of importance (most important first, least important last)
   c. different stages in a circle of events (cyclical)

4. From the following list of topics, choose the type of logical order that fits best
   a. life cycle of a frog: *Cyclical*
   b. history of China: *Chronological*
   c. stages in your English learning: *Chronological*
   d. the members of your favourite sports team: *Order of importance*

5. Which tense is used the most in the Silk Road text? Why, do you think? *Past simple, because the text is about events which were completed in the past. However, if the information report follows the cyclical order or order of importance format, present simple would be more likely to represent facts which are generally true.*

6. Look at the nouns in the text. Are they mostly general (eg Chinese people, thieves) or specific (eg someone's name)? *Mostly general, though there are some specific names.*

Task B | Write an information report ▸▸ SB P. 23

❶ Students choose a topic from the list of topics in the Students' Book, or you can give them a list you generate yourself if other questions are more appropriate to their particular context.

❷ and **❸** A checklist of points about information reports is given in question 2. This is based on the work the students did in Task A. In Question 3, students are encouraged to revise their work, and the concept of drafts is introduced.

LISTENING 1: NUMBERS – PROPERTY AUCTION

Task A | Numbers ▸▸ SB P. 23

Students (and native speakers too) often struggle with numbers when they are spoken rather than written. This listening is to provide students with practice in listening and writing down what they hear. The numbers are sequential because in an auction, they always go up. Students know from the introduction in the recording that the bidding will go up no less than in $10,000 amounts and increments cannot go above $50,000.

Just after the end of the auction, there is another recording of a real auction down south in the USA. The auctioneer speaks extremely rapidly and almost sings the numbers. It's an art form rather like calling a horse race. Students should enjoy it after trying to follow the auctioneer in the listening. It's meant as a humorous ending to a difficult task and to illustrate to them how an auction could sound. Hope you enjoy it.

PRE-LISTENING PRACTICE

- Practise the following numbers with the students. You could read them aloud and ask students to write them before listening to the auction. All the numbers are in thousands, but some are spoken without the 'thousands' added onto them. Students can write what they hear. So, two twenty five = 225; Two hundred and twenty five = 225; Two hundred and twenty five thousand = 225,000
- Explain commas and ask for them to be included.
- Explain and model for students the different stress between the numbers like 15 and 50. = Fif<u>teen</u> but <u>Fif</u>ty
- In sentences, emphasis on the *teen* numbers is usually at the end, whereas emphasis on the *ty* numbers is always at the beginning.
- After the task, ask students to write the $ sign in front of all the thousand statements. eg $225,000; $260,000; $315,000.

Unit 2 Trade | 25

① Students listen and write what you say:

i.	Two hundred and twenty five	225
ii.	Two hundred and fifty	250
iii.	Two hundred and fifteen	215
iv.	Two hundred and fifteen thousand	215,000
v.	Two fifteen	215
vi.	Two hundred and sixty thousand	260,000
vii.	Two hundred and sixteen	216
viii.	Three hundred and fifty	350
ix.	Three hundred and fifteen thousand	315,000
x.	Four hundred and twenty	420
xi.	Six hundred and twenty	620
xii.	Six hundred and twenty thousand	620,000
xiii.	Six hundred and fifty	650
xiv.	Six hundred and fifty thousand	650,000
xv.	Nine eighty	980
xvi.	Nine hundred and eighty thousand	980,000
xvii.	Seventeen	17
xviii.	Twenty two	22
xix.	Eleven	11
xx.	Seventy thousand three hundred	70,300

② Students listen to the auction on the recording and try to fill in the numbers the bidders say.

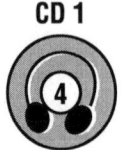

CD 1

ANSWERS

a. Bidder 11: 225
b. Bidder 17: 250
c. Bidder 22: 260
d. Bidder 17: 300,000
e. Bidder 22: 350
f. Bidder 17: 400
g. Bidder 30: 450
h. Bidder 30: 550
i. John: Number 30 offers five hundred and fifty thousand dollars. The sun is shining, it was cloudy, but now it's bright. Let's keep this going and get this beautiful home into a new owner's hands today!
j. John: Ah number 17 Yes! The bid is 550 and you make $600,000. Well done.
k. Bidder 22: 620,000
l. Bidder 11: 670
m. Bidder 17: 700,000
n. Bidder 11: 750
o. Bidder 17: 800
p. Bidder 22: 850
q. Bidder 11: 870
r. Bidder 17: 900, / 900,000
s. Bidder 11: 910
t. Bidder 17: 920
u. Bidder 11: $980,000

Recording script

CD 1, track 4: Trade, Unit 2
(5 minutes, 34 seconds)

Listening 1: Property auction – Trading a property for money!

Narrator: The speakers are standing outside a beautiful house located right on the ocean front. You can hear waves breaking and an auction to sell the house is about to begin. Tony, the real estate agent is a short, fat man and he is going to introduce the auctioneer, John Hedgerow. John is tall and thin with black hair. There is a crowd and different people will bid for the home.

(Ocean waves crashing – then coughing, chatting among selves, general noise of crowd.)

Tony: Now let's settle down out there. Good afternoon and welcome to you all. I see we have both registered buyers and a good general audience here today. We're here to sell this property and let's hope it will be sold!

First, it gives me great pleasure to introduce our auctioneer for this afternoon's auction – Mr John Hedgerow. John has a wonderful credential and he has auctioned properties in Hong Kong, Singapore, Indonesia, New Zealand and America, and is Chairman of the Auctioneers' Chapter of the Real Estate Institute of Old Tat Moor. John used to auction each week, but now, he does only special auctions and we are lucky enough to have him today for this very special property.

This property was inspected and passed. It is ready for sale. So, without further ado, let us begin. I give you Mr John Hedgerow!

(Applause)

John: Thank you Tony, and a warm welcome to you all. Isn't it lovely to be here in this beautiful home? Look at that view! Look at the ocean frontage! We're here today to sell this property and it will be sold! You know the rules and regulations. You bid by raising your card. The bid will be final and you cannot take it back. Each bid will raise by at least $10,000 and not more than $50,000 per bid.

Are we ready?
Do I hear an opening bid of 225

Bidder 11:	225
John:	Yes! You madam number 11 – you say 225 and do I hear $250?
Bidder 17:	250
John:	Bidders, number 17, yes, that's 250.
John:	And number 22 you raise it to 260 and back to you 17 yes? $300,000! That's better – let's get this going now. After all, once you move in, you won't remember what life used to be like without the sound of the sea outside your bedroom window.
Bidder 22:	$350
John:	Yes, 350, now we're moving.
Bidder 17:	400
John:	Number 17? Let's hear 450!
Bidder 30:	450
John:	Ah well done... new bidder. Way to go – let's go – thank you number 30. The bid is 450,000. 22, I see another 50! Alright – the bid stands at half a million. Do I hear $550,000?
Bidder 30:	550
John:	Number 30 offers five hundred and fifty thousand dollars. The sun is shining, it was cloudy, but now it's bright. Let's keep this going and get this beautiful home into a new owner's hands today!
Bidder 17:	600
John:	Ah number 17 Yes! The bid is 550 and you make it 600,000. Well done,
Bidder 22:	620
John:	Oh 22 back in the game. Good, $620,000's the bid.
Bidder 11:	670
John:	And now it's number 11 again with 670. She's not kidding, she means business. Eleven's been very quiet except for the opening and now here you are again. Let's go, let's get this show on the road. Do I hear 700,000? 700,000 for this beautiful home, this seaside paradise?
Bidder 17:	700
John:	Yes! Number 17 – and it's 700,000
Bidder 11:	750
John:	Oh number 11 for 750
Bidder 17:	800
John:	Alright, number 17 800. Back in the game at 800,000. That's the bid. Going once.......Going twice...
Bidder 22:	850
John:	OK number 22, the gentleman in the lime green shirt for $850,000!
Bidder 11:	870
John:	And that's number 11 for 870! Do I hear 900?
Bidder 17:	Yes 900
John:	OK, number 17 for 900,000. $900,000 is the bid. Do I hear 910?
Bidder 11:	910
John:	YES! It's 11 for 910. 17 for 920. 11 for 930. The race is on folks, we will have a sale! 11, madam and your bid? 980! Do I hear one million? Do I hear a million dollars? How about 990 then? 990, alright, the bid is 980, for number 11. It's going to go! Any more bids? 980 to number 11. It's going once, it's going twice, it's going to go! Three times and it's SOLD!!!! *(Auction hammer bangs down)* to the lady in red – Number 11! Congratulations, madam. Ladies and gentlemen, this auction is now officially over. Thank you for your interest, thank you for coming.

(Loud clapping – fades)

Additional listening as mentioned earlier: Crazy auctioneer sings a short auction segment.

LISTENING 2 — IDENTIFYING STAGES – SPOKEN EXPLANATION

Task A | A spoken explanation signalling new stages ▶▶ SB P. 24

❶ and ❷ Students listen to the speaker. The following phrases signal the stages listed in *A Trade Off*. These stages are typical of a spoken explanation. Students tick the phrases in their textbooks as they hear them.

CD 1 — 5

ANSWERS

1. a. Good morning, students. In this unit so far...
   b. Today...
   c. Next...
   d. After that...
   e. You then...
   f. Also...
   g. To finish...

Unit 2 Trade | 27

ANSWERS

Answers to question 2 are underlined (superscript letters are the parts a. to g. of this question)

Answers to question 3 are in **bold** (superscript Roman numerals indicate part i. to v. of this question)

STAGES	SUB-STAGES	EXTRACTS FROM THE TEXT (ANSWERS)
Introduction	Opening	[i] **Good morning**, students.
	Preview of what this unit is going to be about (in this case, a re-cap)	[ii, iv] **In this unit so far**, [a]we introduced trade in some different ways. We began [b]with ...
	Definition of terms	... simple trade [iii]**as** when a child trades ...
Body paragraphs	Stages *(past tense, sequential development)*	Next, [c]you examined retail trade ...
		After that, [d]we moved on to ...
		You then [e]read how it was a major link between ...
		Also, [f]do you remember reading that ...
Conclusion		[v]**To finish**, [g]let me summarise as follows ...

Recording script

CD 1

CD 1, track 5: Trade Unit 2
(2 minutes, 42 seconds)

Listening 2: Information and summary report from a teacher

Narrator: The students in this listening are yourselves, in a way. You are being given a recount or summary report based on this unit – Unit 2, Trade from *EAP Now! Preliminary*.

Lecturer: Good morning, students. In this unit so far, we introduced trade in some different ways. We began with simple trade as when a child trades or swaps a sandwich, a pencil or any item or thing for a different item or thing. For example, Sam has a peanut butter sandwich and Akiko has a honey and banana sandwich, so they trade. They trade because one wants what the other has. Each person then gets an equal and valuable thing.

Next, you examined retail trade in the form of a case study when Kevin returned a broken plate and did not receive quality customer service. Service is at the heart of all business transactions and trade.

After that, we moved on to an historical view of trade with a report about the Silk Road, Asia's famous and ancient trade route. You then read how it was a major link between East and West, and for that reason, it has been very important in history. It spanned two continents and it was used as early as the third century AD to exchange silk for jade, gold and silver. Also, do you remember reading that one of the most important effects of the trade route was that it spread Buddhism from Inda, India sorry, from India to China?

To finish, let me summarise as follows. The word 'trade' has a few different meanings and this unit helped you to understand them. We covered three meanings. There was simple trade between two people, there was retail trade within shops and there was world trade between countries.

LANGUAGE SPOTLIGHT 2 — PAST SIMPLE, USED TO AND PAST PERFECT

Task A | Explanations ▶▶ SB P. 24

1. Students examine explanations of the three ways of expressing past actions and states covered in this section. They are included below as a reminder of the tenses' functions:

Past simple, used to, and past perfect

Past simple: expressing a past action that is completed, ie finished.
Example: I made a profit from my IT shares but I sold them because the company was taken over.

Used to:
Example: I used to have green energy shares.
(**Unspoken meaning** – *but I no longer do.*)

Past perfect: expressing a past action that was completed before another past time or event:
Example: I had ordered those shares before I heard from you. (**Unspoken meaning** – *I wouldn't have ordered the shares if I had heard from you before I did order the shares.*)

ANSWERS

2. Students mark the past simple tense on the *Silk Road* text on page 19. Two instances of past simple passive have also been underlined in that text – however, at this stage there is no need for students to be able to identify these. Passive is covered in the following unit, Unit 3.
3. Student paragraphs will vary. You can check by circulating around the room or ask for the work to be handed in for checking later.

SPEAKING 2: SENTENCE STRESS, COLLOQUIALISMS AND EXPRESSING OPINIONS

Task A | Practising conversations ▶▶ SB P. 25

Students can practise the tenses, past simple, used to, and past perfect, in this conversation. Also, it serves to assist them with intonation and accent. Colloquialisms common in the UK and Australia, such as 'How's it goin?' are introduced and the ellipsed meanings are included on the right side of the table.

Task B | What do you think? Expressing personal opinions ▶▶ SB P. 25

Students read the extracts, form pairs and use 'I agree / that' or 'I don't agree / that/ with…/' to express their own opinion. They use general knowledge on the subjects or you could use this task in conjunction with the internet.

FURTHER PRACTICE: READING, FILMS AND FUN

READING

Johan Norberg (2003), *In Defense of Global Capitalism.* Washington DC: Cato Institute.

Doug Bandow and Ian Vásquez (eds) (1993), *Perpetuating Poverty: The World Bank, the IMF, and the Developing World.* Washington DC: Cato Institute.

Susan George (1988), *A Fate Worse than Debt,* London: Penguin Group.

Green Left Weekly, An Australian Independent Newspaper.

FILMS

There are many films that approach the topic of trade. The following is just a small selection.

The Yes Men, directed by Dan Ollman and Sarah Price. A comedic documentary which follows *The Yes Men*, a small group of prankster activists, as they gain worldwide notoriety for impersonating the World Trade Organization on television and at business conferences around the world. This dark comic satire highlights the worst aspects of global free trade.
Source: Sujit R. Varma (ND), on Internet Movie Database (http://www.imdb.com/title/tt0379593/plotsummary), accessed 6 August 2006.

The Luckiest Nut in the World, written and directed by Emily James. This film is a whistle-stop tour through everything-you-need-to-know about free trade, a no-nonsense guide to trade in the real world using stories from the international nuts trade.

The Corporation, directed by Mark Achbar and Jennifer Abbott. This film takes an in depth psychological examination of the organisation model through various case studies.

The Gods Must Be Crazy, written and directed by James Uys. This film is a visual delight, a classic and a philosophical thought provoking wander around a different world. The ending links to trade.

QUESTIONS

FACTUAL ESSAYS (INFORMATION REPORTS, EXPLANATIONS)

1. Explain the term 'trade justice' as it relates to worldwide free trade agreements.

2. Global capitalism appears to be the goal of the developed countries. Explain the rise of global capitalism since WWII.

OPINION ESSAYS (ARGUMENTS, DISCUSSIONS)

1. Is free trade assisting all countries who are members of free trade agreements? Discuss.

3 DEMOGRAPHICS

'they who live longest will see most'

BY THE END OF THIS UNIT, STUDENTS SHOULD:

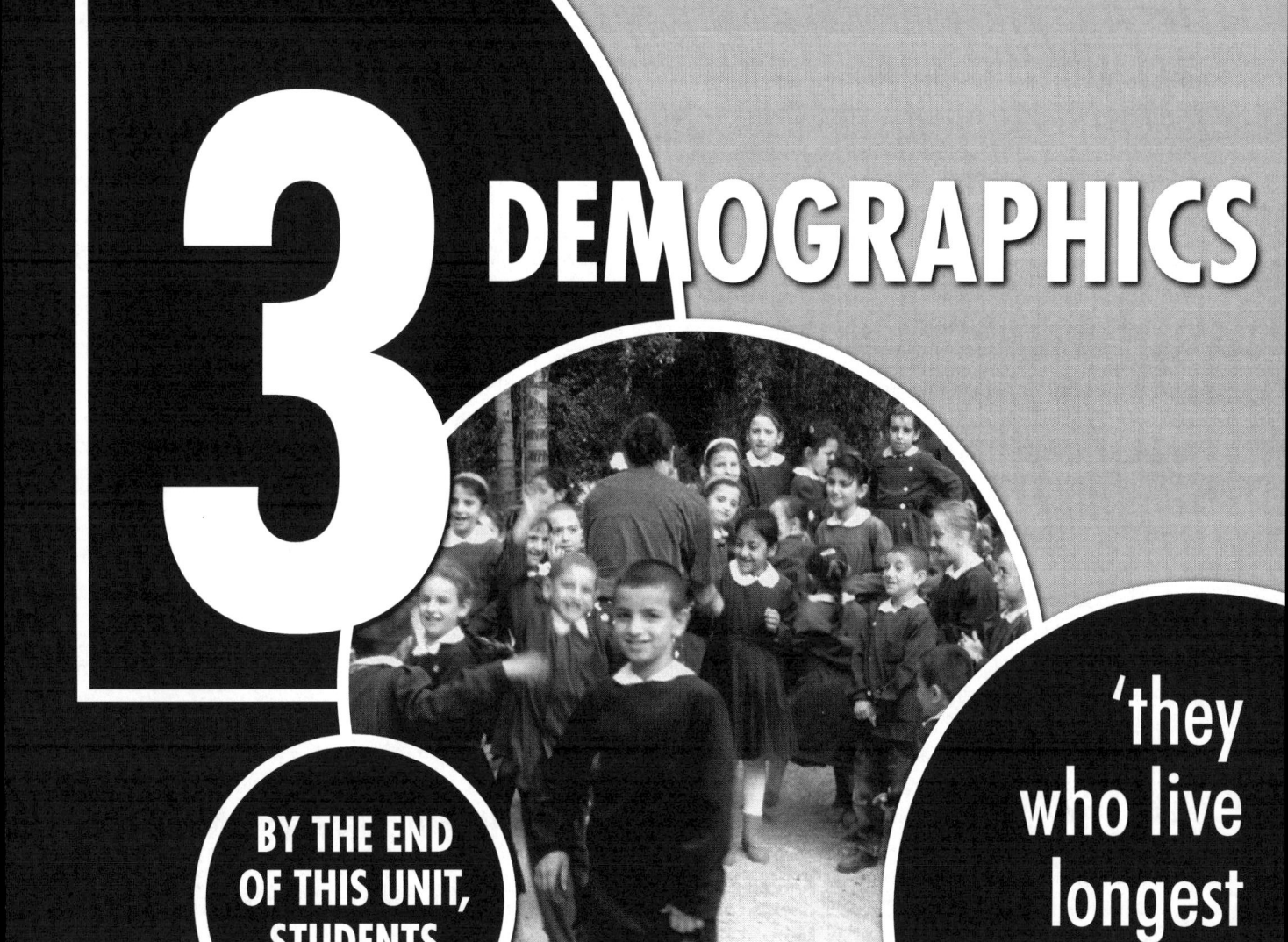

- know more vocabulary for talking generally about societies, people etc. . . . . Speaking 1: Task B **32**
- be more fluent at talking about societies and people . . . . Speaking 1: Task B **32**; Language Spotlight 2: Task C **43**; Reading: Task D **34**
- have improved ability to predict the content of an article from the introduction . . . . Reading: Task B **33**
- have improved ability to find meaning from context in a written text . . . . Reading: Task C **33**
- be able to pronounce many nouns and verbs with the word stress in the correct place . . . . Reading: Task D **34**
- understand why writers choose to use the passive or active voice . . . . Language Spotlight 1: Task B **36**
- know the stages to expect when reading an explanation essay . . . . Writing: Task A **39**
- be able to write a short explanation essay with appropriate staging. . . . . Writing: Task B **40**
- have gained further practice of predicting and brainstorming a topic before listening . . . . Listening: Task A **40**
- have experienced listening to people with different accents. . . . . Listening: Task B **40**
- have improved their ability to take notes while listening. . . . . Listening: Task B **40**
- be able to recognise and talk about general facts (eg using present simple tense and the zero conditional) and temporary actions happening around now (eg using the present continuous tense) . . . . Language Spotlight 2: Tasks A, B and C **42–43**
- be able to ask for clarification when they don't understand something. . . . . Speaking 2: Tasks A and B **43**

DEMOGRAPHIC n., pl. DEMOGRAPHICS [UNCOUNTABLE AND COUNTABLE]: 1 information about a group such as the people who live in a particular area: *the demographics of a newspaper's readership*. 2 [sing] a part of the population that is considered as a group, especially by advertisers who want to sell things to that group: *the 21–40 demographic*.

DEMOGRAPHY [UNCOUNTABLE]: the study of human populations and the ways in which they change, for example the study of how many births, marriages and deaths happen in a particular place at a particular time.

INTRODUCTION FOR TEACHERS

This unit could just as easily be called *Social Change* or *Society*. The aim is to lead students into talking in the general ways that are necessary for academic and less-practical vocational courses (rather than the specific language that normally gets taught up to intermediate level). The topic allows wide-ranging discussion on society as a whole, something that is likely to be of interest to most students, and relevant to the kinds of topics that come up in many international English language examinations.

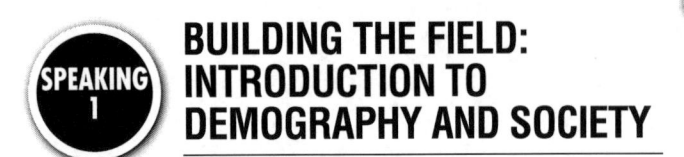

SPEAKING 1 — BUILDING THE FIELD: INTRODUCTION TO DEMOGRAPHY AND SOCIETY

Task A | Discussion ▶▶ SB P. 28

Students look at the pictures of people of very mixed age and race (in Australia) and lots of young children in school uniforms (in Turkey). In small groups, they discuss what they notice about the people, whether they can see similar scenes in their own countries, and the factors behind what they see.

Task B | Vocabulary ▶▶ SB P. 28

❶ In pairs, students help each other to match the words in a list in their book to their closest meanings, also given. They are encouraged to share their own knowledge with a partner, then guess the meanings of words not covered by previous knowledge. If there are words they can't guess, dictionaries can be used at the teacher's discretion.

Numbers against the words have been deliberately avoided here to discourage students from simply writing numbers next to the meanings.

❷ Students are asked what *21–40* means where it says *the 21–40 demographic* in the definition of *demographic* at the beginning of the unit.

ANSWER

People aged between 21 and 40 years old.

SPEAKING PRACTICE

❸ Students tell their partners how the following statistics might have changed in their countries over the last 30 years. (If this is difficult for them, they can be asked to think about things their grandparents told them, and about news reports, or to make an educated guess.)
a. size of families
b. life expectancy
c. the number of the elderly
d. birth rate
e. infant mortality
f. retirement age
g. the age at which couples start families.

READING — PREDICTING; MEANING FROM CONTEXT – AN EXPLANATION ESSAY

Task A | Pre-reading discussion ▶▶ SB P. 28

Students discuss the following questions in small groups.

❶ Think of some products that might be advertised:
a. in a woman's magazine
b. in a sports magazine

ANSWERS

VOCABULARY	MEANINGS
(the) population (of …)	the number of people who live in a particular place (eg a country)
retire	to stop working forever, because of age or health problems
retirement age	in many companies, people have to stop working when they reach this
life expectancy	how many years people live, on average
birth rate	the number of children women have, on average (usually number of births per thousand women)
infant mortality	the number of deaths of babies under one year old, for every 1000 babies born alive each year
the elderly	a polite word for people who are old. This word can also be used as an adjective.
in their early sixties	between around 60 and 64 years old

c. in a tabloid newspaper (a tabloid is smaller, and usually but not always less serious than the other type of newspaper, broadsheet)
d. on commercial TV at 10 am during school term
e. in the same situation as [d] but during the school holidays
f. on TV just after the evening news
g. on TV after midnight.

2 Think of reasons for these differences.

ANSWER

Any reasonable answers are acceptable – the point is to activate prior knowledge and to get students thinking about the topic before they begin reading.

Task B | Predicting from the introduction ▶▶ SB P. 29

Students read the first paragraph only of the text in their books entitled *Market segmentation* (reproduced on the next page), and answer without a dictionary some questions which focus on:
(i) how the introductory paragraph of the essay helps to indicate the focus of the rest of the essay (later this unit will explore stages in introductions to explanation essays, to further clarify this point), and
(ii) finding from context the meaning of some of the key concepts in the essay.

ANSWERS

1. What do you think *market segmentation* might mean?
   Even without already knowing the meaning of segmentation, they should be able to work out from the introduction that it is a reason why different advertisements are shown at different times of day, and that it's related to demographics – so, matching advertising times to demographic would be a good judgment.

2. Why do you think understanding demographics is important for marketing?
   A very specific answer would be: It helps to decide what time to show TV adverts. Students may be able to generalise, eg to say it helps to target the marketing to the best demographic to buy it.

3. What do you think the rest of the essay will explain?
   Even without knowing about the concept of the preview/scope stage of an introduction, students would probably guess that it answers the following two questions: what is market segmentation, and how is market segmentation useful to companies?

Extension: This is a good text for students to see how definitions are constructed, and how to identify them. For example, para 2 of the extract below contains several definitions: *In market segmentation, … [definition]; … [definition] … is known as [word being defined].*

The essay is reproduced on page 34. Underlined italics indicates answers to the next task (Task C). (Bold italics indicates answers to Language Spotlight 1: Passive voice, Task A, Question 2.)

Task C | Finding meaning from context ▶▶ SB P. 29

Students find words in the previous text (*Market segmentation*) that have the same meanings as the following expressions (these meanings are already in the same order in the text as they appear here, and the paragraph number is given to help students know where to look). If they have difficulty finding them, it may help to give a hint about where in the paragraph to find them (beginning, middle or end).

ANSWERS

The words the students are looking for are in the box below and in italics in the text in Task A above.

MEANINGS	WORDS
[a] thought about; speculated (para 1)	wondered
[b] connected with (para 1)	linked to
[c] features; things that make them different from others (para 2)	characteristics
[d] areas of a town or city (para 2)	neighbourhoods
[e] a part of something (para 2)	segment
[f] a way of doing something (para 3)	technique
[g] to make bigger (para 4)	expand
[h] changed (para 4)	modified
[i] the opposite of (para 5)	the reverse of
[j] something with small changes (para 5)	variations
[k] be interesting (para 5)	appeal (to)

Unit 3 Demographics | 33

MARKET SEGMENTATION

① Have you ever <u>wondered</u> why advertisements for babies' nappies *are shown* during daytime TV but not usually at night? Or advertisements for beer and wine only in the evenings? The answer *is <u>linked</u> to* something called market segmentation and is just one of the reasons why an understanding of demographics is important in marketing. So, what exactly is market segmentation, and how is it useful to companies?

② In market segmentation, society *is divided* into groups, based on such things as age, where they live, sex, socio-economic status (their social class and how rich they are) and whether they have children. A group of people (or cohort) having similar <u>characteristics</u>, for example, women in their 30s and 40s with children and who are living in relatively wealthy <u>neighbourhoods</u>, *is known* as a market segment or demographic. A market <u>segment</u> could also include a group of people sharing common interests, lifestyle, attitudes etc.

③ The <u>technique</u> of market segmentation is useful to marketers because it helps them to target their marketing to the right group of people. Clearly sales will be higher, for example, if computer games *are advertised* to young people rather than old people. And different games *might be advertised* in a magazine for teenagers than in a magazine for young adults. Further, new products *may be developed* especially for newly emerging market segments. For example, due to improvements in medical science, people are having a healthier and longer retirement, and therefore a lot more money *is spent* on leisure products for older people than in the past.

④ With an example like computer games, it *can be seen* easily which ones interest different groups. However, it might be less clear with other products. If, for example, a car company wants to <u>expand</u> into a new country by selling a car it already makes, how does it know which demographic to aim at? Different cultures have different characteristics, so the advertising that works for one market segment in one country might have to *be <u>modified</u>* in another country.

⑤ The company must do market research, which can show which kind of people *are interested* in the product and are ready to buy it. Further, different versions of the car, perhaps with different body styles, engine tunings and interior features, *might be produced* for different demographics, and advertising shown where each demographic is likely to see it.

⑥ <u>The reverse of</u> this process is also common. A company might first do market research to find out what the market wants. Then a product *will be designed* that fits the results of this research. Different <u>variations</u> of this product *may be made* to <u>appeal to</u> different demographics.

Task D | Pronunciation – Word stress and shifting stress ▶▶ SB P. 30

This section raises awareness of word stress, and focuses on how the pronunciation of some words changes depending on whether they are nouns or verbs.

❶ In order to provide a speech model, you need to say the following sentences with natural stress and intonation, and ask the students to identify how the word *segment* is pronounced differently in each.
- A good marketing plan *segments* the market
- A good marketing plan divides the market into *segments*.

Students should identify that *segment* as a verb is pronounced with the stress on the final syllable, whereas the stress is on the first syllable when it is a noun.

❷ In this question students predict where the stress falls on the following sentences. They should be able to do this without necessarily knowing the meanings – they can check meanings in Question 3.

> **ANSWERS**
>
> 2. The stressed syllable is underlined.
>   a. *Replay*
>   (i) Does your favourite radio station re<u>play</u> the same music all the time?
>   (ii) Do you like radio stations that have lots of <u>re</u>plays?
>   b. *Retake*
>   (i) Did your school have a policy about exam <u>re</u>takes?
>   (ii) Have you ever had to re<u>take</u> an exam?

34 | EAP Now! Preliminary English for Academic Purposes Teacher's Book

c. *Export*
     (i) What goods does your country ex<u>port</u>?
     (ii) What <u>ex</u>ports is France known for?
  d. *Increase*
     (i) Has your interest in English in<u>creased</u> during this course?
     (ii) During this course, has there been an <u>in</u>crease in interest in English throughout this class?
  e. *Record*
     (i) What other ways are there to keep a <u>re</u>cord of a conversation?
     (ii) Do you re<u>cord</u> conversations to help with your English learning?
  f. *Rebel*
     (i) Please tell me about the biggest <u>re</u>bel in your high school class.
     (ii) Did you ever re<u>bel</u> against your teachers at school? Or in any other situations?

It may be worthwhile to look at how the first vowel in *record* changes between /I/ and /e/, depending on whether or not it is stressed, and the similar change of the first vowel of *rebel* from /e/ to /ə/.

> **Note:** Mostly, words that follow this pattern include a prefix such as re-, in- or ex-. However, not all words with such prefixes involve shifting stress. Words with shifting stress include: decrease, exploit, impact, incline, indent, insert, inset, install, insult, invite, rebound, recall, recap, recoil, recount, recruit, refit, refund, reject, relapse, relay, resit, respray, rewrite, segment.
>
> Words which remain the same as both a noun and a verb but which don't involve a stress shift include: cycle, decline, exercise, exhibit, exit, increment, index, initial, invoice, rebate, rebuff, rebuke, recruit, regard, regret, relish, remain, remedy, repair, reply, report, rescue, resort, respect, result, retort, return, reverse, review, reward, target.

> **Fun extension idea:** The teacher says some of the words boxed above; student says whether it's a noun or a verb. Then, pairs of students take it in turns to do the same.

❸ Students check the meanings of any of the words they don't know (either from you or an English-English dictionary). By asking each other the questions, they then gain some more natural speaking practice (albeit on widely varying topics!) where the words will come up frequently. Focus on ensuring correct placement of word stress.

> **Extension:** This may be an appropriate place to work on shifting stress where the word changes form for different parts of speech, eg <u>pho</u>tograph / pho<u>tog</u>rapher, re<u>vise</u>/re<u>vi</u>sion.

Task E | Discussion ▶▶ SB P. 30

Students discuss the following points with a partner, in order to demonstrate their understanding of the ideas in the text, and to practise some of the vocabulary from this unit.

❶ How do you think a company might do market research? (Think of several ways – you've probably experienced some!)

❷ For the following products, discuss (a) what market segment(s) may be most interested in it, and (b) where/how advertising might reach these market segments. You might be able to think of:
  a. a new design for razors
  b. laptop computers
  c. a new doll to compete with Barbie
  d. a chocolate bar
  e. an English course for people who want to use better English in their office jobs.

LANGUAGE SPOTLIGHT 1 — PASSIVE VOICE

Task A | Identifying passive voice ▶▶ SB P. 31

❶ Students find in the text (*Market segmentation*) on page 29 of their books, paraphrases (using the passive voice) of the following parts of sentences (which use the active voice):
  [a] *... TV companies show advertisements for nappies during the day but ...*
  [b] *Marketing professionals know ... as a market segment, ...*
  [c] *... if companies advertise computer games to young people ...*
  [d] *... we can see easily which ones different age groups will be interested in ...*

Students are then asked to identify the differences between the active voice clauses (in the question) and the passive voice clauses (in the text).

> **ANSWERS**
>
> 1. a. ... advertisements for babies' nappies are shown during daytime TV but ... (para 1)
>   b. ... is known as a market segment, ... (para 2)
>   c. ..., if computer games are advertised to young people ... (para 3)
>   d. ... it can be seen easily which ones interest different groups. (para 4)

In talking about the differences between the active voice and passive voice clauses, students could mention that subject and object are swapped, and that the 'be' verb is added and the main verb changed to the past participle in the versions in the text. (They should be able to identify this pattern even if they are not yet aware of the terms 'passive voice' and 'active voice'.)

In pairs, students then answer the following questions, which guide them through finding out or reviewing a few points about the passive.

② Find other examples in the same text where the writer used the passive voice. Answers can be found below, in the answer box for Question 3 and in the text entitled *Market segmentation* on page 34 of this book, where the passive verb groups are in bold italics.

Note: It is likely to be necessary to work through the form of the passive, and how it is constructed from different tenses here. Depending on the level of your students, it may be good to restrict this to present simple and present modals, as dealt with here, or it could be extended/generalised to a variety of tenses.

As Kennedy (2003) points out, it may be easier to focus on the form of the passive through comparisons with adjective constructions rather than using the traditional approach involving complex word order transformations. For example, the word 'interesting' is usually seen as an adjective, and might appear in a sentence such as:

He was interested in the advertisement

This would normally be seen as a simple construction, which students will be very familiar with:

Subject + 'be' verb + complement.

However, it has exactly the same form as a past simple passive construction, such as:

He was persuaded by the advertisement

Pointing this out to the students can be a powerful technique for making the construction of passive voice clauses appear less daunting.

---

③ Think about the active version of each of the examples you found in Question 2. With a partner, discuss why you think the passive was chosen.

ANSWERS

Clearly, this will be quite difficult for most students, and is really designed to activate previous knowledge/remind students of some of these concepts in preparation for the next task, in which reasons for using passive are made more explicit. With a class new to the concept of passive voice, it may be better to skip this question. However, strong students may gain insight by working out the active forms of the passive voice and then speculating about the reasons for the choice of passive.

are shown (para 1): *because there is no need to mention who shows the advertisements – it's quite obvious anyway.*

is linked to (para 1): *No one actually carries out the link – active is just not possible in this situation as there is nothing to go in the subject position.*

is divided (para 2): *The agent (the subject if the active voice is used) is less important than the action or the object (to mention the agent – marketers – would take focus away from the intended meaning).*

is known (para 2): *same as* is divided *above.*

are advertised (para 3): *the agent is obvious (as well as being less important than the action and the object).*

might be advertised (para 3): *as* are advertised *above.*

may be developed (para 3): *as* are advertised *above.*

is spent (para 3): *as* are advertised *above.*

can be seen (para 4): *again, the agent is less important than the action and the object. Also, if active were chosen here, it would be difficult to find an appropriate word for the agent without the sentence sounding awkward in style.*

be modified (para 4): *again, mention of the agent would detract from the message; it's not important for the message.*

are interested (para 5): *use of passive voice brings the more important idea (interest) closer to the start of the sentence, and also in this case allows the concept to be expressed in a reasonably natural way (cf ... which kind of people the product interest).*

might be produced (para 5): *as* are advertised *above.*

will be designed (para 6): *as* are advertised *above.*

may be made (para 6): *as* are advertised *above.*

Task B | When is passive voice used? ▶▶ SB P. 31

Students answer the following questions. Question 1 is best done orally with books closed to prevent them from looking ahead to Question 2 and finding the answers. To do

Question 1, they need to know that the term *agent* refers to the 'doer' of the action, and is the subject of active clauses, and is sometimes put after 'by' in passives.

① Can you remember (or think of) reasons to use the passive (other than the reasons you looked at in Task A)? *Possible answers are the points with roman numerals in Question 2.*

② Students are asked to look at examples (a) to (g) and match them to the reasons (i) to (vii).

More than one answer may apply to each. However, the most relevant answers have been given below.

ANSWERS

2. **a.** The report will be handed in a little late (cf: I'll hand in the report late)
   v. when we don't want to mention the agent (eg to avoid showing who is responsible)

   b. Surveys are done by the market researchers to find out what the customers think of the product. The results of these are given to the market analysis department. *There are two reasons:* first sentence: *iv. when the agent is less important than the action or the object (both are mentioned, but there appears to have been a deliberate attempt to relegate the agent to a less emphatic position away from the beginning of the sentence;* second sentence: *vii. to make the sentence link better with the previous sentence by bringing the object to the front of the sentence.*

   c. Society is divided into groups.
   iv. When the agent is less important than the action or the object.

   d. The report has been finished (cf I finished the report) As this looks a little unnatural, the most likely answer would be: *vi. to deliberately make the object more important by bringing it to the front of the sentence.*

   e. My mobile phone has been stolen!
   i. when the agent is unknown, and *ii. to avoid vague words like 'someone' or 'people' as the subject.*

   f. It can be seen easily which ones different age groups are interested in (cf It is easy to see which ones different age groups are interested in).
   viii. it can sometimes be used to make writing or speaking sound more formal. (There's simply no other explanation for this!!)

   g. The murderer was arrested.
   iii. when the agent is obvious

Note: If the students have some knowledge of systemic functional grammar, reason vi can be explained easily and effectively through patterns of Theme and Rheme. Please see *EAP Now!* for work based on this.

DISCUSSION POINT
As you probably know, there has been a move to reduce use of the passive in certain academic circles, especially in the US. Some university departments encourage students to reduce use of the passive, partly with the aim of making writing more accessible. Whether to teach this is at the teacher's (or the institution's) discretion. We would suggest that students do cover the passive so they have the option of using it. Of course, it is important for all students to understand the passive voice in reading and listening!

Task C | Practice ▶▶ SB P. 32

① Students rewrite the paragraphs below, changing the underlined parts of each sentence to the active voice. [a] and [d] have been done as examples. Students then answer the following questions:
- What difference do you feel between the active and passive versions of each? For example, did you find it difficult to choose a subject for the active clause?
- Does the active voice make the sentence too informal?
- Does the passive voice help the writer to put the emphasis (first idea in the sentence) on the right idea?

[a] Three distinct generations are often talked about in marketing circles in Western countries: Baby Boomers, Generation X and Generation Y. Each has different attitudes, so [b] marketing is targeted differently to each generation. But, what [c] is meant by these generational terms, and how [d] is marketing strategy affected by the characteristics of each generation?

To answer the first of these questions, [e] demographic changes over the last 60 years have to be examined. After the second world war, there was a sense of peace and prosperity for the future, and people felt secure and optimistic enough that [f] lots of babies were born, hence the term Baby Boomer. [g] This generation was known for being rebellious during the sixties and seventies, for example [h] many were involved in protests against government policy such as the war in Vietnam. [i] The hippy generation and punks are often included as examples of this rebellious trend, though they by no means represented the whole of the generation. However, [j] the Baby Boomers are generally understood to have made Western society more open minded and accepting of differences. Now, they are taking a more adventurous approach to retirement than their parents, because [k] a longer and healthier retirement is expected.

Unit 3 Demographics | 37

[l] The members of Generation X were born from around the early sixties to around 1980, and are a very diverse generation, having a very wide range of different attitudes and beliefs. Only a few trends have become clear so far – people of this generation are getting married later, are having fewer children, [m] jobs and careers are changed frequently, and they are more likely to have higher qualifications than any generation before them. The first of Generation Y (born in the fifteen or twenty years since the early eighties) are now becoming adults, and [n] the changes they bring to society will be observed carefully by demographers and marketers.

ANSWERS

1. a. Given in the Student Book as an example:
People in marketing circles often talk about three distinct generations
– the main point is *three distinct generations*, and passive voice (in the original sentence) allows this noun phrase to go to the beginning of the sentence/paragraph/text for greater emphasis.

b. *People/marketers [or anything with equivalent meaning] target marketing differently*
– it's not important for the meaning of the sentence who does the targeting, just important that it happens.

c. *... what do people [or marketers, or equivalent] mean*
– again, the grammatical subject (people) is awkward and is not the best choice for the main idea of the sentence.

d. Given in the Students' Book as an example:
... how do the characteristics of each generation affect marketing strategy?
– *marketing strategy* is the meaning that the writer wants to emphasise, not the characteristics

e. *... I/we have to examine demographic changes over the last 60 years.*
– *I* is often avoided in academic writing, and is certainly not the main point in the sentence.

f. *... they/the women/female members of this generation bore lots of babies*
– not only is choosing a subject rather awkward (which students may work out), but it also results in rather archaic English, more reminiscent of ancient legends or biblical language (this point will be more difficult for students to spot!)

g. *People knew this generation ...*
– *people* here means people in general. Therefore, there's no need to mention this.

h. *... protests against government policy such as the war in Vietnam involved many [of this generation* can be added to the end, but is normally ellipsed, as in the passive version in the original text*]*
– the connection between *many* in this clause and *this generation* in the previous clause works better when *many* is at the front of the sentence. It can also be argued that *many [of this generation]* should have greater prominence in the sentence by being put at the front.

i. *People/demographers/social scientists often include the hippy generation and punks as examples of this rebellious trend*
– same reason as [b].

j. *... people/demographers/social scientists generally understand the Baby Boomers ...*
– same reason as [b]. Also, it could be that the author just doesn't want to go into the issue of who believes this.

k. *... they [and perhaps society as a whole] expect a longer and healthier retirement*
– same reason as [j].

l. *People/.../... bore the members of Generation X*
– same reason as [f].

m. *... they change jobs and careers frequently*
– this may actually fit better than the active version!

n. *... demographers and marketers will observe carefully the changes they [Generation Y] will bring to society*
– another example of putting the more important point first.

2 For freer practice, students discuss the following topics with a partner. Then, they write a paragraph reflecting the ideas they talked about. This activity can be the brainstorming/preparation for students to write a structured essay in the next section.

The Students' Book points out that the passive voice is used more often in writing than in speaking – this point is made to help students to avoid 'trying too hard' and producing inappropriate language. However, in the paragraph writing stage, they should try to use the passive whenever appropriate.

The topics to talk and write about appear in the Students' Book as follows:
a. Generations in your own country: How is your generation different from your parents' generation? What big events have influenced birth rates, education, people's expectations, etc?

b. Products of your country: what well-known products are made there, exported from there, what has been invented, what films were produced/made/filmed there, what art was painted/sculpted, etc there?

c. Your home town and changes in it since you were a child, eg perhaps many fast food restaurants have been opened there (present perfect passive, for changes between the past and now, is most useful for this).

Students will get more chance to practise the passive when they write an explanation essay later in this unit.

WRITING: STRUCTURE OF AN EXPLANATION ESSAY

Task A | Generic features of an explanation essay ▶▶ SB P. 33

Students are told that the text titled *Market segmentation* earlier in this unit is an explanation essay, and that the main purpose of an explanation is to say how or why something happens, or is done. It usually gives facts, not opinions.

① Students read the text in the following table carefully. It shows the stages in explanation essays.

STAGE	SUB-STAGE	PURPOSE
Introduction	General statement	To introduce the topic of the information report, and to define it.
	Preview/scope (essay map)	To show what ideas will be in the body of the essay
Explanations	*for each main idea:*	
	Theme	To introduce the point
	Elaboration	To give further information about the point

Note: The theme is sometimes a sentence. When it is a sentence, it is often called a **topic sentence**.

② Students are asked to draw boxes around (or colour) the stages from the table onto the *Market segmentation* text on page 29 of their books. The introduction is done for them as an example on page 33 of their books. If this is the first time they have done an activity like this, be prepared to give them plenty of help.

ANSWERS

Market segmentation ← *General statement*

1. Have you ever wondered why advertisements for babies' nappies are shown during daytime TV but not usually at night? Or advertisements for beer and wine only in the evenings? The answer is linked to something called market segmentation and is just one of the reasons why an understanding of demographics is important in marketing. So, what exactly is market segmentation, and how is it useful to companies? ← *Preview/scope: the writer is going to talk in the body of the essay about what market segmentation is, and how useful companies find it.*

Theme ↘

2. In market segmentation, society is divided into groups, based on such things as age, where they live, sex, socio-economic status (their social class and how rich they are) and whether they have children. A group of people (or cohort) having similar characteristics, for example, women in their 30s and 40s with children and who are living in relatively wealthy neighbourhoods, is known as a market segment or demographic. A market segment could also include a group of people sharing common interests, lifestyle, attitudes etc.   ← *Elaboration*

Theme ↘

3. The technique of market segmentation is useful to marketers because it helps them to target their marketing to the right group of people. Clearly sales will be higher, for example, if computer games are advertised to young people rather than old people. And different games might be advertised in a magazine for teenagers than in a magazine for young adults. Further, new products may be developed especially for newly emerging market segments. For example, due to improvements in medical science, people are having a healthier and longer retirement, and therefore a lot more money is spent on leisure products for older people than in the past.   ← *Elaboration*

Theme ↘

4. With an example like computer games, it can be seen easily which ones interest different groups. However, it might be less clear with other products. If, for example, a car company wants to expand into a new country by selling a car it already makes, how does it know which demographic to aim at? Different cultures have different characteristics, so the advertising that works for one market segment in one country might have to be modified in another country.

Unit 3 Demographics | 39

> 5. The company must do market research, which can show which kind of people are interested in the product and are ready to buy it. Further, different versions of the car, perhaps with different body styles, engine tunings and interior features, might be produced for different demographics, and advertising shown where each demographic is likely to see it. ← *Elaboration continued from para 4*
>
> *Theme →*
> 6. The reverse of this process is also common.
> 7. A company might first do market research to find out what the market wants. Then a product will be designed that fits the results of this research. Different variations of this product may be made to appeal to different demographics.
>
> ← *Elaboration*

Task B | Write your own explanation essay ▶▶ SB P. 33

In this task, students are guided through the process of writing an explanation essay.

① Students choose one of the topics from Task C, Question 2 of the previous section (any other topic that they are passionate about is OK – but students should check with you before starting with a different topic, just to make sure the topic lends itself to explanation rather than another genre).

② Students write a plan for their essays, giving (a) the main idea that the essay is going to explain, and (b) each of the points to be included in their explanations.

③ Students write a first draft, following guidelines in the Students' Book: The point they wrote as part (a) of their essay plan should become the end of the General Statement, and each point in part (b) of their plan should be mentioned in their Preview/Scope, and should also be a Theme/Topic sentence of a paragraph in the body of the essay.

   Try to look at all the essays during the lesson, first to ensure that everyone is on the right track, and then to help with any problems.

④ Students finish the first draft of their explanation essays for homework, and hand it in to you as soon as possible.

⑤ This step of the Students' Book instructions would need to be carried out in a later lesson, after you have had time to comment on each draft. In this later lesson time, students read the comments carefully and start writing a second draft while you monitor and help.

LISTENING: PREDICTING, NOTE-TAKING AND DIFFERENT ACCENTS – EXPLANATIONS

Task A | Prediction ▶▶ SB P. 34

In this section, students will listen to some people from different countries talking about the consequences of demographic change in their countries. First, though, they look at some of the points that the students might hear on the recording and, in pairs or small groups, predict some of the consequences they might hear. Make sure the class knows the vocabulary in each of these points. The points listed in the Students' Book are:

1. The birth rate is declining and life expectancy is increasing rapidly
2. People have to pay for their own retirement – the government doesn't provide pensions except for very poor people
3. The birth rate is very high and infant mortality is falling rapidly
4. There is a very large movement of people from the countryside to the cities, because the cities are getting richer very quickly but not the countryside.

It may help the students to work through the first as an open class activity.

> **Extension:** A class with good general knowledge can be asked to guess which country each statement represents.

Task B | Listening and note-taking (different accents) ▶▶ SB P. 34

① Ask students to write the headings in their notebooks that are given in the Students' Book (one for each speaker). They should leave plenty of space for writing notes below each heading – perhaps half an A4 page for each heading.

CD 1 (6)

   Then students listen and take notes – they will almost certainly have to listen several times. Depending on your class, note-taking advice such as the need to write ideas rather than sentences, and for students to focus on meaning rather than vocabulary, may have to be emphasised.

   It may help to remind students about the language of change that they studied in Unit 2 (increase, decrease, etc).

② In the same groups as Task A, students talk about any similarities and differences between the predictions made by the speakers on the recording, and those they themselves made in Task A.

Recording script

CD 1 — CD 1, track 6: Demographics, Unit 3
(5 minutes, 34 seconds)

Listening: Students report about their own countries' birth rates – research

Narrator: You will hear a lecturer and then four students. The students will give very short talks that they have researched and prepared for homework. This is taking place in a tutorial, and the talks are
5 about the demographic issues facing the countries. Notice how different the countries are!

[Lecturer] *English accent*
Good morning, everyone. As you'll all remember, I'm sure, today's the day you'll present your own short reports about the demographics in your own
10 countries. Kate, would you begin, please.

[Speaker 1] *Southern US accent but talking about Japan*
(0 minutes, 53 seconds)
Mmm, yeah, mm, yes, since we heard about my country in the lecture yesterday, the US, I've researched a different country, Japan. In Japan, the birth rate's already declining. Also, life expectancy
15 is increasing very rapidly, and the number of old people is increasing all the time. Err, traditionally, if parents need looking after in their old age, it's the oldest son's responsibility to do this. As a consequence, women don't want to marry oldest
20 sons! But nowadays, companies transfer their workers to other parts of the country, and if the old people don't want to move, the, the tradition is broken. Consequently, the government's spending more and more to look after the old people. But
25 in the future there will be fewer people of working age who can pay taxes, due to the declining birth rate. Now, if the government doesn't do something soon, the consequences will be that the younger generation will have to work much harder than
30 the current generation, or pay much more tax than at the moment. This problem is known as the demographic time bomb, and similar problems exist in many countries.

[Speaker 2] *Russian accent*
(2 minutes, 33 seconds)
Russia is going through some very unusual
35 demographic changes. Since the early 1990s, the population has been declining, because the birth rate is falling and unfortunately more people are dying, often at an earlier age. Now, there are only three births for every five deaths, and the population
40 is falling by three quarters of a million people each year. This all started soon after the fall of communism, so it might look as though the cause of these problems is political change. However, I'm told that this trend was beginning before the end
45 of communism, and is more to do with the baby boomer generation getting older. This means there are just fewer women of childbearing age. However, there is hope for the future – women are beginning to have more children, and life expectancy is
50 beginning to increase again.

[Speaker 3] *Australian accent*
(3 minutes, 49 seconds)
Australia has introduced an interesting way to help cope with the economic consequences of the demographic time bomb. Since the early nineties, all companies have had to pay a percentage of
55 each employee's wages into a special fund, called a superannuation fund, held for that person. This fund is like a private pension – the money is invested for the person and, if all goes well, it will provide an income in retirement. The problem is – the
60 percentage of wages paid into the fund is too low at the moment, and the average fund will provide less than half the income needed when people retire. If the employee wants, he or she can pay in some of their own money. However, not many people do this.

[Speaker 4] *Chinese accent*
(4 minutes, 45 seconds)
65 China has changed radically over the last 20 years. The economy in the cities is booming, but in the villages, things haven't changed so much. If young people have a choice of staying in a village with few opportunities, or going into the big city where there is the chance
70 of making their fortunes, most just go to the cities. Consequently, most of the people living in many places are middle aged and elderly. Already, it is a major problem that the cities are growing so rapidly – development can hardly keep up with the increase in population, and
75 certainly there is very little planning in the new suburbs.

Task C | Discussion ▸▸ SB P. 34

Students discuss the following questions in relation to their own countries (preferably in small groups of mixed nationality – if teaching a monolingual group, try to include as much mixture of previous life experience as possible in each group).

This will be a challenging task for many students, so students will need as much support in this discussion as possible. Depending on your students, it may be necessary to do it quite quickly in open class.

ANSWERS

a. What demographic changes can you predict in your lifetime? *Answers will vary.*
b. What kinds of people or organisations need to make predictions about future demographic trend? *From previous work in this unit, students will be able to suggest marketing departments of many companies. Other answers could include: government departments concerned with planning for the future, especially services such as health, education, transport, planning etc. Also, anyone involved in long-term planning for companies – demographic change would be just one of the areas that they would need to consider for future planning.*
c. Why do they need to make these predictions? *Companies: to help with future planning, gaining or maintaining a competitive advantage even while society changes. Governments: for future planning, eg so that railway lines and hospitals are built in the right place, etc.*
d. How accurate can these predictions be? *'Far from perfect' would be a good answer!*

LANGUAGE SPOTLIGHT 2: PRESENT CONTINUOUS, PRESENT SIMPLE AND ZERO CONDITIONAL

Task A | Identifying use ▶▶ SB P. 34

1 Students listen again to the people talking about the effects of demographic changes in various countries. While listening, they fill the gaps in the following sentences taken from the recording script.
CD 1, track 6

ANSWERS

Japan
a. In Japan, the birth rate's already declining. [lines 13–14]
b. Also, life expectancy is increasing very rapidly … [lines 14–15]
c. … the number of old people is increasing all the time. [lines 15–16]
d. … if parents need looking after in their old age, **[e]** it's the oldest son's responsibility to do this. [lines 17–18]
f. … if the old people don't want to move, **[g]** the tradition is broken [lines 21–22]
h. Consequently, the government's spending more and more to look after the old people [lines 23–24]
i. … similar problems exist in many countries [lines 32–33]

Russia
j. Russia is going through some very unusual demographic changes. [line 34]

k. … the population is falling by three quarters of a million people every year. [lines 39–40]

Australia
l. If the employee wants, **[m]** he or she can pay in some of their own money. [lines 62–64]

China
n. The economy in the cities is booming, but … [lines 64–65]
o. If young people have a choice of staying in a village with few opportunities, or going into the big city where there is the chance of making their fortunes, **[p]** most just go to the cities. [lines 67–70]

Some of these, eg [e], also test the students' skill with identifying weak forms in pronunciation (if they can't work out the missing word from prior grammatical knowledge!).

2 Students answer questions, in pairs, if it is difficult individually. They refer to the clauses in Question 1 [a] to [p] above. Here, they should be activating and reviewing what they have learned earlier in their English study—these tenses should not be new to them.

ANSWERS

a. Which clauses are used for something happening around now, but not true forever (a temporary situation)?
 [a], [b], [c], [h], [j], [k], [n]
b. Which clauses are used for actions that are happening now but which are probably not temporary (ie happening over a long period of time)?
 [d], [e], [f], [g], [i],
c. Which clauses are used for points that can happen regularly, again and again?
 [l], [m], [o], [p]
d. Which clauses are present continuous?
 [a], [b], [c], [h], [j], [k], [n].
 Which are present simple?
 [d], [e], [f], [g], [i], [l], [m], [o], [p] (if students don't notice that [f] is present simple, it's best not to bring it up except with a strong class that can cope with the passive at this point).
e. In what situations do both clauses of an *if* statement use present simple?
 To express the regular (or non-temporary) consequences of regular events or non-temporary events (the 'general' conditional). In other words, when the main clause would use present simple anyway, the 'if' clause usually also uses present simple.

Task B | Practice ▶▶ SB P. 35

Students fill the gaps with the most appropriate form of the verb in brackets.

Many companies nowadays [1] are noticing a great opportunity, which is to sell to retired people. This demographic [2] is increasing in size at an enormous rate, because life expectancy [3] is getting longer but the retirement age [4] is staying about the same, thus people [5] are spending much longer in retirement. Further, better health treatment [6] means that retired people are generally more healthy. When people [7] have more free time, they generally [8] spend more money, and the elderly [9] are no exception. The leisure industry [10] is seeing great benefits – if people have more leisure time, companies can expand their business if they [11] give people something to do in this time.

Another booming field is the provision of health care. If people [12] live longer, they [13] need more medical services, home care services and aged care homes, and the number of companies providing these services is increasing.

So, if you [14] buy shares in companies that target the elderly, [15] expect to make a lot of money!

Task C | Personalised practice ▶▶ SB P. 36

In this task, students have some questions that act as points for them to compare social and demographic trends in their own countries.

In a monolingual class, there may still be sufficient differences of opinion and knowledge for this to be interesting, even if they are talking about the same country.

While students work on this activity, monitor especially for appropriate choice between present simple and present continuous, including third person 's', etc.

Students can also be encouraged to use the passive where appropriate.

SPEAKING 2 — CLARIFICATION

Task A | Expressions for requesting clarification ▶▶ SB P. 36

❶ Elicit from students some expressions they use to ask for clarification (or check understanding) when they don't understand something. Provide corrections as necessary. This step is best done orally before students open their Students' Books.

❷ In the Students' Book, there are several expressions for requesting clarification with the words jumbled up. In pairs, ask students to rewrite each expression with the words in the correct order.

❸ Students answer some questions about the politeness and appropriate context of some of the expressions in Question 2.

ANSWERS

1. Answers will vary.
2. a. *So, do you mean ...*
   b. *I'm not sure what you mean by ...*
   c. *I'm not sure I understood you when you said ...*
   d. *Hold on a minute, I didn't catch what you said about ...*
   e. *Sorry – could you say that again please? I'm afraid I didn't quite catch it.*
   f. *Sorry, I missed that bit about ...*
   g. *Excuse me, could you explain again what you said about ...?*
3. (i) Which is not so polite (only for close friends)?
   d. *Hold on a minute, I didn't catch what you said about ...*
   (ii) Which is more suitable for tutorials (more formal with lots of people)?
   g. *Excuse me, could you explain again what you said about ...?*

Task B | Practice ▶▶ SB P. 36

Ask students, in pairs, to talk about the topics given in their books. Encourage them to give extended answers – and also to ask for clarification, using the expressions from Task A, whenever possible. When students are answering the requests for clarification, insist that they paraphrase rather than simply repeat, so that they practise this important skill as well.

Expressions that students can learn through context from this activity are: *compulsory education, mature student, factors* and *gap year.*

You may want to add more questions, tailored to the particular interests of your students.

At the end of the activity, encourage students to practise the clarification expressions at every opportunity.

FURTHER PRACTICE: READING, FILMS AND FUN

READING

There are several articles about demography, demographics, social change and market segmentation on the English version of **Wikipedia**: http://en.wikipedia.org.

The **United Nations** produces a very interesting wall chart showing populations for all the countries in the world. It includes populations in 2005, and predictions for 2015 and 2050. Just go to: **http://www.un.org/esa/population/publications/WPP2004/wpp2004.htm** and click on 'Wall Chart'.

FILMS

Brassed Off, written and directed by Mark Herman. This is a very funny comedy featuring a rarely shown side of British society.

Not One Less, directed by Zhang Yimou. This is a moving story about children, set against the background of some of the demographic issues in China. Use the English subtitles!

QUESTIONS

1. What differences can you see between your lifestyle, and the lifestyle your parents talk about having when they were the same age as you?

2. (For students outside their home countries only.) What differences can you see between the lifestyles of your home country and the country where you are now living?

3. Think of a product that you are interested in (eg sports shoes or cars). How are different varieties of the product designed to appeal to different market segments? For some products, it may be better just to talk about one company's product range; for others, you may have to talk about a variety of products.

4 ENERGY

'corporations have neither bodies to be punished nor souls to be damned'

BY THE END OF THIS UNIT, STUDENTS SHOULD:

- understand and be able to use various meanings of energy .... Speaking: Tasks A and B **46**
- understand *For* or *Against* and have a concept of 'issues' .... Speaking: Task C **46**
- find definitions in context and the 'clues or signals' that locate those definitions .... Speaking: Task D **46**
- be able to read a graph and work in the present tense to describe it .... Speaking: Task D **46**
- locate stages in an argument and write topic sentences .... Reading: Task A **47**
- write an argument using staging .... Writing: Task A **49**
- differentiate verb forms and functions in phrases (participle, gerund, infinitive) ... Language Spotlight: Task A **51**
- compose an argument and speak using signposting for the listener .... Listening: Task A **52**

ENERGY n., pl. ENERGIES [UNCOUNTABLE AND COUNTABLE]: 1 (habitual) capacity or habit of vigorous activity. 2 the actual exertion of power; operation; activity. 3 power as exerted. 4 ability to produce action or effect. 5 vigour or forcefulness of expression. 6 *Physics.* The capacity for doing work which exists in various forms, as kinetic energy, nuclear energy, etc.; the derived SI unit of energy is the joule.

SPEAKING

BUILDING THE FIELD: INTRODUCTION TO THE TOPIC OF ENERGY

Task A | Understanding energy ▶▶ Sb P. 40

In this task students examine the pictures on page 40 of their books and describe them. This is an introduction to the field of energy and introduces the idea that some different kinds of energy exist. You might point out that the energy used by the person is a different kind from the other six and is measured in joules or calories. It also comprises an exercise common to some English language proficiency exams, for example, IELTS (International English Language Testing System) one to two minute stand-alone speaking practice with a one minute preparation time to make notes.

Task B | Recognising an issue ▶▶ SB P. 40

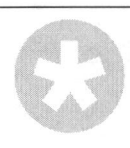

Definition: issue – subject/problem. A subject or problem that is often discussed or argued about, especially a social or political matter that affects the interests of a lot of people.

❶ Explain to students the definition of an issue using the one above plus the explanation in the Students' Book. The students then determine which statements from [a] to [j] are issues and which are not. One way to help identify an erroneous or contentious thing is when the word 'always' appears. Rarely, if ever, is anything as definite as *always*.

ANSWERS

a. no	f. yes
b. no	g. yes
c. yes	h. yes
d. yes	i. yes
e. yes	j. no

❷ Students then explain to their partners why they knew the correct answer.

Task C | For or against ▶▶ SB P. 40

Each statement around nuclear energy is either for or against it. Students should read the extracts below and decide which side of the argument the statements represent.

ANSWERS

A. Against
B. For
C. Against
D. For
E. Against

Task D | Definitions in context ▶▶ SB P. 41

Students look for the definitions in context. They practise so they recognise when a definition is offered rather than panicking if they don't immediately know a word.

❶ Students must find the definitions of particular words in the texts A-E from the previous task (Task C). Most of the definitions have parenthesis ( ) around them or are signalled by the following introductory words or punctuation: *which means*; *that means*; *which are*; and *commas*.

Students write the definition next to the word in the table and include the 'clues' within it. You should point out the signals or workshop them before and after the task.

For example: **A.** toxic: (very poisonous, deadly)
environment: (the living world around).

ANSWERS

1. **A.** toxic: (very poisonous, deadly)
   environment: (the living world around)
   B. toxic: *which means* it can kill you
   C. waste: tailings
   contaminated: *that means* people cannot drink or bathe in the water
   D. ballistic nuclear missiles: *which* are powerful weapons that can travel a long distance, fly up into the sky and then back down to earth where they explode
   cruise missiles: (*these are* missiles that fly close to the ground and go for hundreds of miles) and *parenthesis*
   E. poison: neutrons
   place: the facility
   levels of radiation: isotopes
   green kryptonite: a rock
   exposure: the time near the source
2. The photograph of the five yen coin (found in Task C) tells us about the physicists in Tokai, Ibaraki, Japan. The physicists used the 5 yen coin to measure the level of poison that went into peoples' houses after a nuclear accident happened.
3. Students are given a cloze passage to assist with their explanation. The key to explaining the graph is to recognise the sequential markers and connectives and work in the present tense.

46 | EAP Now! Preliminary English for Academic Purposes Teacher's Book

> First radioactive materials are released into the __air__. Then, they go __three__ ways. They go into the __soil__. From the soil, these radioactive materials move to __crops__ and __plants__ and they __move__ to animals too. From animals, they __move__ or go into milk and __meat__. Finally, humans __drink__ the milk and __eat__ the meat. After that, humans absorb the __radioactive__ __materials__.

4 Students work in pairs to discuss nuclear power and uranium mining. They can use Figure 4.1 to help them. This is a personal response question to encourage critical thinking. Answers will vary.

5 Students to respond to the questions: Are there different opinions in their group or class about nuclear energy? How will they discuss this issue in English? Task E gives students some signposting phrases.

Task E | Signposting in speaking/talking about an issue ▶▶ SB P. 43

Students use the signposting phrases to help them in speaking about an issue. You could change the issue from nuclear energy if there is something more relevant to your individual class.

Monitor talks and encourage the use of the signposts. Listeners may make an outline in their notebooks of Introduction, Points and Conclusion, then take notes when they think the speaker in their group is speaking in that section. This will promote active listening and speakers will need to organise their talks to include the stages then signal the stages with the signpost phrases.

STAGES IN ARGUMENT, DEFINITIONS IN CONTEXT, TOPIC SENTENCES AND LOCATING POINTS IN ARGUMENT
READING

Task A | Staging – The outline, the schema, the map ▶▶ SB P. 43

The reading promoting clean energy is an *argument*. In this task, students read the text; *Clean energy is possible* and analyse its stages using the information provided.

In Question 3 they are asked to find definitions in context. (*You may wish to do this either before, during or right after the reading prior to staging if you are working with your students reading aloud.*) Then the students must locate the topic sentences in body paragraphs and locate supporting statements for the topic sentences in each paragraph.

1 Students read the text (you could do the definitions at the same time or just read for general meaning the first time).

2 Analyse stages: Staging in arguments
You could photocopy this for students and put it on an OHT. The Students' Book outlines Introduction, Body, and Conclusion requirements. They can match the text to those requirements by boxing the stages as shown on the next page.

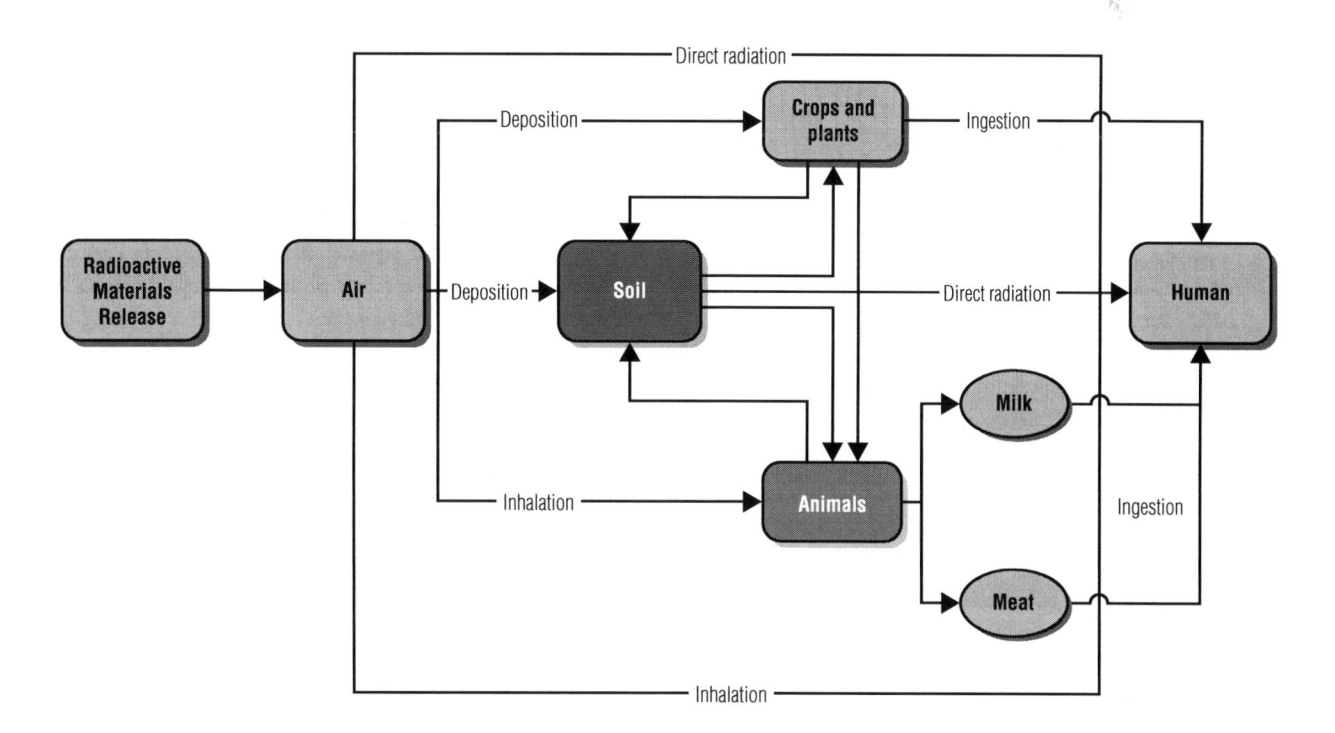

FIGURE 4.1 | Graph of Radioactive Materials Release

ANSWER

Clean energy is possible

Introduction to the field – first sentence in general introduction

1. I'd like to present you with an argument against using energy that ruins our environment and with an argument for using energy that is healthy. There are energy sources that do not cause so much destruction as oil, coal, nuclear and wood, which are dirty energies. Clean energy is energy that uses wind, water or sunshine. It's just that simple. Clean energy is energy that does not pollute our earth as much as dirty energy. Energy that works with nature instead of against nature, energy that doesn't ruin the earth, doesn't pollute the earth as much as what we are using now in the 21st century. A name for this energy is renewable. It's renewable energy. Since renew means to make new again, energy that is renewable can be made over and over again without using up its source.

Definition stage

2. Clean energy is not necessarily perfect. Nothing is perfect. Clean energy does pollute in some ways, for example, wind turbines may kill migrating birds or they may make too much noise when placed near homes. Some say they look ugly and that is eye pollution. Water or hydro energy may ruin land because of dams. The dams flood existing areas and farmers may lose farms. People may have to move from their homes. As for sunshine, that is, solar energy, there do not seem to be any polluting effects. However, dirty energy always pollutes. There are several arguments against that type of energy.

Preview or scope of what the essay will be about.

3. Firstly, to define dirty energy, we are looking at wood, coal, oil and nuclear. Wood and coal burning causes a great deal of pollution in the atmosphere. There is no argument to refute that. That is, there is no way to deny that fact. Coal burning is dirty. It is smoky. Oil burning is dirty, too. Oil makes petrol, of course, and cars burn petrol (gasoline). This is also causing pollution in every major city of the world.

> The shaded areas paras 3 – 5 are **the Body paragraphs** and offer arguments to support the preview statement – *However, dirty energy always pollutes. There are several arguments against that type of energy.*

4. Next, nuclear power, which starts with uranium mining, is supposed to be clean, but can actually be very dirty. There are three parts to using nuclear power. The first is mining it, the second is processing it and the third is using it in a power station. Nuclear supporters advertise nuclear power as clean energy. Advertising is not always truthful. Nuclear energy is only clean until there is an accident, and accidents happen. In fact, there is no industry that has no accidents. In addition, getting the uranium out of the ground to process into plutonium for nuclear power stations is a very dangerous, risky business for workers. Uranium mining often causes terrible poisoning of people and land. Nuclear power stations, when there are leaks, also cause the same problems: cancer, death, food supplies destroyed.

5. Another argument against nuclear is uranium mining. Uranium is also mined for the purpose of making nuclear weapons. These are weapons that have the power to destroy the entire world and everyone in it. Why mine such a dangerous material? Why not leave it in the ground?

   If each country in the world began to use wind, water and sunshine for their power needs, and to drive cars and machinery, even in small quantities, then we would see an improvement in our atmosphere. Soon we would see less smog. Our cities would have clean air and birds instead of filthy air and people wearing masks over their faces.

(para 6) and para 7 Conclusion stage – summary

6. If governments around the world put money into research, we would soon have solar powered cars, solar powered heating, both water and home heating. We could improve wind energy. All technologies improve over time and with research. Look at computers!

7. The question is – why don't governments put money into researching and using clean energy? Why are they continuing to use dirty energy that pollutes our cities, our countries, and our earth? Can you answer that question? We should ask it in the right places and work together for clean energy.

Recommendation stage in Conclusion

③ This question is about locating the textual clue signalling the definition in each of the paragraphs. They do this by writing out the sentence or paragraph and drawing arrows forwards or backwards to the words and their corresponding definitions. For example:

[a] **dirty energies**
Para 1, sentence 2 – There are energy sources that do not cause so much destruction as

oil, coal, nuclear and wood, **which are** dirty energies.

> **ANSWERS**
>
> 3. a. **dirty energies** (as above)
>   b. **clean energy**
>
>   Para 1, sentence 3
>
>   *Clean energy* **is** energy that uses wind, water or sunshine.
>
>   c. **renewable energy**
>   Para 1, sentence 7
>   Energy that works with nature instead of against nature, energy that doesn't ruin the earth, doesn't pollute the earth as much as what we are using now, in the 21st century. *A name for this energy* **is** *renewable*. (This refers back to the previous sentence. It is anaphoric referencing – referencing can refer forward as well as backwards.)
>
>   d. **solar energy**
>   Para 2, sentence 6
>   As for sunshine, **that is**, *solar energy*,............
>
>   e. **to refute that**
>   Para 3, sentence 3
>   Wood and coal burning causes a great deal of pollution in the atmosphere. There is no argument to refute that. **That is**, *there is no way to deny that fact*.
>
>   f. **nuclear weapons**
>   Para 5, sentence 2
>   Uranium is also mined for the purpose of making *nuclear weapons*. **These are** weapons that have the power to destroy the entire world and everyone in it.

> **ANSWERS**
>
> 4. Here students locate topic sentences in body paragraphs.
>   Para 1 – *I'd like to present you with an argument against using energy that ruins our environment and with an argument for using energy that is healthy.*
>   Para 2 – *Clean energy is not necessarily perfect.*
>   Para 3 – *Wood and coal burning causes a great deal of pollution in the atmosphere.*
>   Para 4 – *Next, nuclear power, which starts with uranium mining, is supposed to be clean, but can actually be very dirty.*
>   Para 5 – *Another argument against nuclear is uranium mining.*
>   Para 6 – *If governments around the world put money into research, we would soon have solar powered cars, solar powered heating, both water and home heating.*
>   Para 7 – (here the topic sentence is both the first sentence and the concluding sentence or recommendation stage) *We should ask it in the right places and work together for clean energy.*

5 Students now locate supporting statements for the topic sentences in each paragraph.

Each paragraph has supporting statements after the topic sentence. Almost every sentence supports the main idea in each paragraph. Paragraph 2 offers an 'against' argument around clean energy. It pre-empts arguments by saying that 'nothing is perfect'. When the word 'However' occurs in the next to last line, we have 'dirty energy always pollutes' and the argument against non-renewable energies or dirty energies is re-established.

All the paragraphs argue *against* dirty energy and *for* clean energy after 'establishing the terms of reference', ie giving definitions of what the writer believes to be 'clean' and 'dirty'.

WRITING

AN ARGUMENT

Task A | Staging in an argument ▶▶ SB P. 46

Students are provided with schema/a map/stages that they can use as a guide for producing their own, written argument on the topic of clean air. They use the lines next to each indicated stage as a guide. If they don't research this topic, then, obviously, the writing is going to be basic and drawn from experience and general knowledge. The topic around 'clean air' has been kept within the field of 'clean energy' so that students will not have to grapple with another field of knowledge in addition to writing an argument.

Unit 4 Energy | 49

With regard to formatting, tell students to skip two lines for each new paragraph. Their introduction will probably consist of one paragraph. There are three body paragraphs and then the conclusion, ie five paragraphs in all. This is similar to written language exam tasks such as those found in IELTS or Cambridge. They are asked to use the stages to write an argument for an educated reader **for** the following topic:

Governments around the world need to spend money on ways to make the air cleaner

Students are provided with the following vocabulary. You could workshop more vocabulary with your individual group and ask them to give examples from their own country about the environment in the body paragraphs in order to strengthen and personalise their arguments.

pollution (dirty air from factory emissions, car exhaust fumes, coal and wood burning); government funding; pristine (very clean); respiratory diseases (lung diseases like asthma and cancer); populations; government legislation; and any vocabulary they find useful from Reading: Task A.

This is an **example essay** written at *Intermediate level* using the schema provided in the Student Book. It has 566 words which is about double what an Intermediate student will be able to accomplish. Italicised words in parenthesis indicate higher lexis which more proficient level students may use.

SCHEMA/ A MAP/ STAGES

INTRODUCTION

Introduction to topic or introduction to the field:	→	Around the world today, there is an increasing issue concerning clean air within countries. Although populations may wish for this to change, it is largely up to governments to spend money on ways to make the air cleaner. (This will require legislation and other measures.)
Definition of terms:	→	Clean air means air that is comfortable to breathe and is not polluted to the extent of being dangerous. There are many capital cities in the world today where the air poses a danger to people (or populations).
Preview or scope:	→	Air is definitely getting dirtier, populations want change and there is no reason for governments to resist this change. They need to spend money on ways to make the air cleaner. There are ways in which they can do this. (*accomplish or achieve this aim*)

BODY PARAGRAPHS
Body paragraph 1

Topic sentence – the main idea:	→	At present, every major city has dirtier air than it did ten years ago.
Topic sentence explained:	→	I remember Wollongong, Australia, where I come from, when the horizon over the sea was a clear line. Today, there is a band of grey, brown air that originates in Sydney and stretches across that horizon.
Provide an example or elaborate (say more) OR contrast and compare using only the idea in the topic sentence:	→	This pollution is visible and when the wind blows in from the sea, we must be breathing it in. The Steel Works are in our city so the air has always been in question. But it is worse now.
Introduce or lead into next argument for:	→	Wollongong, like Sydney, has a lot of people with asthma (very high amount of respiratory illness such as asthma; a high incidence of…). Surely, the government doesn't want its population to be ill.

Body paragraph 2 **Topic sentence – the main idea:**	→	Respiratory illness is on the increase around the world and if governments don't want ill populations, then they had better begin to do something about it (address the problem).
Topic sentence explained:	→	Governments have the power to act in this matter in several ways.
Provide an example or elaborate (say more) OR contrast and compare using only the idea in the topic sentence:	→	One way they can assist is to sign the Kyoto Protocol, which is designed to reduce green house gas emissions around the world. Many governments have signed this document, but not all.
Introduce or lead into next argument for:	→	Some of the causes of green house gases are exhaust fumes from cars, CO2 emissions from factories and methane gas.
Body paragraph 3 **Topic sentence – the main idea:**	→	It is well known that car exhaust fumes are harmful. Governments could spend money on (fund or finance) projects that move away from typical fossil fuels like oil.
Topic sentence explained:	→	Oil is not the only resource for producing fuel.
Provide an example or elaborate (say more) OR contrast and compare using only the idea in the topic sentence:	→	For example, hybrid cars that run on less fuel and use another source for energy are a good idea. Also, pure electric cars are now for sale and they produce zero emissions. In other words, no pollution at all! Government spending on both research and tax breaks for companies that produce 'clean air cars' could change the air throughout the world in a fairly short time span.
CONCLUSION **Lead in discourse signal:**	→	In conclusion,
Write a brief *summary* of what you have been saying in the beginning and body of your argument essay:	→	The air in our world is becoming increasingly dirty and polluted. Even cities within Australia which are supposed to be renown for relatively clean air are becoming worse. (*Teacher please note – from Body para 1*) One result of this is that respiratory illness is on the increase. (*Teacher, please note – from Body para 2*) Using fossil fuels like oil to run cars is one cause of major pollution as it contributes to the overall problem of green house gas emissions. Governments do have the power and means to address this problem. (*Teacher, please note – from Body para 3*)
Make a *recommendation* or *suggestion* for the future:	→	Governments *should* encourage big business to start investing in renewable fuel sources, and finance their own government research agencies in their quest for cheap (inexpensive) useable (viable) energy as well as sign the Kyoto Protocol, then clean air would become a normal fact of life once again.

LANGUAGE SPOTLIGHT: VERB FORMS AND FUNCTIONS

Task A | Gerunds and infinitives ▶▶ SB P. 47

Students learn the difference between '*–ing*' endings on participles and gerunds.

> **Gerunds** end in *–ing*: gerunds are used only as *nouns* (and can be modified)
>
> **Participles** end in *–ing*: participles are used as *adjectives*

① Students underline the nouns and/or noun phrases and write the function of the gerund. For example:
Watering and tending a garden /can be fun.
(*Gerund* used as subject)

> **ANSWERS**
>
> a. <u>Writing</u>/is required at all levels of school. (Gerund used as subject)
> b. My family/attended the annual <u>running (of the bulls in Spain)</u>. (Noun gerund modified by the adjective 'annual')
> c. <u>The cat's meowing</u>/woke me at 4 am, so I got up and opened the door for her. (Subject)
> d. The lazy student finally/got motivated and <u>began working</u>. (Direct object)
> e. I prefer/<u>eating quickly</u>. (verb phrase, gerund noun modified by adverb)
> f. <u>That baby's loud crying</u>/needs attention. (Subject, gerund modified by adjective – loud)
> g. Students think of four sentences of their own using gerunds. Answers will vary.

② Students underline the infinitives and write their function in seven sentences in their books (a–g).
Infinitives are the base form of verbs. They usually have the marker to: to be, to come, to think. Infinitives can function as nouns, adjectives or adverbs. They modify either the noun, or verb in a sentence when functioning as nouns or verbs. In the sentence I'm happy *to meet you*. To meet you functions as an adverb. It's an infinitive phrase modifying the predicate adjective 'happy'.

> **ANSWERS**
>
> a. <u>To love</u> is to learn (noun)
> b. I like <u>to drive</u> carefully. Do you? (adverb)
> c. <u>To think</u> is a process. (noun)
> d. The process of thinking can be rewarding or it can cause you <u>to go</u> crazy. (verb)
> e. If you want that computer <u>to work</u>, you'll have <u>to turn</u> it on first. (verb); (verb)
> f. I'm ready <u>to see him now</u>. (adverb)
> g. The work <u>to be done</u> cannot be avoided. (adjective modifying *work*)

③ Students underline the infinitives, participles and gerund phrases in the following text.

> **ANSWER**
>
> I always believed her <u>to be</u> my friend. I'm afraid I found out differently <u>seeing her</u> at the movies with another guy. <u>To think I was wasting</u> all that time on her for months. <u>I was spending</u> money every day on her as well. <u>I prefer thinking</u> she still likes me but <u>to tell</u> the truth, I'm not so sure. <u>She's avoiding me</u> all the time <u>when seeing me</u> on campus. To me, that means she isn't interested anymore. <u>I'm looking at you</u> and <u>wondering</u> what <u>you're thinking</u>. <u>Are you going to discuss</u> this with me?

> **Infinitives** are the base forms of verbs. They usually begin with *to*, eg *to be, to go, to work, to drive, to think, to love*
>
> **Infinitives** function as **nouns, adjectives** or **adverbs**

LISTENING

ENERGY TO BURN

Task A | Listening for meaning and content ▶▶ SB P. 48

① Students listen to the recording for meaning and content first and answer true or false to a list of statements.

CD 1 (7)

② On second listening, they listen for the word 'energy' and to identify how the one word may have differing meanings.

③ Third listening is focused listening – listening for a specific phrase – and is grammar based. Students listen for 'what …'. and note down eight uses of 'What' in the listening.

④ Students write the full sentences that used the 'What' forms noted in the above question.

Recording Script
CD 1

CD 1, track 7: Energy, Unit 4
(2 minutes, 14 seconds)

Listening: Dialogue between three friends

Narrator: In this listening, Jess drops in to Miki's flat in Sydney, Australia. They talk for a bit and then Allan arrives as well.

Jess:	Hi Miki,
Miki:	Hi Jess, how are you going?
Jess:	Good, you?
Miki:	Yeah, alright.
Jess:	Wow! What was that?
Miki:	A new song by my boyfriend. It's pretty high energy, isn't it? He and his band just recorded it.
Jess:	Sure is. Hey, why are you wearing that coat?
Miki:	What do ya mean?
Jess:	Just what I said. Why are you wearing a coat when it's a hot as hell today.
Miki:	I'm cold.
Jess:	How can you be? *(pause)* You're too thin, that's why.
Miki:	Shut up, I'm not.
Jess:	Well, I hate to tell you but you are. That's why you've got no energy and you're always lying around.
Miki:	What about you, Jess? You're skinny, too.
Jess:	Yeah, but I don't need a coat on a bloody hot day like today.
Allan:	What's up you two? Howzit goin'?
Miki & Jess:	Hi, Allan.
Allan:	What's with the coat, Miki?
Miki:	Not this again, please …
Jess:	I know, I was just saying something about that to her, it seems she's cold.
Allan:	What – on a hot day like this? I think you'd better eat something. You've obviously got no energy and that's why you're cold. Here, want some chips?
Miki:	*(Repulsed)* Yuck! God no… but thanks anyway.
Allan:	What about a banana? or an apple? Or … How about some crackers and cheese? Here's an orange, *(rustling noise of searching in bag)* down the bottom – they're in my bag. I always carry food so I don't run out of energy.
Jess:	What else have you got in there? A chicken?
Allan:	Funny you should mention that … as a matter of fact …
Jess and Miki:	*(Laughing loudly – one squeals out)* Oh my god! You <u>do</u> have a chicken in there! *(Laughter all around …)*

ANSWERS

1. **a.** F, **b.** F, **c.** T, **d.** F, **e.** T
2. **a.** energy, **b.** energy, **c.** energy, cold
3. What was; What I; What do; What about you; What's up; What's with; What about; What else.
4. **a.** What was that?
   b. Just what I said.
   c. What about you?
   d. What's up you two?
   e. What's with the coat, Taki?
   f. What – on a hot day like this?
   g. What about a banana?
   h. What else have you got in there?

Unit 4 Energy | 53

FURTHER PRACTICE: READING, FILMS AND FUN

READING

Suzuki, D. & Dressel, H. (1999) *Naked Ape to Superspecies*. Toronto, Canada: Stoddart Publishing Co.
http://www.zpenergy.com/index.php

FILMS

An Inconvenient Truth: This film is a documentary about how our planet is changing due to huge amounts of carbon dioxide released into the air. It was created by Al Gore who once ran for President of the USA. It is causing a lot of interest and controversy. Hope you get to see it.

Million Dollar Baby: A high energy boxing film with a young woman as the star.

QUESTIONS

ESSAY

① Research any kind of renewable energy, for example solar or wind and write an argument in favour of its use.

DISCUSSION

② Read the true text below and discuss. Do you think it's possible that in the future, the big oil companies will be a thing of the past and cars will run on water and hydrogen? What other kinds of future energy are possible?

1994 Ford Escort gets 100 miles

A scientist named Klein just patented his process of converting H_2O to HHO, producing a gas that combines the atomic power of hydrogen with the chemical stability of water. 'It turns right back to water. In fact, you can see the H_2O running off the sheet metal.' Klein originally designed his water-burning engine for cutting metal. He thought his invention could replace acetylene in welding factories. Then one day as he drove to his laboratory in Clearwater, he thought of another way to burn his HHO gas. 'On a 100 mile trip, we use about four ounces of water.' Klein says his prototype 1994 Ford Escort can travel exclusively on water, though he currently has it rigged to run as a water and gasoline hybrid.

5 COMMUNICATION

'whispered words are heard afar'

BY THE END OF THIS UNIT, STUDENTS SHOULD:

- know more vocabulary for talking about communication.... Speaking 1: Task A **56**
- be more fluent in talking about communication............Speaking 1: Task A **56**; Reading: Task E **59**; Writing: Task A **59**
- have further practised reading for main ideas and reading for detail.. Reading: Tasks B and D **56–57**
- be aware of the differences in formatting and language between informal emails, formal emails and formal letters .... Writing: Task B **59**
- be able to write informal emails, formal emails and formal letters with appropriate formatting and choice of language.. Writing: Task C **61**
- have further practised listening for specific information................................ Listening: Task A **61**
- know more vocabulary on the topic of telephoning .... Listening: Task B **62**
- have improved accuracy in using *will* for instant decisions .... Language Spotlight: Tasks A and B **65**
- have improved accuracy in using conditional expressions for real possibilities .... Language Spotlight: Tasks C and D **65–66**
- have practised making telephone enquiries .... Speaking 2: Task A **66**
- have improved accuracy, skill and ability to adjust the level of politeness in making requests... Speaking 2: Task A **66**

COMMUNICATION n. [UNCOUNTABLE]: the process by which people exchange information or express their thoughts and feelings: *Good communication is vital in a large organisation.* | *Radio was the pilot's only means of communication.*

SPEAKING 1 — BUILDING THE FIELD

Task A | Types of communication ▶▶ SB P. 52

❶ Students match words from a list in their books with pictures to introduce them to thinking about different types and aspects of communication. Emphasise that there may be more than one possible answer – however, students should choose the *best* set of answers.

> **ANSWERS**
>
> Written communication: *Picture 1 (man reading newspaper)*
> Gestures: *Picture 2 (woman with thumbs up)*
> Telecommunications: *Picture 3 (telecommunications dishes)*
> Mass communication: *Picture 4 (TV, DVDs etc)*
> Visual communication: *Picture 5 (traffic lights)*
> Other answers may be possible, but those above are the best fits for all five of them.

❷ Now students brainstorm different kinds of communication using the categories given in their books, in pairs. The following vocabulary may have to be pre-taught: *body language, facial expressions, digital, disabled.*

> **ANSWERS**
>
> The following are suggestions – many more ideas are possible.
> **Telecommunications:** TV, radio, telephone, mobile phone
> **Gestures, body language and facial expressions:** smile, frown, shrug, point, wave, bow, cringe, smirk (students may use these gestures, with the teacher supplying the vocabulary)
> **Visual communication:** traffic signs, warning signs, fire exit signs, toilet door signs (male/female), road crossings (zebra crossings), etc
> **Written communication:** books, newspapers, magazines, instruction manuals, notices, advertisements etc
> **Mass communication:** TV, radio, Internet, rallies and demonstrations, advertising
> **Digital communication:** DVDs, CDs, Internet, email, Internet chat
> **Communication systems for the disabled:** Sign language, Braille.

READING — MAIN IDEAS & SPECIFIC INFORMATION – EXPLANATION ESSAY

Task A | Discussion – Communication and miscommunication ▶▶ SB P. 52

❶ Ask students to think about a time when they were involved in a breakdown of communication. Perhaps introduce this with an example from your own experience. The students should be given time to prepare what they are going to say, and should focus on:
- What happened
- The reasons for the communication breakdown
- What would have made the situation better.

Following the preparation period, students work in small groups. After each speaker has finished, the other students in the group should ask follow-up questions.

When all the students have talked about their experiences, change the groups around so that each student is working with a different student, and then ask them to do Questions 2 and 3.

❷ Students make a list of reasons why communication sometimes doesn't work – from what they heard from the other students, and from other ideas they think of.

❸ Students think of ways in which people can prevent these problems, that is, to help communication work well.

If some of your students are heading for vocational education and training courses, you may want to point out that much of the content of the reading text in this section is relevant to units such as Business Communication in many college courses.

Task B | Reading for main ideas ▶▶ SB P. 52

Ask students to read the text (*Effective communication!*) on page 53 of the Students' Book, thinking about the main ideas of each paragraph as they read it. Then, point out to students the statements in this task (in the Students' Book), and ask them to write the number of the paragraph that best matches each statement in the boxes provided.

> **ANSWERS**
>
> 7 Active listening
> 5 Good place, good time, good situation
> 2 Listening and speaking are equally important
> 3 Different understandings
> 4 Not just words
> 6 All areas of life

56 | EAP Now! Preliminary English for Academic Purposes Teacher's Book

Task C | The five questions for reading any text ▶▶ SB P. 54

Students look at the five questions that are provided (the same as those used with the readings in other units of this book), then read the following text *Effective communication!*

① They answer the questions about the reading text for this unit, *Effective communication!*

> **ANSWERS**
>
> a. **What is it?** *A web page / An explanation (of effective communication)*
> b. **What is the source?** *University of New North Scotland, Faculty of Business, Centre for Professional Communication (bottom of the webpage – a common place on web pages for source information)*
> c. **Who is the writer?** *Information not given – but presumably someone from the Centre for Professional Communication*
> d. **What purpose does the writer have for writing it?** *To provide information to the general public, to help them – according to the bottom of the website. There may also be some 'hidden' purpose, such as to create publicity for the university, but there is no apparent evidence.*
> e. **Who is the intended audience?** *The general public, according to the bottom of the web page.*

Task D: | Reading for detail ▶▶ SB P. 54

① Ask students to scan the text (*Effective communication!*) for words and phrases that appear in a list in their books. It's a good idea to clarify to the students that this question is not the 'reading in detail' aspect of this task – it is just a lead-in to the main part, Questions 3 and 4.

> **ANSWER**
>
> The highlighted words in the text on the next page are the ones the students are scanning for. This could be photocopied onto an OHT.
>
> | benefits | barriers |
> | --- | --- |
> | express | technique |
> | extrovert | conflict (two places) |
> | assume | paraphrasing |

② Ask students to write the words and phrases from Question 1 next to the closest meanings in the list in their books. They should use context to find the meaning, not a dictionary.

> **ANSWER**
>
> | MEANINGS | WORDS |
> | --- | --- |
> | communicate | express |
> | a special or clever way of doing something | technique |
> | say something in different words | paraphrasing |
> | argument | conflict |
> | make a guess that something is true | assume |
> | a person who enjoys spending time with other people; usually someone who talks loudly and a lot | extrovert |
> | advantage, improvement or help that you get from something; something good | benefits |
> | a rule, problem, etc that prevents people from doing something, or limits what they can do | barriers |

③ A summary of the *Effective communication!* text appears in the Students' Book, with gaps. Students must fill the gaps in the text, using words from a boxed list in their books.

> **ANSWER**
>
> Note: Missing words are **bold underlined**.
>
> A good [a] **communicator** does much more than just [b] **talk**. Listening is also very important, as is avoiding the kinds of problems that might stop the message from being [c] **understood** in the way the speaker wanted. One such problem is when people make assumptions about what the other is thinking, or assume that something [d] is **common sense**. To solve this, it is useful for the listener to say what he or she thinks the meaning is, and to ask if this is correct.
>
> Non-verbal communication is also very important, especially when communicating [e] **feelings**. [f] **Body language** and expressions on the face are important for this. It can also help to move to a [g] **quiet** place or arrange a better time if the message is important. These techniques are useful in all situations, including [h] **informal** situations.
>
> Active listening includes many of the techniques listed above, and can help to make [i] **relationships** stronger. Using active listening can mean that everyone can become a very effective communicator.

Address: http://www.unns.edu/fob/cpc/effective.com.html

University of NNS   Faculty of Business   Centre for Professional Communication

Home | About Us | Mission | Research

EFFECTIVE COMMUNICATION!

1. Many people think that communicating is nothing more than talking a lot and speaking clearly. However, in reality, good communication is far more complicated than that.

2. One of the most important points in good communication is that listening is just as important as speaking. If someone isn't listening, the message is lost just as surely as if it wasn't given in the first place.

3. It is dangerous for a speaker to **assume** that the listener is thinking the same way they are thinking. Something that is common sense to one person may be illogical to another, especially if they are from a different culture. It's surprisingly common for major communication breakdowns to occur when the listener understands one thing from the speaker's words and the speaker actually wanted to **express** a very different meaning. Therefore, it is very useful for the listener to check that their understanding is the same as the speaker's, especially in formal discussions such as those during business meetings.

4. Also, communication can be helped considerably if the listener makes an effort to understand the speaker's feelings. It's useful to remember that non-verbal communication such as body language and facial expression is very important in this, although the degree of its importance depends on the situation. Many websites and books say that over 90% of communication is through non-verbal communication. Although this is only partially true – the research that this idea is based on applied only to the communication of emotions and feelings, not facts – it's an important point nevertheless. An example will demonstrate this: if someone tells you that they are interested in a programme they are in the middle of watching on TV but their eyes are looking elsewhere, their facial expression looks bored and their intonation is flat, would you believe their words?

5. In situations where accuracy in communication is important, for example where there might be a possibility of **conflict**, sometimes the simplest of things can make a big difference. **Barriers** to good communication are obvious: noisy rooms, frequent interruptions from other people, and situations where one person is concentrating on something else, for example, when driving. Just moving to a different place, closing the door, or waiting until another time to hold the discussion are all things that people often forget, but which can cause a very different result.

6. It may sound as though these techniques are mainly for formal situations such as business meetings and interviews, but in reality they are also useful in every situation in life, whether at a bar, chatting with neighbours, or talking with partners, children and other family members.

7. Many of the skills mentioned above are used in a **technique** called active listening. This can be used in almost any situation – it is a good idea to try to always be an active listener. There are several parts to this technique. Firstly, an active listener will try to understand from the speaker's point of view, thinking about what there is in the speaker's experience that might affect how something is understood. Also, he or she will watch the facial expressions and body language of the speaker carefully, and try to understand these. The active listener will also give the speaker time to think as well as to talk and, depending on culture, will make eye contact with the speaker. Most importantly, the active listener will check that he or she understands correctly, by **paraphrasing** what he or she understands that the speaker has said. **Benefits** of active listening include stronger trust, fewer **conflicts** and, ultimately, better relationships and thereby greater happiness.

8. In conclusion, there's a lot more to good communication than simply talking at length. Active listening techniques and avoidance of factors that will cause the message to become confused are all things that a good communicator will try to do. Sometimes a quiet person who listens carefully and puts thought into how they express themselves can be a more successful communicator than even an **extrovert** who doesn't pay attention to the other speakers' ideas, feelings and way of thinking.

University of New North Scotland, Faculty of Business, Centre for Professional Communication

This site is provided as a service to the public by the university
Last updated 14th January 2007

(4) Students see in their books some statements about communication. For each statement in the list, they should write **T** (for True) if the statement is confirmed by the text on page 53 of their books, **F** (for False) if the statement is contradicted by the text, and **NG** (Not given) if it is neither confirmed nor contradicted by anything in the text.

Mention to students that they should only use information from the text for this type of question, not information from their own knowledge or even commonsense.

> **ANSWERS**
>
> **Answers and commentary**
> a. *Communication is just saying many things clearly.* **F (False)**: this is denied in the second sentence of the first paragraph
> b. *Over 90% of meaning is expressed in ways other than words.* **F (False)**: para 4 says in relation to this statement 'this is only partially true'.
> c. *Concentrating on other things can be a barrier to communication:* **T (True)**: para 5
> d. *Active listeners don't need to paraphrase what the speaker said:* **F (False)**: para 7
> e. *Active listening can make people happier.* **T (True)**: para 7
> f. *Active listening is difficult.* **NG (Not given)**: nowhere is this stated. Paragraph 4 mentions that good communication involves 'making an effort' but this does not necessarily mean that something is difficult.
> g. *Introverts are better communicators than extroverts.* **NG (Not given)**: the question implies introverts are always better communicators, but the text says introverts can be better communicators, that is they are sometimes better but not always. Therefore, T is not possible. F is clearly not possible because the statement can be true according to the text. NG is the answer, as no information is given about whether introverts are always good communicators.

Task E | Discussion ▶▶ SB P. 55

The reading section is wrapped up with six discussion questions in which students respond to the text.

> **ANSWERS**
>
> 1. Answers will vary.
>
> 2. Theoretically, it can be applied to almost all situations.
>
> 3. Some students may mention that active listening would be harder to use during lectures, where interaction is difficult.
>
> 4.–6. Answers will vary.

WRITING: FORMAL AND INFORMAL EMAILS; FORMAL LETTERS

Task A | Reasons for writing emails and letters ▶▶ SB P. 55

(1) In order to introduce the topic and make it feel relevant to the students, students tell each other in pairs how often they write the following:
[a] informal emails
[b] formal emails
[c] formal letters to companies, organisations, etc.

(2) Students should now be asked to think of as many purposes as they can for writing each.

(3) This question asks the learners to predict reasons and purposes for which they might write formal letters and emails during the time they prepare for, or undertake, their course of further study.

> **ANSWERS**
>
> Answers will vary, but could include the following:
> - to complain
> - to request information (eg about a course, accommodation, travel or holiday information, how to join a club or society ...)
> - to inform (for example, about sickness, ...)
> - to confirm (information, bookings, etc).

Task B | Conventions for emails and letters ▶▶ SB P. 55

(1) The Students' Book contains examples of a formal letter, a formal email and an informal email. Students are asked to identify which is which.

> **ANSWERS**
>
> a. a formal email: *Example 2*
> b. an informal email: *Example 3*
> c. a formal letter: *Example 1.*

(2) This question guides the students through finding out or activating knowledge about some of the conventions of formatting and forms of address used in letters and emails. They do this by reading the example correspondence and completing a table about the conventions they notice. (This can be done individually or in pairs.)

ANSWERS

CONVENTIONS	FORMAL LETTER	FORMAL EMAIL	INFORMAL EMAIL
Sender's address and contact details at top right hand corner	X		
Sender's address and contact details below sender's name, at bottom		X	
Receiver's address on left, above date, lower than sender's address	X		
Date below sender's address, above salutation	X		
Date and time appear automatically		X	X
Topic is on a line after the salutation, starting with *Re:*	X		
Formal salutation	X	X	
Informal salutation			X
Paragraphs are used	X	X	X
First paragraph gives the purpose of the message	X	X	
Paragraphs after the first give more detail	X	X	
Formal ending	X	X	
Informal ending			X
Signature included	X		
Sender's full name at the end	X	X	
Sender's given name (only) at the end			X
Formal vocabulary (eg *request* instead of *ask for*)	X	X	
Contractions (eg *I'm* instead of *I am*)			X

3 Students see speech bubbles in their books containing salutations and endings for formal and informal correspondence. They have to mark each with one or more of the following codes:
- FL if it's used in formal letters
- FE if it's used in formal emails
- IE if it's used in informal emails.

Students may need a reminder of the following:
- Mrs can only be used with married women
- Miss can only be used with women who have never been married
- Both of these are being replaced with Ms – nowadays this is less likely to cause offence, though some women still prefer the use of *Mrs*.

- Titles (Ms, Mr, Dr, Professor etc) are never used in formal letters with the given name alone. For example, someone called Mr Peter Hallam is never formally referred to as Mr Peter.

This is also a good time to point out to students that, conventionally, *Yours faithfully* is used when the writer doesn't know the addressee's name and thus is common when the letter begins *Dear Sir/Madam*; whereas *Yours sincerely* is used when the name is known by the writer. This convention is falling out of use, but if students can follow it, they will create a good impression.

Yours truly is generally used only in North American varieties of English.

ANSWER

> **Salutations**
> Dear Mr Whitehurst – **FE, FL**
> Dear Dr Peter Hallam – **FE, FL**
> Hi Fred – **IE**

> **Endings**
> Best wishes – **IE**   Take care – **IE**
> Yours sincerely – **FL** Love – **IE**
> Yours faithfully – **FL** Lots of love – **IE**
> Regards – **FE**   All the best – **IE**
> Kind regards – **FE**   Cheers – **IE**
> Catch you later – **IE** Thanks – **IE**
> See you – **IE**   Talk to you soon – **IE**
> See ya' – **IE**   See you soon – **IE**

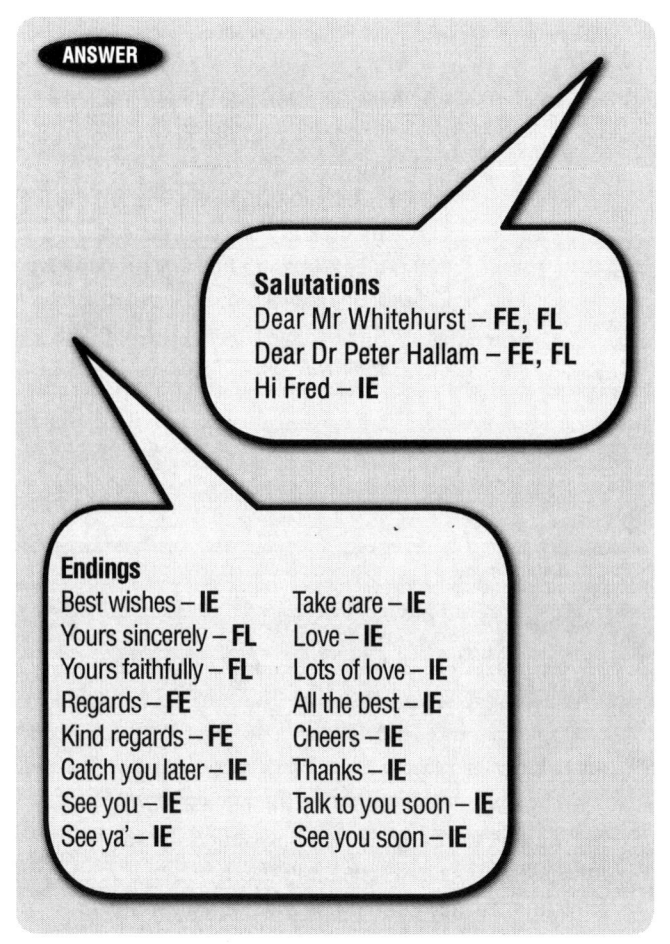

Task C | Write your own correspondence ▶▶ SB P. 57

① Students are directed to write a formal letter, a formal email and an informal email in this task, asking for information. They can choose to write to (a) the institution at which they want to do the further study for which they are preparing, and a friend who is studying there already, to ask for information about the institution, or (b) the tourism authority where they want to study, and a friend who lives in the same area, about the facilities in the region.

② The Students' Book asks the learners to check their letter and emails using the table they completed in Question 2 of Task B as a checklist. Depending on the students and their relationship with each other, it may be effective to do this as a peer review activity, in which students swap their work with a friend. They check each others' work, then give feedback to each other, commenting on the positive aspects of the other student's work and especially in areas they could use in their own future writing.

> **Extension:** The emphasis in the Students' Book is on formatting and polite forms. However, work could also be done on changing the writing style according to the level of formality, for example with more noun groups, more formal lexis and more polite phrasing of requests in the more formal correspondence.

LISTENING — SPECIFIC INFORMATION – TELEPHONE CONVERSATIONS

Task A | Listening for specific information ▶▶ SB P. 57

Students listen to the recording and write the correct word in the gaps in the script in their books.

Recording script

CD 1, track 8: Communication, Unit 5
(2 minutes, 5 seconds)

Note:
- Only the conversation parts appear in the Students' Book, not the narrator's part.
- **Bold underlining** indicates the answers to this task.
- *Italics* indicate answers to Task B, Question 1, later in this listening section (scanning activity).
- Circled expressions indicate answers to Task A, Question 1 of the Speaking 2 section on page 66 of this book (request and offer expressions).

Listening 1: Leaving a message

(Telephone ringing)

Narrator: Brendan Whitehurst, an overseas student from Canada, is travelling in England, and is thinking about studying in England. Here he telephones a university to try to arrange to visit to find out more information. Unfortunately the person he needs to speak with, Martha Billington, isn't answering her phone, so he has to leave a message.

Receptionist: Hello, Newham University Admissions Office
Brendan: (Could I) speak to [1] **someone** about doing an undergraduate, er, biology degree?
Receptionist: Are you an international student or a local student?
Brendan: I'm from overseas.
Receptionist: (Can I) put you on [2] **hold** while I see if there's an international student officer available?
Brendan: No problem

(Telephone music on hold)

Receptionist: Hello again, er, she doesn't seem to be at her [3] **desk**. Would you like to leave a message on her voicemail?
Brendan: That'll be fine.
Receptionist: I'll just *put you* [4] ***through***. Her name's Martha.

(Click and change of background hum)

Martha (recorded voice): This is Martha Billington. I can't [5] **answer** my phone right now. You can leave a message on my voicemail *after the tone*, or if you *press zero* you'll get *back to* [6] **reception**.

(Ding)

Brendan: Ah, hello, it's Brendan Whitehurst here. I'm thinking of [7] **applying** to do a biology degree, and I was wondering whether I could pop in and [8] **visit** the department, and perhaps speak with someone. Would you be able to *call me* [9] ***back*** on 07740 942 563, otherwise I'll *try again* later. Thanks, the number again was 07740 942 563.

Task B | Scanning and finding meaning from context ▶▶ SB P. 58

1 Ask students to find the phrases in List A below in the telephone script (Task A above) and mark them. They should have a limited time to do this – one minute or less.

List A	
put ... on hold	get back to
put ... through (to)	call me back
after the tone	try again (later)
press zero	

ANSWER

Answers are indicated with *italics* in the recording script in Task A above.

2 and **3** Ask students, in pairs or small groups (perhaps with preparation by themselves first), to match up each of the words they found in List A in Question 1 with its meaning given in List B in Question 2. They should use the context of the words in the recording script, and each other's prior knowledge, to complete this. Then, students should also try to match the words from List C in Question 3 to the meanings in List B. These don't appear on the recording but are also useful.

ANSWERS

2 and **3.**

LIST A	BEST MATCH FROM LIST B
put ... on hold	let you wait (on some phone systems, you listen to music while you are waiting)
put ... through (to)	allow you to speak to another person
after the tone	after an electronic sound
press zero	push the button with 0 on it
get back to	allow you to speak to the person you first spoke with
call me back	call me later
try again (later)	call the same person again later

LIST C	BEST MATCH FROM LIST B
after the beep	after an electronic sound
hold the line	let you wait (on some phone systems, you listen to music while you are waiting)
would you mind holding?	ask if someone wants to wait on the line
press hash	push the button with # on it
press star	push the button with * on it
ringing tone	a sound that means the telephone you are calling to is ringing
engaged tone/busy tone	a sound that means someone is already using the telephone you are calling
receiver	the part of the telephone you pick up
handset	the part of the telephone you pick up
the dial	the part of the telephone with numbers that you press
dial a number	press buttons on a telephone to call someone
make a call (to)	call someone

Point out that "busy tone" is North American English.

4 Ask students to read the conversation again and mark other expressions they think might be useful. This is good practice and students should do this with any text after they have gained an overall understanding.

Task C | Listening for specific information ▶▶ SB P. 58

1 Tell students they are going to listen to Brendan calling Martha back. Ask them to predict what he will say.

> **Extension:** Students could, in pairs, write out a possible conversation between Brenda and Martha, and then refine it (eg by changing vocabulary and other expressions) after listening to the recording and completing the rest of the work in this listening section.

2 Ask students to fill in the blanks in the form in their Students' Book while they listen. (It is a form that Martha might complete during the phone conversation, to be passed to the lecturer later.)

ANSWER

Note: Accept any recognisable spelling for the names!

APPOINTMENT REQUEST

Name:
Brendan Whitehurst

Person to see:
Dr Pennington

Day:
Wednesday

Time:
3 pm

Purpose:
talk about possible future study in the univeristy biology department

Recording script

> **Note**: Braces are used to intended forms where conversational slips occur. For example, if the script says *They goes {go} to the party*, the correct form is *They go to the party*.

CD 1, track 9: Communication Unit 5
(2 minutes, 57 seconds)

Listening 2: The call back

Narrator: A few hours later, Martha returns Brendan's call.

Martha: Oh, hello, could I speak to Brendan, please?
Brendan: Yes, speaking
Martha: It's Martha Billington here, from Newham University, returning your call. How are you today?
Brendan: Very well, thanks. And you?
Martha: I believe you wanted to arrange a time to speak with one of our lecturers about the course, is that right?
Brendan: Yes, that's right.
Martha: Well, we've just missed the open day, unfortunately, it was last week, but I might be able to book an appointment with Dr Pennington. How does next Wednesday at 3 pm sound?
Brendan: Yep, that sounds fine. Sorry I couldn't make it to the open day, I only arrived in the country yesterday. 3 pm sounds fine. How will I know where to go?
Martha: How are you getting to Newham?
Brendan: I'll probably take the train.
Martha: It's probably easiest to get a taxi to the entrance to the science site. It's not far – it'll be only about three pounds or so. The taxi can take you right into the science site, and then just follow the signs. If you ask to be dropped off at the library, you shouldn't go too far wrong. Then when you get to the biology department, just let reception know who you are and who you want to see.
Brendan: Thanks very much, Ms Billington.
Martha: You'll also get a chance to look around the campus and the city and see if you like it.
Brendan: Yep, that's the plan! I'm looking around a few universities while I'm here.
Martha: Well, hope we can have {hope we have} the course for you! Good luck with everything. Just give us a call or send an email if you have any questions.
Brendan: Thanks, I will. I'd better take down your email address then.
Martha: No problem, it's M Billington, all one word, no punctuation, at b d h dot a c dot c o dot u k
Brendan: So that's M Billington at b h d dot …
Martha: no, b d h
Brendan: …oh, ah, at b d h dot a c dot c o dot u k
Martha: That's right. Good luck with everything, and have a smooth journey.
Brendan: Thank you, bye.
Martha: Bye.

3 In their Students' Book, students fill in the gaps in some notes made by Brendan, as they listen again. You may have to explain the pronunciation of the £ symbol if you are doing this outside the UK.

ANSWERS

Directions

Taxi – about £3

<u>Science</u> site

Drop off at <u>library</u>

Follow <u>signs</u>

Go to <u>reception</u> when arrive there.

Email: <u>mbillington@bdh.ac.co.uk</u>

Alternative: Students could be asked to close their text books and take their own notes about directions.

Task D | Role plays ▶▶ **SB P. 59**

Put the students in groups of three and ask them to practise conversations similar to the ones on the recordings in this Unit. Their aim should be to try to use as much of the new vocabulary from this section as possible. In each group, two of the students should practise the conversation, and the third should count the number of new words the other two use. When finished, the roles should be rotated. This activity will work best if the students don't refer to the recording scripts in their books.

When all have finished, the students in each group decide which pair used the largest number of the new words.

This activity could be repeated as a warmer/review activity in a later lesson.

LANGUAGE SPOTLIGHT: WILL (INSTANT DECISIONS); FIRST CONDITIONALS

Task A | Uses of *will* ▶▶ SB P. 59

① Ask students to match clauses [a] to [d] in their course books to the best choice of the situations listed in i, ii or iii. Clauses [a] and [b] are in the script from the recording in Task A of the Listening section, so students can look back in their books (pages 57 and 58) to see the context of these. However, the others are from the second listening for this Unit (Task C), so it would be useful to play this again while students listen to the context of [c] and [d].

CD 1 / 9

Will is also frequently used for promises, though this aspect of usage isn't covered here. Another commonly stated usage is for offers – though in most cases offers with *will* are a kind of 'instant' decision.

> **ANSWERS**
>
> a. *I'll just put you through* – **Situation ii**: speaking at about the same time as deciding to do the action ('instant decisions').
> b. *I'll try again later* – **Situation ii**: speaking at about the same time as deciding to do the action ('instant decisions').
> c. *I'll probably take the train* – **Situation iii**: no fixed decision made yet.
> d. *It'll only be about £3 or so* – **Situation i**: making a prediction or guess about the future.

② This question directs students' attention to how *will* can have its degree of certainty affected by other words.

> **ANSWER**
>
> *Probably* used in conjunction with *will* indicates lack of certainty. Alternative ways of expressing this idea, using modal verbs, are covered in the Language Spotlight section of Unit 6.

Task B | Instant decisions ▶▶ SB P. 59

① Ask students to write responses to the prompts in their books, which give examples of situations where decisions are made quickly. Point out if necessary that the contraction *'ll* is more commonly used in conversation than the complete word '*will*', and that saying '*will*' can in fact create the impression of emphasis when none is intended. For example, depending on context, *I will go tomorrow* can sound like a promise, while *I'll go tomorrow* may sound more neutral.

> **ANSWERS**
>
> These are suggestions only – students' answers may (in fact, should) vary.
>
> **A:** It's hot in here!   **B:** *I'll open the window.*
>
> **A:** It's so noisy!   **B:** *I'll close the window / I'll ask those people to keep their voices down.*
>
> **A:** Can I speak with a customer service representative, please?   **B:** *Sure, I'll put you through.*
>
> **A:** I can smell burning – I think there's a fire!   **B:** *I'll call the fire brigade / I'll go and check.*
>
> **A:** I think I'm going to drop these books!   **B:** <u>*I'll give you a hand*</u>.

Task C | Real conditionals – Form and use ▶▶ SB P. 60

Ask students to look at the four sentences in the Students' Book (the first sentence is from the second listening of this Unit, which you may want to play again to provide a context). Alternatively, for a different focus, the sentences could be put on OHT or written on the board. Either way, students should match each sentence with one of the statements of probability given, either (i), (ii) or (iii), then answer Questions 2 and 3, which direct students to look at the tenses in these conditionals. It may be helpful to point out to the students that the main clause is the clause that doesn't include *if*, and that the *if* clause is the other clause, a subordinate clause (students did work about main and subordinate clauses in Unit 1).

> **ANSWERS**
>
> 1. In all the sentences except [e], the answer is ii – the situation in the *if* clause is reasonably likely. For [e], the answer is iii – the situation in the *if* clause is very unlikely, given the last clause of the sentence ("I guess you're too far away").
> 2. In all the sentences except [e], the tense in the *if* clause is present simple. The *if* clause in [e] uses a past tense (in fact, a past modal).
> 3. In the main clauses of sentences [a] to [d], a variety of present modal verbs is used, most commonly *will*. In [e], *would* is used, ie a past modal.

Discuss with students the following points about real conditionals (the ones here are often called *first conditionals*):

- Real conditionals are conditionals in which the *if* clause is reasonably likely to happen (not where it is very unlikely).
- They usually use present simple tense in the *if* clause and a modal verb in the main clause (most often *will*, but *may, might* and *could* are also common).

Unit 5 Communication | 65

- Other tenses are also possible in the main clause, eg present continuous or *going to*, eg *I'm going to take the students out on an excursion tomorrow if the weather is good*
- Where the *if* clause comes first, there is a comma between it and the main clause; where the main clause comes first, it is not necessary to separate the clauses with a comma.

Task D | Real conditionals – Practice ▸▸ SB P. 60

Students now undertake personalised practice by:

1 Completing real conditional sentences to make them true for themselves.

2 Talking in pairs about some hypothetical but quite possible situations, which naturally lead to use of real conditionals.

If students start going into unlikely possibilities, it may be an opportunity to step in and point out the use of *would* in the *if* clause and past tense in the main clause to indicate unreal ('second') conditionals (see Unit 9).

> **Variation:** This variation could be done as a warm-up or review activity in a subsequent lesson, or as a bit of fun to wrap up a lesson. Students get into groups of around three people. One student starts the game by completing sentence [a] orally. The next student takes the main clause of the sentence the first student said, and makes it into the *if* clause of a new real conditional sentence. The chain continues until the students get stuck. For example,
> - First student may say: *If it rains at the weekend, I'll stay in and watch TV.*
> - Second student continues: *If I stay in and watch TV, I'll probably eat more than I should.*
> - Third student: *If I eat more than I should, I might put on weight*
> - … and so on …

SPEAKING 2 — MAKING REQUESTS

Task A | Requests ▸▸ SB P. 60

1 Ask students to look again at the script in their books from the first listening of this Unit (at pages 57–58). They should circle the expressions used for requests, plus one used for an offer.

> **ANSWER**
> Please see Task A of the Listening at pages 61 to 62 where the requests are circled.

It may be worth summarising the request and offer structures and eliciting others that could also be used. The structures from the recording are:

Requests
Can I + *infinitive without 'to'*
Could I + *infinitive without 'to'*
Would you be able + *infinitive*
I was wondering whether I could + *infinitive without 'to'*

Offer
Would you like + *infinitive*

2 Ask students to hypothesise about which request phrases are more polite. (They may already have a good awareness of this from previous learning).

> **ANSWER**
> The list above has the sentence starters in approximate order of politeness, going from informal to very polite.

3 Students practise the request structures through role-plays, in pairs, using information given in the situation boxes in Appendix 4 of their books (pages 162 and 164). They take turns being both the caller and the person who answers the call.
   There are three situations. The information they need is provided in the situation boxes. To ensure that students don't just read the boxes, the information provided to the caller is in a different order from the information provided to the student answering the call, and is in a form that forces them to change the word forms to fit the grammatical structures they are using.
   Students should be encouraged to add their own ideas – but they must not contradict the printed instructions.
   Some vocabulary and concepts that are mentioned in the boxes which students may need to know before they begin the task are:
   – orientation week
   – insurance
   – university clubs (known as university societies in some countries).

> **Extension:** Activity 3 above will almost certainly provide good examples of language from students that could be focused on afterwards in open class, with a view to providing expressions, collocations etc to make it sound much smoother and more natural.

66 | EAP Now! Preliminary English for Academic Purposes Teacher's Book

FURTHER PRACTICE: READING, FILMS AND FUN

The ideas below are provided in the Students' Book for further reading, discussion and writing practice.

READING

- You can read some interesting ideas about communicating well (including active listening) at: **http://www.mindtools.com/page8.html**
- The Wikipedia article on communication is an interesting place to start exploring this topic. It is at **http://en.wikipedia.org/wiki/Communication**

FILMS

Rain Man, directed by Barry Levinson, starring Dustin Hoffman. Two sons of a millionaire spend time together. One has trouble communicating – but for the first time, the other feels he needs to communicate something very important.

Ace Ventura: Pet Detective, directed by Tom Shadyac; *Ace Ventura: When Nature Calls*, directed by Steve Oedekerk and both starring Jim Carrey. Comedies about a vet with an amazing ability to communicate with animals.

QUESTIONS

1. Explain some barriers to communication, and say what can be done to stop them.

2. What skills are important for good communication?

3. What are the advantages of mobile phones for everyday life? What are the disadvantages?

4. For people who have lived in at least one country other than their own:

   Do differences in non-verbal communication (eg body language, facial expressions) between cultures cause communication difficulties? Provide examples to show your ideas on this topic.

6 POLITICS

BY THE END OF THIS UNIT, STUDENTS SHOULD:

'never discuss politics or religion'

- be able to recognise a prefix and a suffix .... Language Spotlight 1: Task A **70**
- know how to critically examine an issue like war and be able to express an opinion by agreeing or disagreeing when speaking in a group .... Speaking 1: Tasks A and B **70**
- be able to recognise features of individual paragraphs within a longer text; discussion .... Reading: Task A **70**
- understand some of the features of a discussion essay .... Reading: Task B **71**
- be able to map an essay .... Writing: Task A **71**
- be able to use modality and present simple tense when talking about future predictions .... Language Spotlight 2: Tasks A, B and C **73–74**
- understand probability; possibility; certainty and the language that they signal .... Language Spotlight 2: Task B **73**
- have practised agreeing and disagreeing .... Speaking 2: Task A **74**
- have listened for and recognised some importance markers based upon intonation, stress and emphasis of the speaker .... Listening: Task A **75**

POLITICS n. [UNCOUNTABLE]: 1 ideas and activities relating to gaining and using power in a country, city, etc.

LANGUAGE SPOTLIGHT 1

PREFIXES AND SUFFIXES

Task A | Greek and Latin into English! ▶▶ SB P. 64

Students are introduced to relevant prefixes and suffixes from Latin and Greek. Prefixes: *olig, mono, demo, bureau*, and suffixes: *archy, cracy*. They should attempt definitions of the words one through to four in their list using the above prefixes and suffixes. Dictionaries are not essential if students apply common sense and reasoning along with the given explanations. Students' answers can be simple so long as the gist is there. The Teacher's Book answers are formal definitions.

ANSWERS

1. *oligarchy* – a form of government in which the power is vested in a few, or in a dominant class or clique. The few ruling collectively.
2. *monarchy* – supreme power or sovereignty wielded by a single person.
3. *democracy* – government by the people; a form of government in which the supreme power is vested in the people and exercised by them or by their elected agents under a free electoral system.
4. *bureaucracy* – government by officials against whom there is inadequate public right of redress; excessive governmental red tape and routine. (<u>bureaucrat</u> – an official who works by fixed routine without exercising intelligent judgment.)

SPEAKING 1

BUILDING THE FIELD

Task A | Thinking for yourself and talking about it ▶▶ SB P. 64

❶ Students look at their books and identify the photographs of various 21st century politicians or leaders from around the world.

ANSWER

A The Queen of England, Queen Elizabeth;
B Government officials; C The Royal Guard.

❷ Students read the statistics (below) about the human cost of occupation in Iraq. They offer their personal opinion concerning the war and by so doing they have entered the mine field of this unit – politics. They are provided with phrases to help them to agree or disagree.

Task B | What is politics? ▶▶ SB P. 65

Students begin this unit with critical thinking using their own knowledge and experience of their culture to activate their background knowledge for the work following. In groups, students examine three questions.

❶ They explain what sort of government is in power in their home country;

❷ What they think is meant by 'politics'

❸ Whether they agree or disagree with the following statement – *People should never talk about politics or religion.*

READING

DISCUSSION ESSAY

Task A | Form and comprehension – Features of individual paragraphs ▶▶ SB P. 65

In this section, students become familiar with discussion as a genre. They read an essay about politics and religion and examine each paragraph for features of a written essay,
  Students are tested (multiple choice) on their understanding of the content.

THE HUMAN COST OF OCCUPATION FROM THE BEGINNING OF THE WAR IN IRAQ UNTIL 6 FEB 2006

US military casualties in Iraq

Since war began, 19 Mar 2003	2552 dead
Since 'Mission Accomplished' speech by Bush, 1 May 2003	2115 dead
Since capture of Saddam, 13 Dec 2003	1785 dead
Since US handover to Iraq, 19 June 2004	1386 dead
Since Iraqi election, 31 Jan 2005	816 dead
US wounded (official count)	16,549
Iraqi death toll (est.)	30,000–100,000
Average cost of war per day	US$300 million
Rumsfeld '05 estimate of duration of war	12 years

Source: http//:antiwar.com

Within the features of each paragraph, form and function are mixed. Form, including language and grammar, is combined with structure or schema to illustrate how the two combine to make meaning in the written genre of discussion.

Students then match the stages of a discussion to the actual text.

> **ANSWERS**
>
> Features of each paragraph.
> a. para 2
> b. para 1
> c. para 3
> d. para 5
> e. para 3
> f. para 7
> g. para 4
> h. para 6

SCHEMA or MAP of a discussion essay (on next page; SB P. 65)

INTRODUCTION
- introductory sentence which restates the topic question
- sentence explaining how the writer will tackle the discussion – preview or scope
- definition of term with page number from dictionary (cited)
- explanation of the writer's position (beliefs) so the reader knows what the writer is thinking
- restatement of what the essay will be about

(All these features appear in para 1 and 2 and constitute the introductory phase of the writing.)

The final sentence in para 2 – *From that, it will be seen that there are times to discuss politics and there are other times when you probably should not* – is the preview or scope at the end of the introduction. It is a statement of what the essay will be about.

SUBSEQUENT BODY PARAGRAPHS
- background information
- both sides of discussion
- concrete supporting evidence to back up statements

CONCLUSION
- summary of the whole
- no new information introduced
- position restated
- recommendation to the reader

The recommendation stage is the following sentence which appears at the end of the text – *Choose the right time and place and discuss freely so that information can be shared and people have the power of knowledge from your discussions.*

Task B | Understanding ▶▶ SB P. 67

This task involves the discussion essay that follows and is to assist students with comprehension and expand their vocabulary. It is meant to increase general knowledge and help students to focus on main ideas within paragraphs.

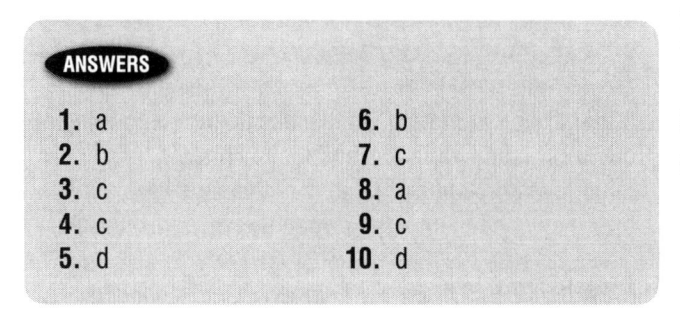

> **ANSWERS**
>
> 1. a
> 2. b
> 3. c
> 4. c
> 5. d
> 6. b
> 7. c
> 8. a
> 9. c
> 10. d

WRITING

DISCUSSION GENRE

Task A | Map or schema of discussion essay ▶▶ SB P. 68

You may have heard the statement: *'People should never talk about politics or religion'*. Shorten this statement to *'People should never talk about politics'*. Discuss.

Students are asked to examine the reading – *Discussing politics and religion* – and draw the following stages on it.

DISCUSSING POLITICS AND RELIGION

[INTRODUCTORY STAGE – This first stage consists of three (sub) stages: the introduction stage, the definition stage and the preview or scope stage.]

[Introduction stage – This stage restates the question. It provides an opening general statement.]

1. It is often said that people should never discuss politics or religion. It may be because discussions of this nature might begin as pleasant conversations but then become heated arguments and even turn into violent fights. For the same reason, some say that people should never talk about politics. However, 'never' is a difficult word. Perhaps there are times when it is OK and other times when it is not OK to discuss politics.

[Definition stage]

2. First, what is politics? According to *Longman's Dictionary*, politics is a noun and it means *ideas and activities relating to gaining and using power in a country* (p 1265). Thus, politics involves people – the people who gain power in order to either represent or control the rest of the population. Everyday, we read about politics and see the result of politics, such as political decisions on the television. Every single person's life is affected by politics everyday. Since politics are a huge part of everyone's life, it would be foolish to say you should 'never' talk about politics. However, if politics are discussed, you have to be prepared to take the possible consequences.

[Preview or scope stage – Here the writer says what he or she will write about in the essay.]

> Following are two consequences that happened when politics was discussed in my country. It is also about my own personal experience. From that, it will be seen that there are times to discuss politics and there are other times when you probably should not.

[BODY STAGE – Here, the writer writes exactly what s/he has said s/he will do in the scope stage. Each paragraph must have a topic sentence and concrete, supporting evidence to back up the topic or theme of the paragraph.]

3. **In my country, there was a political figure who caused many discussions between friends about politics.** ← *Topic sentence*
She also caused the news to discuss her and her views and opinions. In both these cases, discussing politics had a negative effect (was bad). This woman was definitely a racist in her views, although she always pretended not to be. My country is a country where most of the population comes from other countries. It is multicultural which means there are many different kinds of people. All these people love their new home while they sometimes speak their own language, eat their favourite foods and follow some customs and religion that is their tradition. Most of the time, people get along together and respect each other while enjoying this country which is a democratic one.

4. **This woman became a leader of a little party in our country.** ← *Topic sentence*
This job meant she could speak in public to the press. She spoke badly about others and the media put her face on television a lot. Other media around the world seemed to find her interesting too and we heard that she was in newspapers in Japan, China and Indonesia. Her opinions influenced tourists not to come for a holiday, so discussing politics in the media had a very bad effect. Tourism lost money because visitors changed their minds about visiting this country. Some students of English decided to go to other countries and not come here. She did not represent the majority of people and their thinking but her open discussion of her own personal views caused a lot of trouble and misunderstanding.

5. **There are definitely times when discussing politics is inappropriate.** ← *Topic sentence*
Here is another example. One night my friend came over and brought her father and mother too. Her parents came from the same town that this political figure, the woman, came from. They began to talk about her and they said they liked her a lot. They said they agreed with many of her views. I said I did not agree with her and that I didn't like her at all. The father became very angry with me and he and his wife stood up and left quickly. It was embarrassing for everyone. It was quite terrible and my friend and I did not speak for a little while. I wrote her a letter and apologised in the end. If you are the host or hostess for a party and the conversation is getting dangerous, like that example, then maybe it is a good idea to guide the conversation away from the topic of politics.

6. **However, discussing politics means you are thinking. It means more than one view can be talked about.** ← *Topic sentence*
A discussion needs more than one point of view, rather like an argument. To discuss politics is to bring out information, opinions and facts. This can be a good thing. Even though people may not change their minds, they may open them a little when they hear discussion.

[CONCLUSION STAGE – Remember, that in a conclusion, no new information is ever introduced. You must summarise what you have already said and recommend / suggest something.]

7 In conclusion, perhaps it is better to 'never say never' rather than say 'never discuss politics'. It is important, however, to choose the time and place if it involves friends or family. A happy social occasion is probably not the best time to discuss important political things. Choose the right time and place and discuss freely so that information can be shared and people have the power of knowledge from your discussions.

TALKING ABOUT FUTURE PREDICTIONS (GOING TO), MODALITY (PROBABILITY), PRESENT SIMPLE TENSE

Task A | Future predictions – *Going to* ▶▶ SB P. 68

Students look at some sentences containing future predictions using 'going to':

> You can express future by using the present continuous – *I'm ....ing*; but you can also use *to be + going to* 'intentions'. For example:
> - *I'm going to lose weight!*
> - *Really! I'm going to try to gain some, myself.*
> - *You're both silly, I'm going to stand for government and forget all about weight!*

1 Students are asked to write five sentences talking about things they're *going to* try to do in the future.

2 Students must fill in the gaps in the following dialogue. In pairs, they should speak (or read aloud) the dialogue first before writing any answers. (Answers are in bold type.)

ANSWERS

Jess: *What are you doing tonight?*
Sveti: *Well, I haven't really decided yet. But, I think I'm **going to** the movies.*
Jess: *What do ya' want to see?*
Sveti: *Again, I haven't decided yet.*
Jess: *Well, that's a coincidence, because I'm **going to** go.*
Sveti: *Do you know what you're **going to** see?*
Jess: *Yep! I'm **going to** see a foreign film at the Independent.*
Sveti: *Sounds pretty good to me. I'm **going to** come with you. Alright?*
Jess: *Yes, of course, that's fine. We're **going to** have a good time.*

Task B: Modality – *Probably* or *possibly* ▶▶ SB P. 68

In order to express *probability* or *possibility*, this section examines the **modal auxiliary**. An auxiliary verb is a verb that combines with the main verb. In order to form certain tenses, the main verb must be combined with an **auxiliary verb**. There is a difference between regular auxiliaries and modal auxiliaries. They differ in more than meaning. They differ both (1) in their own form and (2) in the verb that follows them.

Having said that, however, the modal auxiliary does NOT change the tense of the main verb it combines with; rather, it changes its emphasis or meaning. Modals are used to express *possibility, ability, obligation, permission or changes in emphasis*. For students in this section 'talking about the future', we will use 'possibility'; *might, may* and *could*.

Modal auxiliaries do **not** change the tense ending of the main verb (are not inflected):
- *I might go; he might go; she might go; they might go*
- *I could come; she could come; he could come*
- *I may apply; we may apply; she may try; she may not try*, etc.

> Students need to see the difference between the **regular auxiliaries** *be* and *have* because they **do** change their form (are inflected) in order to agree with their subjects.
>
> - *I am ....ing (coming, laughing)*
> - *They have ....ed (succeeded)*
> - *You are ....ing (going)*
> - *He has .....ed (tried)*

The purpose of Task B, Question 1 is for students to observe how regular auxiliaries change their form (are inflected) and agree with their subjects. The verb 'to think' has been used to illustrate how the subject changes. Contractions show common usage.

ANSWERS

1. **a.** thinking – thinking
   b. thinking – thinking
   c. thinking – thinking
   d. thinking – thinking
   e. thinking – thinking
2. It changed by getting 'ing' added to it. (ie the main verb changed).
3. No, nothing happened to the main verbs. They stayed the same.

4. Students may read the following text aloud and choose the missing modal auxiliary as they go, then write the answers.

(might, may) (might)
Al: *I _____ have a party next week and I _____ invite you, if you're lucky.*

(might, could, may)
Max: *Well, that's nice of you and I just _____ come along, if you ask me nicely.*

Al: *What do you think I should buy for food and drink?*

(could)
Max: *Hmmmm, depends on who's coming. You _____ buy a lot of different things to suit a lot of different tastes.*

(could, might)
Al: *Yeah, and I _____ be a millionaire, too.*

(might, may)
Max: *HAH! You _____ have to stay within your budget then.*

(may, might, could)
Al: *Yeah, but I _____ lash out and really go crazy with this one.*

(might, could, may)
I love having parties. I _____ try and do an extra shift and get more money.

(could)
Max: *I _____ put a little cash in too, mate.*

Al: *You're a good friend, you know.*

Task C | Present simple tense ▸▸ SB P. 69

Present simple tense is used to express routines or habits; when something is true and it will remain true (facts); and when things stay the same over a long period of time.

❶ Students are asked to underline each example of the present simple tense in the following texts. The verbs in simple present tense are underlined in the text below and for the students the first one is done for them as an example.

Present simple tense

[a] *For routines or habits* – Sylvia washes her hair everyday. She sets her alarm for 7, gets up and washes her hair in the shower. Then, she brushes her teeth, makes a cup of tea, drinks it and heads for the university library. She almost never varies this pattern. It's her habit.

[b] *When something is true and it will remain true. It is always true* – The clock strikes midnight every twenty-four hours. That's a fact. It's also a fact that a match burns when you light it, sand makes glass, and in winter I see my breath. Another fact that lends itself to the present simple is that birth and death happens to everyone.

[c] *Things that stay the same over a long period of time* – Rory Lee goes to accountancy classes. He's been going for two years and he has to keep going another two years. He goes with his roommate just about every day. He attends each class, never misses a lecture and remembers his laptop as well.

❷ Students write a paragraph, using present simple tense, about their own habits or routines. Answers will vary.

❸ In the extract below *students are asked to complete the following tasks*:
a. underline the tense – *present simple*;
b. double underline all forms (tenses) using *going to* and
c. broken line any words they think show *probability*. Probability means 'maybe' or 'it's possible that'.

ANSWER

My uncle runs for the local Green Earth Party every year. He's going to do so again this year and may do so next year too, if he loses again. One day, he might win. We hope he does. I mean, he could win. He just needs a few more votes. We vote for him. We always vote for him. His wife, my aunt, goes to the polls, casts her vote and walks away. Each time she does it, she hopes this will be the year he may win.

SPEAKING 2

AGREEING AND DISAGREEING

Task A | Discussion – Future of government ▸▸ SB P. 70

This task attempts to activate the language that students have been taught within the Unit by discussing the following question.

74 | EAP Now! Preliminary English for Academic Purposes Teacher's Book

Do you think there will be a world government one day? Something like the United Nations but not controlled by one, large, industrialised country? Rather, it might be organised as a proper League of Nations or Democratic World Group that would work together to make the whole world a better place. Do you think it's possible? Do you think there will be other planets discovered and governments to run those planets in space?

It is also a critical thinking activity. Students are to:
- Think about the question.
- Form an opinion.
- Express their opinion.
- They can use the information provided in the Students' Book to do this. There is a speaking box on page 70 with expressions to help them give opinions.
- Discuss their thoughts.
- In pairs or groups, students find a person or persons with an opposite opinion to theirs. They write down three points each, based upon the points in the paragraph above concerning the 'Future of Government' that they wish to discuss or debate. They then tell one another what they think. This should lead to interjections and expression of opinions if you keep the groups small. Four people are sufficient for each group.

LISTENING: MINI-LECTURE, GOVERNMENT AND POLITICS, NOTE-TAKING FROM LISTENING

Task A | Importance markers – Intonation, stress, emphasis ▶▶ SB P. 71

❶ Students listen to a mini lecture and tick the markers in Column B in the Students' Book. The purpose is to focus students' listening on the spoken cues that denote importance. In other words students learn to recognise when the speaker is going to tell them something they need to write down, as if they were in a lecture/note-taking situation. This should also prove helpful when listening to news reports, documentaries or in other listening situations where primarily one person is doing the speaking.

❷ Students then identify the purpose of the markers by filling in a table. Are the words signalling an upcoming definition? Did they listen sufficiently to hear the second or third thing in a list of three? Was an explanation about to ensue?

❸ Finally, students listen for intonation and stress and match up words and sentences that carry this meaning.

- Teachers could use the transcript as a visual aid while the students listen the second time. Print and use highlight pens as you talk the students through the functions of the terms.
- Examine especially 'there' and 'this' and 'that' each time an explanation is offered. Ask students to listen carefully for what follows those words. If you provide them the transcript, then read each section that follows the underlined words.

ANSWERS

See marked up text below.

KEY
DARK BLUE – redundancies, reiterations, things not essential to the topic within the talk
UNDERLINING – the signal (importance marker) that tells the listener the importance of the utterance. Often signals a definition or further explanation.
LIGHT BLUE – central to topic

Recording script
CD 1

CD 1, track 10: Politics, Unit 6
(8 minutes, 03 seconds)

Listening: Mini lecture: Lecture about politics and government
(General coughing, scraping of chairs, papers rustling, background chatter, then room falls silent.)

Lecturer: Good afternoon, students. <u>Today's talk is about</u> politics. I want you to feel free to ask questions, even though it is a lecture. Today's lecture is, um, pardon me, quite informal in the sense that I welcome your curiosity and – if you do ask a few questions, then at least I know you're listening and not asleep.

(Group laughter.)

Lecturer: So, to begin. I guess anytime we're talking about something, we'd better know, that is you have to know what it is you're talking about. I want to outline some different government types for you and, ah, well, actually, <u>I said I would define politics</u>. <u>So</u>, politics roughly means any ideas and activities related to the gain and use of

Unit 6 Politics | 75

power in a country. But there are politics in every walk of life, if you know what I mean. You hear employees complaining about politics in the work place. It has to do with power and how power is used. But anyway, we are concerned today, really, with countries because politics is about government generally, and, government is about politics.

Lecturer: I see a hand up there, very good, yes, Miss?

Russian student: Can you please explain the difference between government and politics ... If there is a difference?

Lecturer: Very good question. And it does need explaining. And, yes, there is a difference. Alright, we said that politics was about the gain and use of power in a country. Government, though, when we're talking about government ... is really about the group of people who govern, well, that's not too helpful...ah, I mean who control, you know, um, make the decisions for all the people in a country or state. So the government is the controlling body and politics are how the people behave who have that control. I'll/ I'll give you brief overviews of what I think are some different types or kinds of governments to make it clear.
 Now then, government, as I said before, has to do with governing or controlling and making decisions for people in a country or state. Roughly, I'll outline three major kinds of government. There's government that believes people have a right to make some decisions for themselves. This form of government is elected by people in a state or country. This type of government, the election type, is supposed to represent people's wishes. It's supposed to be democratic.
 Now, a second type of government is made by the military. You could say that this form of government is based on power and strength. If a military group is strong and can form government or support government by force, then this is how they rule or govern. Sometimes they support a dictatorship; sometimes they are a military junta. A junta is a small group of people and they could be elected too. Usually a junta means a small group of ruling people who have come to power after some sort of revolution.
 Yes, yes, what's your question?

South American student: Thank you. Well, I thought I heard you say that a junta can be elected. Is that right?

Lecturer: Well, yes, according to the dictionary, it is possible. It simply says a small ruling group, either elected or self-chosen. Which is a nice way of saying, ah, to choose yourself is to put yourself in power.

South American student: Well, in Venezuela where I come from at the moment there is a bit of every thing. People voted for the current President which as you said fit into what is democracy, but at the same time, there is a military based in some way from power and strength.

Lecturer: ...Thank you, that is a very good example of government and politics.
 A third type of government is one based upon family. There is the idea that who your parents are makes you fit to rule – your parents and their parents, mother and father and their mother and father before them and so on and so on. You are chosen to rule by blood, the blood that is in your veins. This rule is blood-line rule and the Queen of England with Charles and then his children and/ and so forth ... is a good example and, uh, so is Tonga for that matter in the South Pacific islands.
 Yes?

Student's voice: Can you please spell TONGA?

Lecturer: Ah sure ... T. O. N. G. A. You'll find it in a World Atlas between the Hawaiian islands and ah, Samoa, the Samoan islands. There's quite a long line of kings in Tonga.
 So, we come to the question of politics and what that is. I think I said before that, um, politics is about governing, that is about the people who govern and how they act, how these people in power conduct themselves. I want you to think of all the meanings around politics. There is to be politic, which is to be careful and polite and to consider sides of an issue and maybe consider other people's feelings. Then ... there is the noun – political animal which is not as attractive. It means a person who acts ... a person who has power in politics and then they act for their own good and not thinking of the good of the people, state or country they ... represent. A political animal acts for their own survival in office. They want to keep their job more than they want to do a good job. It usually refers to

> a politician who knows how to stay in office. They might lie, they might go behind other people's backs – that is connive. Yet another colloquial meaning around political is political football. You can think of a football as being tossed back and forth and in politics that's kind of what it's like. The football is an issue, or it stands for an issue, it represents an issue, usually an important issue used to gain advantage in politics. Often that issue has social importance.
>
> Now … to match various forms of government with different countries …
>
> *(Voice fades off.)*

② Students add the purpose and function of the language using phrases from a list.

ANSWERS

COLUMN A	COLUMN C – Purpose
Today's talk is about	5
that is	1,4
define	2
so	4
we are concerned with …	3
Government is about …	2
I'll give you …	3
Now then …	3
This type of …… is	2
This form of …… is	2
Think (used as imperative, directed at listeners …)	3
…… means	2
then this …… is	2
A third type …… is	2
There is ……	2
A second type …… is	2

③ Students listen for intonation and stress in the talk.

ANSWERS

Group A
1. louder – volume increases in voice
2. softer – volume drops in voice
3. upwards in the voice
4. downwards in the voice
5. less confident or a little insecure in voice

Group B
A. __1,3__ Because it adds emphasis
B. __1,3__ Because it is important
C. __2,4,5__ Because it is less important
D. __2,4,5__ Because it is an aside – not really important at all.

Unit 6 Politics | 77

FURTHER PRACTICE: READING, FILMS AND FUN

READING

Booktopia Political Science:
http://booktopia.com.au/books/political-science/0/

Xing Lujian, *Rhetoric in Ancient China, Fifth to Third Century BCE: A Comparison with Classical Greek Rhetoric*, Uni of South Carolina Press. (A surprisingly accessible dissertation that illustrates some of the similarities between ancient Chinese politics and that of the classical Greek.)

FILMS

The Yes Men: A modern documentary that combines humour and fact to expose the way corporate power rules the world.

Crash: A look at racist issues and politics in America.

Bowling for Columbine: A satirical documentary about a sad event. Michael Moore, writer and film maker, produced this film as a political comment on what makes the sort of country that produces high school massacres.

QUESTIONS

1. What sort of government is in your home country? Describe the current government and explain how it came to power.

2. Politics in English and the Western world are linked to Greece and Rome. Research early politics in one of these countries and discuss how it relates to present day democracy.

7 MEDIA

'remember to distrust'

BY THE END OF THIS UNIT, STUDENTS SHOULD:

- know more vocabulary for talking about the media....... Speaking 1: Task A **80**
- have increased their fluency in talking about the media ..... Speaking 1: Task A **80**;
  Listening 1: Tasks A and C **85–89**; Speaking 2: Task A **91**
- have improved their skill at identifying different kinds of procedural text ... Reading: Task A **80**
- be more aware of some forms of cohesion in English................................. Reading: Task D **81**
- be able to interpret some nominalisations .... Language Spotlight: Tasks A and B **81–82**
- be able to use imperatives and other structures for giving instructions and
  advice .... Language Spotlight: Tasks C and D **82–83**
- be able to write one kind of procedural text............................... Writing: Tasks A and B **83–85**
- be aware of one style of note-taking .... Listening 1: Task B **86**
- have practised following and taking notes from a lecture .... Listening 1: Task B **86**
- have practised understanding instructions .... Listening 2: Task A **90**
- have practised listening for specific information.................................. Listening 2: Task C **91**
- have practised fluency in speaking by completing a survey .... Speaking 2: Task B **91**

MEDIA n., pl. [UNCOUNTABLE]**:** all the organisations, such as television, radio, and newspapers, that provide news and information for the public, or the people who do this work.

SPEAKING 1: BUILDING THE FIELD

Task A | The range of media ▶▶ SB P. 74

Students ask each other, in groups, some questions aimed at brainstorming the topic of media which should bring out some vocabulary that is useful for talking about the topic.

ANSWER

Students give various answers.

READING: IDENTIFYING TEXT TYPE; COHESION – ADVICE AND INSTRUCTIONAL TEXTS

Task A | Identifying text type ▶▶ SB P. 74

Students are asked to look at three texts and try to identify what type of publication each comes from. They select from a list, and then think back about the clues that helped them decide.

ANSWERS

	ANSWER	REASON
Text 1	Magazine	From the choices, only the magazine article has the cheerful, chatty style of Text 1.
Text 2	Instruction book for something in the house	This is the only one that uses the grammar for direct instructions (imperatives). It is written in a brief style that helps people to find information and understand quickly.
Text 3	Student essay	Formatting – longer paragraphs; Writing style – formal, with long sentences; Not a text book as it mentions it's an essay.

Task B | Meaning behind the words ▶▶ SB P. 76

(1) Ask students to read Text 1 again, thinking about whether it is formal or informal, and what makes it so. Students may have to put forward some hypotheses, to be confirmed by you.

ANSWERS

It's quite informal. Some features that contribute to this impression are:
- Sentences beginning with *and*.
- The use of *get*, eg *get your photo on the front page of …* instead of *have your photo published …*; *get your hair cut* instead of *have your hair cut*
- Short paragraphs
- Other informal vocabulary: *hit the big time, better off,*
- Repetition of words: *talk, talk, talk.*
- Contractions: eg *it's, you're* etc.
- Abbreviations: eg *adverts* for *advertisements*.

(2) Ask students whether they find Text 1 amusing and, if so, what makes it funny. Again, they might have to hypothesise here.

ANSWER

Some of the features they might be led towards noticing include:
- The ironic tone – for example, one would expect that developing acting ability would be more important, but this is relegated to almost the last-mentioned point.
- On a similar note, the emphasis on whom you meet being the most important, looks being more important than talent, and the complete failure to mention any industry knowledge all contribute to the focus on the superficial; a further hint to the irony.

Task C | The five questions for any text ▶▶ SB P. 76

As in other units of this book, students answer five questions about a text (in this case, Text 1, but students could do the same with the other texts as well). These questions appear later in the Reading section than in some units, because in this case the answers in Task B above will help students answer Question 4.

ANSWERS

[a] **What is it?**
A magazine article.
[b] **What is the source?**
A magazine.
[c] **Who is the writer?**
Agnes Daydrew, a member of the magazine's staff.
[d] **What purpose does the writer have for writing it?**
Almost certainly to entertain rather than inform, as the 'advice' appears rather superficial.
[e] **Who is the intended audience?**
Most likely readers of celebrity magazines who are interested in the glamorous world of Hollywood movie stars.

Task D | Cohesion ▶▶ SB P. 77

Teachers should explain to students that cohesion is the way in which a text is joined together, and that methods of cohesion vary between languages, just as grammar is different. Two types of cohesion are looked at here. Understanding these will help in reading, and using cohesion in writing can make a learner's texts feel more natural.

❶ Anaphoric referencing (using words that refer backwards to ideas mentioned previously in the text). In this exercise students are asked to write in their books what some referencing words in Text 1 (*How to become a film star*) stand for.

ANSWERS

a. **that** (line 4): becoming a film star, star – the glamour of Hollywood, the fame, the money, the excited fans and mixing with the most talked-about people in the world

b. **there** (line 14): Southern California

c. **them** (line 19): (eye catching) business cards

d. **this** area (line 23): making yourself as beautiful or handsome as possible

e. all of **this** (line 34): being in the right place, meeting the right people, looking good (ie all the ideas mentioned in previous paragraphs)

f. **this** (line 50): going to classes and practising

Note: there is also an example of cataphoric referencing here (using words that refer forward, to ideas mentioned later in the text): para 1, line 6: *these tips* refers to the tips that are mentioned in later paragraphs.

❷ Ellipses (missing words out to avoid too much repetition). Students fill gaps with words that have been missed out (ellipsed) in Text 1.

ANSWERS

a. **better off** (line 12) means better off than in a place like the north of Scotland/a place where there are no producers or casting directors

b. **even more careful** (line 31) means even more careful than in any other job

c. **far more difficult** (line 59) means far more difficult than becoming a film star in the way explained in the rest of the essay.

LANGUAGE SPOTLIGHT: LONGER NOUN GROUPS

This Language Spotlight focuses on building awareness of the use of nominalisations, but students are not expected to produce their own nominalised forms at this stage. Unit 12 reviews unpacking nominalisations.

Task A | What is nominalisation? ▶▶ SB P. 77

❶ Students look back at Text 3 in the Reading section at page 76, the beginning of a student essay (*Advertising and children*). They mark the groups of words that have the same meaning as those in the following list (the first has been done for them). The meanings of some vocabulary are given, as follows:

> **eating** = consuming (vb); consumption (n)
> **junk food** = food that is mostly fat and sugar – it isn't healthy
> **very fat** = obese (adj); obesity (n)
> **less** = reduce (vb); a reduction (n)
> **show** = expose (vb); exposure (n)

This activity also makes use of some of the vocabulary for describing changes over time that was introduced in Unit 2 (eg *reduce, increase*).

Note: there is an argument that using 'action' verbs instead of nominalisations creates a more readable style, but the point of this activity is for students to be aware of what nominalisation is and to be able to understand it receptively as they will no doubt be exposed to nominalised forms in their further reading. There is more work for the students on producing nominalisations in our other book, *EAP Now!*

ANSWERS

a. the number of overweight children has increased dramatically
Answer given in Students' Book as example: *a dramatic increase in the number of overweight children* (line 1)

b. children are eating more junk food
the increased consumption of junk food by children (line 4)

c. exercising less
a reduction in exercise (line 6)

d. childhood obesity is increasing
an increase in childhood obesity (line 6)

e. the food companies argue against this
arguments against this from the food companies (line 7)

Unit 7 Media | 81

f. showing less advertising of junk food to children
a reduction in the exposure of children to junk food advertising (lines 9–10)
g. they will become healthier later in life
an improvement in their health later in life (line 10)

② Students now complete a table by matching words or expressions from Question 1 in this task to those with the same meaning in Text 3. The aim is for students to notice that the language in the text is more formal. It conveys meaning through nouns and noun groups (nominalisations), while the equivalents in Question 1, which sound more conversational and which the students are more likely to be more familiar with, convey meaning through verbs and verb groups. Point out to students that this pattern is typical. Ensure students understand that this process is called nominalisation, and that it doesn't just involve single words being transformed from verbs (or adjectives) to nouns, but whole groups of words.

Note: Nominalisation can also involve changing adjectives to nouns.

ANSWERS

	TEXT 3 (academic)	QUESTION 1 (less formal)
[a]	increase (n)	increase (vb)
[b]	the increased consumption of …	eating more (answer to this question given in Students' Book as an example)
[c]	a reduction in exercise	exercising less
[d]	an increase	is increasing
[e]	arguments	argue
[f]	a reduction in the exposure of … to … advertising	showing less advertising
[g]	an improvement in the health	become healthier
	The main words here are mostly **nouns** / verbs / adjectives	The main words here are mostly nouns / **verbs** / adjectives

The *Text 3* column contains more formal, written-style expressions. The expressions in the *Question 1* column are more informal and conversational. One reason for this is that the written version conveys more meaning through nouns and spoken language often conveys more meaning through verbs.

Extension: Students rewrite Text 3 using a less formal, more conversational style.

Task B | Understanding nominalisations ▶▶ SB P. 78

Students are asked to convert the following nominalisations to clauses with verbs. The first has been done as an example.

This task also helps students to develop the skill of paraphrasing.

The meanings of the following words are glossed in the Students' Book: halt, gradual and desire.

ANSWERS

a. his desire for fame
   → *He wants to be famous*
b. the danger of traffic accidents
   → Traffic *accidents are dangerous*
c. instructions on the use of DVD players
   → How *to use DVD players*
d. a drop in mobile phone use
   → People *are using mobile phones less*
e. a decrease in the amount of exercise in children
   → Children *are having less exercise* / children *are exercising less*
f. a gradual increase in the amount of advertising
   → Companies *are slowly advertising more*
g. a halt to the introduction of new products
   → New products *are not being introduced.*
h. a lack of improvement in the quality of mobile phone service
   → Mobile phone companies *are not getting better at giving service to customers / are not improving the quality of mobile phone service*

Task C | Giving instructions ▶▶ SB P. 78

① Refer students back to Text 2 from the Reading section (*DVD instructions for use*, page 76 in the Students' Book), and ask them to answer the questions for this task.

ANSWERS

a. For each sentence, can you see a subject? *No, we can't*
b. What form of the verb is used? *Infinitive without to, otherwise known as the base form, eg press, put, close, use.*

The Students' Book next gives information about the imperative in a note box.

2 Students are now referred to Text 1 (*How to become a film star*), which also gives instructions, but does so in a less direct, gentler, more conversational, more polite style. This question helps students see how this is done. If students find this difficult, give them some of the answers as hints until they see the pattern.

ANSWERS

a. Circle all the other instructions/advice in that text, except imperatives. See Text 1 on the next page.
b. Put the instructions you found in [b] in the table below, in columns according to the headings. The first two have been done for you as examples.
c. What is the most common verb form? *Infinitive with 'to', eg 'to hit'.*
d. Underline the imperatives in Text 1, Why do you think they don't sound as direct as they do in Text 2? *In Text 1, the imperatives are used in a context where a friendly, humorous, chatty style has already set the scene.*

SENTENCE STARTER	INFINITIVE OR GERUND	REST OF SENTENCE
The first thing is	to make sure	you're in the right place
it's no good trying	to hit	the big time in the north of Scotland
You're much better off	going	to southern California
You will need	to present	yourself well
they have	to be	the best quality they can be
it's important	to dress	well
you have	to be	even more careful
All of this will help you	to get	an agent
you'll have	to use	the contacts you've made
It's also useful	to make sure	your acting skills are good

Task D | Practising giving instructions ▶▶ SB P. 79

Put the students in pairs. One person from each pair tells the other to do something. (There is a list in the Students' Book – or you and/or your students can make your own list if you like.)

The 'listener' mimes what they have been told, exactly as they were told it.

Note: Students get further practice in giving instructions and advice in the writing section, coming up next.

WRITING
PROCEDURAL GENRE

Out of the wide variety of sub-genres of procedural texts (such as recipes, institutional procedures and games instructions), only one is used here – an advice article. Not all procedural texts have the preview/scope structure, which is emphasised here mainly to get students accustomed to the 'say what you're going to say, then say it' rhetorical style common in a wide variety of English-language text types.

A basic model of a procedural text without an introduction is Text 2 in the reading section, instructions for operating a DVD player. Students could be asked to write their own instructions for other items such as a TV, a computer game or a mobile phone.

Task A | Stages in an advice article ▶▶ SB P. 79

If necessary with your students review the staging of introductions (General Statement and Preview/Scope) discussed earlier in the Writing section of Unit 3, page 33 of their books. Also review discourse signals that signal new stages or paragraphs in an essay (see Writing section of Unit 4, page 46 of the Students' Book).

Then ask students to answer the questions in their books. This allows them to apply their knowledge of essay stages to Text 1.

ANSWERS

1. Draw a box around the General Statement and Preview/Scope in Text 1.

    General statement: introduces the topic

    > Everyone wants to become a film star – the glamour of Hollywood, the fame, the money, the excited fans and mixing with the most talked-about people in the world – wouldn't that be wonderful! We know that's not easy, but, if you follow these tips, you just might get your photo on the front pages of the celebrity magazines!

    Preview/scope: the writer is going to give tips in the body of the essay about achieving fame in Hollywood, which is the topic of the text.

Note: Imperatives are underlined; other instructions/advice is circled; double underlining indicates answers to Task A, Question 2 of the Writing section.

TEXT 1

HOW TO BECOME A FILM STAR

Everyone wants to become a film star – the glamour of Hollywood, the fame, the money, the excited fans and mixing with the most talked-about people in the world – wouldn't that be wonderful! We know that's not easy, but, if you follow these tips, you just might get your photo on the front pages of the celebrity magazines!

The first thing is to make sure you're in the right place – it's no good trying to hit the big time in the north of Scotland where there are no producers to meet or casting directors to give you a job. You're much better off going to southern California where all the action is.

And when you're there, do all you can to meet the right people. Go to as many parties as you can, get your hair cut at the same places as the stars, do whatever you can to find out what's going on, and talk, talk, talk. Get eye-catching business cards printed, give them out to everyone you meet, and above all, make as many contacts as you can.

Looks are also very important. Make yourself as beautiful or handsome as possible. Any money you spend in this area is a good investment – Hollywood just doesn't want to employ average-looking actors. Almost everyone will need cosmetic surgery to fit into the Hollywood ideal of perfect looks.

You will need to present yourself well. Get professional photographs made – they have to be the best quality they can be. Of course, it's important to dress well, just like any other job … but you have to be even more careful in this image-conscious field by paying attention to fashion.

All of this will help you to get an agent. An agent can help by introducing you to the right people at the right time … but there are thousands of people all wanting the services of one of these people, so you'll have to use the contacts you've made to help you with this. And make lots of copies of your photograph, and mail them together with a carefully-written, exciting-sounding letter to every agent in the phone book.

And don't forget to check the newspapers – there are sometimes adverts for extras and assistant staff members on the film crews. Get as much experience as possible, and take every opportunity to spend time with those important casting directors!

It's also useful to make sure your acting skills are good. Do whatever classes you can, practise whenever you can … the more of this you do, the better.

Regarding personal qualities, the most important points are persistence – keep on trying every day, and patience – it can take a few years before your name is known to enough people.

Good luck! Of course there are other ways – become famous on TV or as a singer first, for example, but these require more than one talent and are far more difficult!

Agnes Daydrew, staff writer

New Celebrity Magazine, March 2007

2. Double underline expressions that signal new stages in Text 1.
   Answers are marked on Text 1 on the previous page, and listed below:
   The first thing ... (line 8)
   And ... (* 2) (lines 14 and 43)
   ... also ... (* 2) (lines 21 and 48)
   Regarding ... (line 52)

   > **Note:** *And* is only used at the beginning of a sentence in informal writing. *Regarding* is used to introduce a new topic

3. List any other expressions you can think of to begin a new stage or paragraph.
   Suggestions include:
   Most importantly
   In addition
   Additionally
   Also important is ...
   It's important to ...

Task B | Write an advice article ▶▶ SB P. 79

In this task, ask students to write an advice article. Possible topics are:
- How to choose a language college
- How to find an apartment/house to rent
- How to become very good at playing video games
- How to look fashionable
- Their own idea!

While writing, students should focus on the following:
- Choice of grammar and expression for instructions/advice (see previous section, Language Spotlight)
- Stages
- Expressions that start different stages.

These are useful points for teachers to focus on when marking.

LISTENING 1 — NOTE-TAKING – LECTURE ABOUT MEDIA REPORTS

There are two recordings in this section. Students at the level the book is intended to cater for might find the first listening difficult. However, if these students are planning to go to college upon completion of this course, this is the kind of lecture/lesson they need to be prepared to cope with in quite a short space of time, hence it is important that work at this level is included in this book. The support given to students in the tasks here should help them to understand much of the content they hear, and give them some confidence in their ability to learn from lectures like this.

It may help to spread the first listening over two lessons. Task A and Questions 1, 2 and 3 of Task B could be done in the first lesson, and the rest of Task B, together with Tasks C and D, in the second lesson.

Task A | Opinions in the media ▶▶ SB P. 80

To lead into the topic of the first listening, students ask each other (in pairs or small groups) some questions about the neutrality or otherwise of the media.

Question 1 is intended to pre-teach the word *bias/biased*. Question 2 asks students to think about newspapers in their own countries, in particular about which sections of the newspaper they are most likely to find opinions, and what the influences on the opinions might be. Question 3 gets students to think about newspaper websites, and additional features that might be provided, such as discussion forums and the ability to submit opinions on news stories.

If some of your students don't usually read newspapers in their own countries, they could talk about how opinion is expressed on TV. Focusing them on the advertisements and trailers should get them thinking about where opinions are expressed in the media, and how bias is introduced.

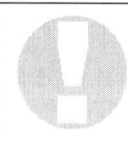

> **Variation for Question 2:** If your college subscribes to a newspaper, you could show that day's edition to your students, and then to go online to see the same stories on the Internet, noting any differences such as articles cut down in size, some articles missing, and the ability to submit comments and discuss the story on the website.

ANSWERS

Answers and commentary
1. Imagine a newspaper is owned by a political party. The newspaper never says anything bad about its owner, but says lots of good things about it. How would you describe the opinions of this newspaper?
   a. neutral   b. biased   c. impartial
   → [a] *biased* (adj). Point out to students that the noun and verb forms of this word are both *bias*.
2. Students are asked to think of a few newspapers in their country. Working with other students they should:
   a. list as many sections of those newspapers as they can.
   b. decide which sections give opinions.
   c. discuss whose opinions they give – the government's, the owners', or the journalists'.
   d. discuss whether the newspapers sometimes show bias.

Some sections in newspapers could include:
- Main news section
- Feature articles
- Editorial
- Letters to the editor (a wide variety of opinions)
- Sports (will give opinions about different teams and sports people)
- Travel (will give opinions about different hotels, destinations, etc)
- Entertainment, etc (will give opinions and reviews of performances)
- Arts (will give also give opinions and reviews)
- Gossip (will give opinions about well-known people)

b. All could give opinions in different ways. Students may mention selective reporting – that is, missing out some stories in order to hide the existence of certain points of view, eg news about protests against the government.

c. and d.
Any reasonable answers based on students' knowledge of the situation in their own countries are acceptable.

3. Students are asked about the difference between online news and print newspapers.

Any reasonable answers are acceptable. These could include the addition of surveys, links to relevant external websites, links to other articles or stories on a similar topic and discussion forums in the online version. The newspaper could include more detail – often the online version of the story is shorter than the print version, at least where the online content is free.

Task B | Listening and note-taking ▶▶ SB P. 80

Tell students they are going to listen to part of a lecture taken from a Diploma of Media Studies course.

① In the Students' Book are some notes that could have been made by a student in the lecture. Students should read those notes, making sure they understand the vocabulary – point out or elicit that some of the words are abbreviated, eg *mrktng* for *marketing*, and other common abbreviations are used, for example *cf = compared with*. The following words are those the students are most likely to need help with from the teacher: *blog* (a web page, like a diary, with the newest entries at the top), *discussion forum* (web page where online discussions take place), *moderator* (person who checks discussion forum posts to make sure they follow the rules of the forum, eg they don't contain offensive language), *censor/censorship/ censoring, consequence, disguised, trivia, make up stories*.

Mention to students that reading ahead (as in this activity) is very useful in exams and for real college and university lectures. In exams, they should read the questions as thoroughly as possible before the listening starts, to help orientate them to the topic, to help them know what they are listening for, and to help reduce their reading workload while they are listening. At college and university, reading any lecture notes they are given before the lecture starts will help them understand the lectures.

② Ask students to follow the notes as they listen. They should mark off the points as they hear them – as well as being a good listening exercise in itself, marking the points is also a good exam technique, to help maintain concentration. Play the CD only up to where product placement is mentioned (to 7 minutes, 29 seconds). There are three mistakes in the notes – students should try to identify and correct those mistakes. They can also annotate and thereby extend the notes in the book with their own notes.

CD 1 (11)

ANSWER

The mistakes in the notes are as follows:
- under the 'Types of texts – features' heading, 'focus on two major issues' should be 'focus on one major issue'
- under the 'Electronic media' heading, 'only small media companies here' should be 'only main media companies here'.
- under the 'Electronic media' heading, 'blogs – like adverts …' should be 'blogs – like editorials …'

③ Students now answer some questions which focus on the formatting of the notes and the rationale behind it.

ANSWERS

a. Which ideas are on the left hand side of the page – main ideas or supporting ideas?
→ *Main ideas are on the left*
b. Which ideas are on the right hand side? → *Supporting ideas are on the right – basically, ideas get smaller and more detailed as you go from left to right across the page.*
c. What is the advantage of this format when looking at notes quickly? →
Can quickly see the main ideas; can quickly locate an area of interest.

④ and **⑤** Students now listen to the rest of the recording and complete the notes. Students could be encouraged to use similar formatting – there are many other ways of taking notes, but before students can really decide which is best for them, it's advisable for them to try different ways.

They may need to listen several times. Between listenings, they can compare their notes with another student.

ANSWERS

4 and **5.** Here are some suggested notes.

HOW TO SYSTEMATICALLY RECOGNISE BIAS

(from before – look at: <u>kind of text</u>, <u>topic</u>)

<u>Audience</u> – who? eg time of day, of school, work

<u>Author</u> – but could be owner's opinions

<u>Purpose</u> – eg   to make pple buy,
             make –ve opinion of gvrnmnt
             be interesting → increase viewers, sales
             – may lead to emphasis on trivia, making up stories

<u>Other possible viewpoints</u>
         – things not stated

<u>SO:</u>
– when know topic, predict opinions & arguments
– if these missing, maybe bias.

Variation 1: *For stronger students.* Students look at the notes in their text books, as in Question 1 above, but close their books before listening. While listening, they take notes, afterwards comparing the notes they write with the ones in the book, at that point identifying any mistakes.

Variation 2: *High level students only.* They listen without seeing the notes in the book, but take notes while listening. The CD could be stopped from time to time, with students summarising what they heard either in open class or in small groups, after each stop.

Recording script

CD 1

CD 1, track 11: Media, Unit 7
(11 minutes, 18 seconds)

Listening 1: Lecture about media reports

Narrator: This listening is from a small lecture in a college course on media. The lecturer will tell the students some of the ways to find out if there is bias in media, that is, if only one point of view is shown more strongly than other points of view.

(0 minutes, 35 seconds)

Lecturer: Good morning students. Lovely day, yes?

Students in unison: Mmmmm, yeah ... beautiful
(Laughter)

Lecturer: Well, everyone, as you know, the media provide sources of information that we are all exposed to every day, but, in this lecture we'll look at how we can protect ourselves from being influenced by what we hear. By that I mean, how to deal critically with what we hear and read. Let's start off by thinking about the things we ... to watch out for when listening, or reading critically. Who can think of something to watch out for when interpreting media reports. ... yes, Mohammad:

Bangladeshi student: Bias.

Lecturer: Yes, and how do we detect bias?

Russian student: Mmm, we look to see if the argument is one-sided, that is, if more emphasis is given to one side of the argument than the others.

Lecturer: Yes, that's one way of doing it. Anything else we can look out for?

Student: How about if the journalists have to follow the opinion of the owner of the media?

Lecturer: Yes, that can happen a lot, especially with the mass media. Anyway, those are all good points, but we'll look next at a systematic, a fixed approach to media messages. First, we have to think about what types of media there are. For print media, such as newspapers and magazines, texts generally come from several different varieties such as news articles, feature articles, editorials and advertisements. News articles are obvious, feature articles are longer and focus on one major issue, and both of these should, at least in theory, cover all sides of the issue. If you feel they haven't done this, you've probably found a sign of bias. Editorials on the other hand are intended to give a one-sided opinion. They can be quite useful in predicting bias, as reading a few of these can give clues as to the publication's political viewpoint. In some media organisations all journalists have to follow the opinion of the publication, while in others, they are given much more freedom to write what they like.

(2 minutes, 56 seconds)

Electronic media have opened up a whole new can of worms. For the moment, we'll talk only about websites of the main media companies. Often the content is identical to that of the organisation's print material, the main difference being the extras such as blogs and discussion forums. Blogs tend to be more like editorials in nature and can be quite biased, although the same publication may have bloggers with a range of political opinions. On the other hand the thing about discussion forums is that anyone can say anything. Often, very biased opinions from all sides appear, and strong opinions on one side will be met with equally strong ones on the other side ... but, it's rarely possible to tell how much, if at all, the moderator is preventing ideas he or she doesn't agree with from appearing on the site. And, more frighteningly, sometimes false information can be given, for example, by companies trying to use the media to make people think more positively about their products. A good example might be ..., well, ... say, there's some research on news about hamburger meat causing people to get fatter. Then a fast food company employee posts a message that says there are problems with the research, mentioning that he's a food scientist but not mentioning his company's name. Who's to know what's behind his opinion? The information that we need to have before we can understand the message properly is missing. It's true that there are usually moderators, people who can choose which messages to allow online and which to delete, but it's not usually possible to tell how many messages they stop.

(5 minutes, 1 second)

Moving on now to broadcast media, TV and radio. Because these have a much wider range of content, you have to be more aware of the different techniques for how bias can be introduced. For example, drama may show negative consequences for one set of actions, and positive consequences for others. For a long time, TV has been used by governments as a means of teaching morals to children, often through the choice of consequences of actions that are shown in children's programs, but this technique can also be used to create political bias.

(5 minutes, 42 seconds)

It's worth spending some time to look more closely at advertisements, because identifying them might be more difficult than it seems at first sight. Sometimes, an advertisement looks just like a newspaper article and is written in the same style. However, instead of being written by journalists, who traditionally are trained to look at all sides of the issue and write a balanced report, the authors are sales and marketing people, and the article will say good things about the product without mentioning the bad points. The aim, quite simply, will be to sell.

On television as well, people from some countries may be familiar with shopping shows, which are heavily sponsored. A few minutes are spent on each of several 'featured products', which are presented in a very positive way, and alternative products, such as those produced by rival companies, are not mentioned or only mentioned briefly. Of course a critical listener will detect these quickly due to the unusually positive opinion of the product. However, they must be influencing a large number of people, because the companies wouldn't continue to use these programs if they didn't boost sales. Basically, these programs are just long advertisements, often with other advertisements inserted into the middle.

Sometimes, also, advertising can get into movies and {TV} drama through techniques such as product placement, but that's a separate issue. You'll find out more about that as part of one of your assignments.

(7 minutes, 29 seconds)

So, let's get back now to looking at how we systematically recognise bias. Once we've found out the kind of text, we have to look at the audience it is intended for. You can probably do this very easily – it often depends for example on the time of day – for instance, children's programs are usually broadcast before and after school, and programs for middle-class office workers are shown after business hours.

And, remember how with written texts we usually try to find out who the author is? Media often complicate things, because the author is often employed to represent the opinions of the TV station or newspaper rather than their own opinion. So, we have to look at who the owner is and what the policy about editing is as well.

All of this helps us with the next step, understanding the purpose of the text, how the text is intended to affect the audience. For example, is it intended to persuade the viewer to buy? Is the purpose to get the reader to form a negative opinion of the government? Or, a common situation with mass media, is it to make you feel the publication helps you learn very interesting things and therefore makes you want to buy it again and again to find out more? This is especially the case with celebrity magazines such as *Hello* and *OK!* and with many tabloid newspapers. The danger here is that there may be a tendency to emphasise less important points, and ignore more important points, or even to make up stories completely.

Then, another very important thing is to think about what other viewpoints and opinions could exist but aren't stated, or what evidence might be presented but which you didn't hear. One trick for dealing with this is, as soon as you know the topic, try to predict the arguments and opinions that could appear. If several of these don't appear, then this may, but it isn't definitely a sign of, bias.

(9 minutes, 42 seconds)

So, there we have it. To summarise, the first thing to do is to decide what kind of media text it is, watching out especially for advertisements that look like something else. Then, predict from the introduction, the headline, any pictures or even the trailers what the topic is and the way the topic looks like it's going to be approached, for example through what opinions are mentioned as going to be presented, and try to think of as many ways, from your own knowledge or from logic, of presenting and supporting the main ideas that you can. Next, think about the most likely audience or audiences. After that, consider the owner of the media – you may have to look it up at first, but before long you'll get to know all the major players in the industry. Then, try to think of other points of view and supporting ideas that you haven't heard, and finally use all these clues, and your knowledge of persuasion techniques, to look at the bias and attempts to persuade.

Now, let's look in more detail at … *(fade out)*

Task C | Discussion ▶▶ SB P. 82

Students have a discussion in groups, using the following questions as prompts, to wrap up this listening.

1. Do newspapers in your country have editorials? Letters pages?
2. Do newspapers in your country usually follow the government's ideas, or do they often have different opinions?
3. Do you prefer reading the news online, or in newspapers? Or do you prefer to watch the news on the television?
4. Do you have shopping programs like those described in the lecture in your country?
5. Is it possible for media to be completely neutral, that is, to have no bias at all?

LISTENING 2: LISTENING TO AND FOLLOWING INSTRUCTIONS – MAKING A FILM

Task A | Making a film ▶▶ SB P. 82

Next, students listen to a talk about how to make a film. This is an oral equivalent to the kind of instructional/procedural texts they read earlier in this unit, containing imperatives and other instruction/advice structures as covered in the Language Spotlight section.

To activate prior knowledge about this topic, students discuss in small groups what they know about film making (questions in the Students' Book).

Task B | Order of stages ▶▶ SB P. 83

1. Students read a list of some of the steps in making a film, and from prior knowledge try to put the stages in order. Students should put the stages in approximately the right order before they listen, thus helping to build confidence in using the strategy of prediction. Go over any vocabulary that is causing difficulty if they aren't able to work it out from context.

2. Next, students should listen to the recording, writing numbers in the boxes provided to indicate the steps.

CD 1

ANSWERS

1 and 2.

1. Decide story/plot
2. Write screenplay
3. Choose actors
4. Choose locations
5. Get permission to use locations
6. Start filming
7. Add special effects
8. Editing

Note: Adding special effects and editing could be said to occur at the same time and it is quite possible to choose locations before the actors!

Recording script

CD 1

CD 1, track 12: Media, Unit 7
(3 minutes, 8 seconds)

Listening 2: How to make a film: a procedure

Narrator: Many people dream about how wonderful it would be to make their own film. Now we have some instructions about how to do this!

(Film clicking noise / whir – countdown.)

Instructor: Well, to make a movie, first, you need to decide on the story, or at least a plot. Next, unless there is already a screenplay, you need to find someone to write one. This isn't as easy as it sounds, because a screenplay has to use the right words to create the right feeling – in written stories, feeling can be described, but in spoken stories feeling has to come from the words the characters say, and perhaps the music and sound effects.

Then, choose the people. It's important to choose actors who fit the personality, age and appearance of the characters well. The director is one of the most important roles. He or she must tell the actors his or her vision for how he or she wants them to play the character, although this is often discussed with the actors themselves. Also, he or she gives feedback on their performance, guiding them to adjust what they do if it isn't right the first time. Then, of course there are the camera operators, sound recordists and people to help.

Next, choose locations and make sure that you can get permission to use them. It's no good deciding to shoot in the middle of a shopping centre if management feel it will interrupt trade to the shops, and therefore don't grant permission. Another thing to do before starting to film is make sure the right equipment is available – it can be hired if the people working on the film don't already own it.

There are a lot of details to organise to make sure everyone is ready with the right equipment in the right place at the right time.

During the filming, everyone has to listen to the director. There may be some discussion, but usually because of the cost of the actors' time, hiring of equipment, that sort of thing, things have to be done quickly, so there isn't time for too much talk.

After filming is finished, the post production work starts. This can be much more time-consuming than many people expect. A sound engineer will make sure that all the sound flows smoothly and matches the video, and will also add special effects. The editor cuts out parts and sometimes rearranges things, also to ensure that it appears very smooth in the final version. With the director, the editor also has to ensure the film is well balanced, and this may mean cutting out some very good parts of it.

When all this is finished, you have your own wonderful film!

Voice with authority yells: CUT!

Task C | Listening for specific information ▶▶ SB P. 83

Students listen again and complete sentences in their books with words they hear. They shouldn't write more than three words for each.

ANSWERS

1. A screenplay is more difficult to write than a novel because feelings can't <u>be described</u>
2. In a film, the feeling has to come from the character's words, the music or the <u>sound effects.</u>
3. The person in charge during filming is <u>the director</u>
4. Make sure you have permission to <u>use the locations</u>
5. During filming, there isn't much time for discussion because of <u>the cost</u> of everyone's time, equipment hire, etc.
6. Post production work can be very <u>time-consuming</u>
7. The purpose of editing is to make sure the final version of the film is well <u>balanced</u>

SPEAKING 2 — SURVEY – PREFERENCES AROUND MEDIA CHOICES

Task A | Discussion ▶▶ SB P. 83

In this section, students prepare and conduct a survey to 'research' the media topic of their choice. First though, in this task, they discuss the topic of media use, in order to start thinking about the topic, using some questions in their books as prompts.

Task B | Survey ▶▶ SB P. 83

Students form groups in which they will remain for the duration of this task (which can range from a couple of hours to a full-scale mini research project spread over a few weeks).

❶ In groups, students should choose a question about media use to research. Some potential questions are given in their books as examples, but it is preferable if they choose their own ideas of interest to them, perhaps springing out of the discussion in Task A.

The list of research questions in the Students' Book is:
- Is the Internet taking over from TV?
- Are DVDs taking over from cinemas?
- What do people use the Internet for the most, browsing, Internet chat or emailing?

❷ In the same groups, ask students to work out some questions (at least 5) that could go in their survey. It may be interesting to look at age group and/or gender.

❸ Students conduct the survey. This could be just with other groups in the same class, visits to other classes, or going outside the college and interviewing members of the public.

❹ After collecting sufficient answers, students help each other to draw conclusions from the answers (eg by averaging numbers of hours, counting *yes* and *no* answers, etc).

❺ Students prepare a short talk (2–3 minutes) about the results. This doesn't have to be elaborate – a quick introduction followed by their findings would sufficient. A time should be set for the class to come together and present their findings to each other.

FURTHER PRACTICE: READING, FILMS AND FUN

As with every unit, here are some ideas for further reading, and some suggested questions for discussion and writing practice. The ideas below are as they appear in the Students' Book, page 84.

READING

For some of the celebrity magazines mentioned earlier, look at **http://www.hellomagazine.com/**, **http://www.ok-magazine.com/**

For some very different opinions on the media, look at **http://www.adbusters.org/home/**

FILMS

The Truman Show, directed by Peter Weir, starring Jim Carrey. This film is about a man who lives for television – but doesn't know it!

Shattered Glass, directed by Billy Ray, starring Hayden Christensen. This film tells the story of a newspaper reporter who makes up his own stories.

Also, many films have a 'making of' documentary, showing how the film is made. These would follow on nicely from the second listening of this unit. Often, you can find them as an extra track on the DVD of the movie.

QUESTIONS

1. Some people say TV is bad for children because it discourages them from having exercise and from communicating with other children. However, others say it stimulates the mind and gives children knowledge of the world. Overall, is TV good or bad for children? Give reasons.

2. Should TV companies be stopped from showing violent programs in case children watch them? What should be the limits (if any)? Give reasons for your answer.

3. Should journalists be free to write about views that are different from the opinion of the owner of the publication?

4. Some people say that a journalist's main responsibility is to tell the truth. Others say that journalists should help their newspaper or TV station make a profit by making the news sound more dramatic than it really is, so that more people listen to the news programs or buy newspapers. Which of these views do you agree with?

5. The media should be stopped from giving opinions against the government. Do you agree with this opinion? Give reasons.

8 ART

'there are pictures in poems and poems in pictures'

BY THE END OF THIS UNIT, STUDENTS SHOULD:

- have increased their general knowledge about art and recognise that it is part of everyday life .... Speaking: Task A **94**
- have learned vocabulary including nouns and verbs, and verb tenses used in reviews .... Speaking: Tasks A and B **94**; Reading 1: Task A **95**
- have improved their ability to locate definitions in context ....Speaking: Task B **94**
- know how to locate grammar in context and know how it functions to create meaning in a review .... Reading 1: Task A **95**
- be able to think critically about a subject or experience and know how to offer a review of it ....Reading 1: Task A **95**
- know how to handle the grammar and verb tense changes around reported speech; reporting direct speech .... Language Spotlight 1: Tasks A and B **96**
- know how to scan text for a specific purpose... Reading 2: Task B **97**
- know how to use tag questions and answer tag questions (such as *do you? don't you?*) appropriately; recognise and use intonation that indicates tag certainty or uncertainty ....Listening: Task A **98**
- have practised using voice intonation in tag questions ....Language Spotlight 2: Tasks A and B **100**
- have learned to write a review .... Writing: Task A **100**

ART n. [UNCOUNTABLE]: 1 the use of painting, drawing, sculpture to represent things or express ideas: *an example of Indian art \ contemporary/modern art the Museum of Modern Art* → ART FORM, FINE ART, PERFORMANCE ART. 2 pl., objects that are produced by art, such as paintings, drawings etc: an *art exhibition \ an art critic \ an arts and crafts fair \ The exhibition features 175 works of art.*

SPEAKING

BUILDING THE FIELD

Task A | Discussion and vocabulary ▶▶ SB P. 86

In small groups, students tell each other as much as they can in answer to the following questions. Questions 1 & 2 could be teacher led and a guided discussion. Students answer Questions 3 to 6 in a more personal way.

ANSWERS

1. *What do you think of when you hear the word, 'art'?*
   Students to gain an understanding that art could include as many areas as painting, sculpture, ceramics, bronze casts, shadow puppets (like those of Indonesia), clocks, stone lintels, maps, decorated manuscripts, coffins, music, architecture, technology and design, quilts, embroidery.
2. *When do you think art began?*
   Perhaps the earliest art is cave drawings and paintings (Pre-historic – 40 000 to 3000 BC). These would be in Africa and depictions of the Dreamtime in Australia. Depending on your culture, answers as to the earliest art are arguable. For Western art the Palace of Knossos with its frescoes and bull leaping is often cited as the beginning of classical art moving to Hellenistic, Etruscan and Roman in the 4th century. Maps of the world such as the Psalter World Map (1260s) combines art, Christian religion and technology as do the Egyptian pyramids (Ancient – 3000 to 331 BCE). It's safe to say that from around 300 AD forward, there is evidence of art around the world: India, Mexico, China (618 AD), Japan (1180 AD), Mexico and Peru.
3. *What kind of art do you like?* Answers vary.
4. *Do you have a favourite piece of art you have seen or know about?* Answers vary
5. Students examine the photographs and discuss them.
6. *What is a 'griffin'?*
   A griffin is a mythological creature or monster that has the head and wings of an eagle and the body of a lion (Picture 7). This picture is of a frescoe from the wall of the Palace of Knossos in Crete.

VOCABULARY

Text

[1] Artisans, or skilled craftspersons, work very hard. Some create objects made from clay and once they have glazed them, these objects become beautiful [2] ceramics. Another thing artisans do is [3] casting. It's dangerous, in a way, because hot liquid metal can be pretty difficult to handle.

I like [4] oil painting myself. I've even tried it. I enjoy mixing the pigment to get just the right colour. When not painting, I also often study a [5] motif within a work of art for hours. One motif I have seen repeated is that of figures carrying wine or other offerings to a central place, like a temple, for example. Often these are wall paintings, or they are embroidered on cloth or tapestry. Sometimes, they are carved in relief out of stone. They are [6] rituals because they occur over and over again and they seem to have special meaning. There is a lot of meaning there and I think they help people with the [7] afterlife, in other words, their souls after they die.

Students read the text and glean meanings from the context. All words are defined or explained within the text. You can either explain the definitions or write them out after students locate them in their books.

ANSWERS

1. **artisan** – a skilled craftsperson.
2. **ceramic** – objects made from clay, usually glazed and fired or baked.
3. **casting** – when hot liquid metal (bronze, for example) is poured into a pre made mould.
4. **oil paint** – a paint that is not made from water; it is made by mixing pigment (colour) and oil together.
5. **motif** – the theme or main design of a work of art.
6. **ritual** – processes that honour special events such as weddings or funerals; repeated actions over time that have special meaning.
7. **afterlife** – the life of the soul after the body dies.

Task B | More vocabulary fun ▶▶ SB P. 87

Students complete the crossword below.

		¹S	H	²A	R	D				
				D				³C	U	T
				M				O		
				I		⁴M		L		
			⁵C	R	E	A	T	O	R	
⁶I				E		N		U		
D	⁷A		⁸P			N		R		
E	R		O			E				
⁹A	R	T	I	S	T					
			T			Q				
						U				
	¹⁰I	M	P	R	E	S	S	I	O	N
			R			N				
			Y							

94 | EAP Now! Preliminary English for Academic Purposes Teacher's Book

ANSWERS

ACROSS

1. A piece of pottery usually ancient. *shard*
3. Said by the director of a film to tell people to stop acting, filming. *cut*
5. Someone who made or invented a particular thing. Creation/something that has been created. *creator*
9. Someone who produces art, especially paintings or drawings. *artist*
10. Something you say, write or do that shows what you think or feel. *impression*

DOWN

2. To look at something and think how impressive or beautiful it is. *admire*
3. Shade, hint, hue. *colour*
4. A model of the human body used for showing clothes in shop windows. *mannequin*
6. A plan or suggestion. *idea*
7. The use of painting, drawing or sculpture to represent things or express ideas. *art*
8. An object hand shaped from clay. *pottery*

READING 1 — A REVIEW

Task A | The five questions for reading any text ▸▸ SB P. 88

① The students look at the reading, which is a review of Van Gogh's painting 'Irises'. It is called *Looking at Art*. As per all readings, students should begin by scanning the information, looking for who wrote it, what the title is and so forth.

ANSWERS

[a] **What is it?**
It is a review.
[b] **What is the source?**
The source is the title, 'Looking at Art'. It is most likely from an art magazine, or it might be from a newspaper.
[c] **Who is the writer?**
The writer is Charlene C Rose (fictitious, produced by the authors, but students are to use the name as the writer).
[d] **What purpose does the writer have for writing it?**
The purpose of a review. It informs readers about something and gives an opinion of it so that readers can make up their own minds whether to watch, visit, read go to an event.
[e] **Who is the intended audience?**
Readers of the art world or anyone interested in art.

② Students read the review then answer the comprehension questions that link grammar to the content and meaning of the text.

ANSWERS

I. Amazing; absolutely amazing; a wonderful work of art; a beautiful work of art.
II. Yes,
III. Because she calls it amazing, wonderful and beautiful.
IV. Amazing; astonishing; wonderful work of art; deep purple flowers; Lines create a feeling of movement; irises look like they are bobbing about on their long stems; the leaves twist and turn reaching for sun and look like they are dancing; thick dark lines around the edges of the leaves and stems; they are orange and make a beautiful contrast; one, lone white iris.
V. Yes, there are a lot of adjectives in this article.
VI. Because it is a review and that means there will be descriptive words in the text.
VII. Vincent Van Gogh.
VIII. 1889.
IX. Japan.
X. Japanese wood blocks.
XI. The Romantics.
XII. Yes or no – up to the student.
XIII. A critical thinking question … there is no correct answer.

(3) Students then match the list of *nouns* taken from the reading with their meanings by drawing a line.

NOUNS — **MEANINGS**

a print	a printed copy of a painting or drawing
his works	in art, it means the artist's paintings or other art s/he did
canvas	the material artists oil paint upon
in amazement	with surprise
foreground	front
astonishing amount	surprising quantity, surprising level of

(4) Students do the same matching with this list of verbs.

VERBS — **MEANINGS**

bobbing about	moving up and down, like a cork in water
twist	move about in a spiral way, turn from the waist, for example
turn	change direction
praise	say good things about or think good things about a person or thing

Note: The tense used in reviews is present and present continuous when the actual item is being discussed, eg. *'The leaves twist and turn reaching for sun and look like they are dancing'*.

LANGUAGE SPOTLIGHT 1 — REPORTED SPEECH

Task A | Reporting direct speech ▶▶ SB P. 90

Direct speech reporting is always a difficult area for students, as are tag questions. In reported speech the tenses move *back* or *down* a tense. From the Students' Book:

When we talk to each other sometimes we need to tell or report what someone else has said. Look at this example:
- **A.** 'Did Tina say she's (she is) coming to the party?'
- **B.** 'Yes, she said she was.'

Look at what has changed in the two simple sentences. Tina – the noun/name changed to the pronoun 'she'. The verb – present simple tense 'is (she's)'– changed to the past tense 'was'. This is the key to reported statements. There are other changes but practise this one first. Present simple tense verbs become past simple tense.

ANSWERS

a. **Aarron:** 'I think blue mobile phone covers are the best.' (Note: there are two verbs to change.)
Aarron said (that) he thought mobile phone covers were the best.

b. **Gina:** 'I'm going to Hawaii for a holiday this June.'
Gina said (that) she was going to Hawaii for a holiday this June.

c. **Aarron:** 'Well, I'm as tired as a dead snake.'
Aarron said (that) he was as tired as a dead snake.

d. **Gina:** 'I think Hawaii is wonderful.' (Note: there are two verbs to change.)
Gina said (that) she thought Hawaii was a wonderful place.

Task B | Verb tense changes when reporting speech ▶▶ SB P. 90

In the previous task, students practised simple present to simple past tense.

This task shows the tense changes to use where the person you are reporting speaks in the past tense. For example, *I gave mother a present*. How will you report what he or she has said?

PAST SIMPLE > BECOMES PAST PERFECT
'I gave mother a present'

He said he had given a present to mother. (or) He said he had given mother a present.

PRESENT PERFECT > ALSO BECOMES PAST PERFECT
'We have completed our projects', the students told the lecturer.

The students (or they) told the lecturer (that) they had completed their projects

PRESENT CONTINUOUS > BECOMES PAST CONTINUOUS
'I'm working at a restaurant while I'm studying for my exams.'

She said she's been working at a restaurant while she's been studying for her exams.

> **Modals:** Present modals like *can* and *may* change tense too. But past modals like *could* and *would* do not change.
> can > could
> may > might
> shall > should
> will > would

ANSWERS

Ask students to change the verb tense in the following 10 sentences:

a. 'I'm surprised she managed to get a ticket to Hawaii in June.'
He said (that) he was surprised she had managed to get a ticket to Hawaii in June.

b. 'I wished I had booked earlier.'
She said (that) she wished she had booked earlier.

c. 'I wish you'd (you had) booked earlier, too.'
He said (that) he wished she had booked earlier, too.

d. 'My flight leaves at 4 in the morning.'
She said *(that) her flight left at 4 in the morning.*

e. 'I hope it's going to be really good weather that day.'
He said *(that) he hoped it would be really good weather on that day.*

f. 'I'm sure it will be.'
She said *(that) she was sure it would be.*

g. 'I know you're going to have a fabulous time, no matter what.'
He said *(that) he knew she was going to have a fabulous time, no matter what.*

h. 'I think you're very sweet and I'm going to miss you a lot.'
She said *(that) she thought he was very sweet and she was going to miss him a lot.*

i. 'So does that mean you'll go out with me when you get back?'
He asked, *Did that mean she would go out with him when he got back?*

j. 'You'll just have to wait and see, won't you?'
She said *(that) he would just have to wait and see, wouldn't he?*

READING 2 — AN ARTICLE

Task A | Another view of art – *Art as technology* ▶▶ SB P. 91

① Prior to and after reading the text *Art as technology* by Winnifred Smith-Cox (fictitious, by the authors), students look over it quickly, and with your help identify and answer the five questions that go with every reading.

ANSWERS

[a] **What is it?** – *A review, a Sunday piece*
[b] **What is the source?** – *Go Green Thinkers! magazine Jan 2007 (fictitious)*
[c] **Who is the writer?** – *W Smith-Cox*
[d] **What purpose does the writer have for writing it?** – *To convince and to inform*
[e] **Who is the intended audience?** – *Young people and anyone who owns a mobile phone*

② The questions in the Students' Book focus on content (see answers below). For additional interest you could lead a discussion around mobile phones or ask students to ask one another these questions:
- *How old were they when they got their first mobile phone?*
- *How many has each student owned in his/her life?*
- *Did they throw them out?*
- *Have they ever lost a mobile phone?*
- *Do they think there is art in the design of them?*
- *What colour is everyone's phone?*

ANSWERS

I. It refers to the words ' they could be called' – a pun is a play on words
II. Because it can now be used for many other things, such as a TV and for the Internet.
III. Neither.
IV. Large or flip up.
V. Two billion.
VI. Buy a mobile made of biodegradable material.
VII. Soy beans.
VIII. It is biodegradable.
IX. *Dangle* means to hang down from something and *jingle* means to make a small noise, like a little bell, for example.
X. Answers will vary, but according to the article, they save personal pictures as screen savers, and attach things to the phones.

Task B | Scanning ▶▶ SB P. 93

This is a different way to practise scanning. Students search newspapers or magazines for the letters from their own names. You could give them a time limit. But they will not be reading, just searching for their own, individual letters in order to cut them out (or tear them if no scissors are available) and then form their names laying the pieces on paper. Paste if possible, or simply arrange them.

Scan means to look for one thing while moving eyes over text. Students don't read – they scan, search and find.

① Ask the students to create their own work of art using the letters in his or her name. They can make as many names as they like. Students have to scan in this task.

INSTRUCTIONS
- Students scan a magazine or newspaper quickly and look for the letters that spell their name. They can add those of their friends or family later.
- When they find a letter, tear or cut it out and lay it on a clean piece of paper.
- Then they arrange the letters to spell their name.
- Suggest they make it artistic by the way they cut out the shapes around the letters and by the way they arrange the letters next to one another.
- If they have paste, they should stick down the letters.

PRE-LISTENING

OPINIONS

Task A | Thinking about opinions ▶▶ SB P. 93

① Students are presented with four questions and should use these to discuss a television show and/or movie they like. They should try to express a personal opinion about it. The listening is a spoken review between two TV presenters.

In this part, most of the phrases occur in the listening. Students should familiarise themselves with opinion phrases prior to the listening. Answers vary.

② Ask students to circle the following phrases in the following lists which they think *introduce or express an opinion*.

ANSWERS

a. They arrived last night.; <u>I thought</u> …; <u>I mean</u> …; then they …; <u>Frankly, I was rather offended</u> …

b. Yes, that's right; Well, <u>as far as I'm concerned</u> …; I hear what you're saying …

c. but…; <u>it's also quite funny</u> …; <u>that's pretty boring</u> …; <u>it's very weak</u> …

d. <u>it's interesting</u>…; <u>I do like</u>…; Come here.; <u>I'm not sure I</u>…; Who is he? …

LISTENING

REVIEW, OPINIONS, TAG QUESTIONS

Task A | Locating opinions, summarising ▶▶ SB P. 93

The format of this listening is one of a dialogue between two people offering their opinions on a review program designed for the purpose. It would be television. This activity covers a learning cycle for oral skills development, including staging, grammar and vocabulary, cohesion (conversational gambits – question forms), and key grammatical functions. It comprises a baby step towards the more academic oral and written reviews, for example literature reviews, by focusing attention on opinions.

Students listen:
- to figure out how opinions are expressed and how to identify those opinions; listen for opinion markers and adjectives.
- to discover the attitudes and opinions which characterise each speaker.
- globally to discover the differences in opinion between the two speakers.
- to recognise these opinions in a summary form.
- for stages of a review which apply to reading and writing as well as to speaking and listening. They can predict what's coming if they recognise the segment or section of review introduced by speaking. You can point out to students that these 'information units' are highlighted with intonation and in order to introduce new information, question forms are used.
- for when one speaker disagrees with the other.
- for questions and answers (function as well as grammar): tag question forms, such as: *They can't, can they? No, they can't.*

> **Extension:** After listening and completing the tasks, students work in pairs or groups to offer a brief review of a movie, television program or musical piece/artist that they admire or dislike. Students familiar with the same program or other choice weigh in agreeing or disagreeing, expressing their own opinions.

This listening is used again in the Language Spotlight that follows to illustrate tag questions in terms of voice. When there is certainty about asking a question and the questioner is only seeking agreement for what they ask, then the voice drops at the end of the question. You can point this out to students the second time they listen. In the first listening, they should try to understand the different opinions of the two reviewers.

Recording script

CD 1

CD 1, track 13: Art, Unit 8
(4 minutes, 0 seconds)

Listening: Two people giving a review about the latest reality TV show

Narrator: The listening begins with an introduction from a compere who is the host for a television program that reviews other television programs. Oliver and Christine discuss a reality TV show and give their opinions for the viewers.

Oliver: Good evening viewers and listeners. Tonight, on the *All About Television* show, we are reviewing *The Country Cousin* reality TV program that went nationwide to air last night. Christine, I think I'll let you go first. What did you think of *Country Cousins*?

Christine: MMMMM, Oh my God, Oliver, where to start. A bit shocking in some ways.

Oliver: I know … But we had better be clear for our audience about what we mean. What exactly was shocking about it, do you think?

Christine: Well, really, for me, I suppose the only thing was… , first of all, I thought the nudity was a bit over the top. I mean, it is on prime time viewing so children can easily be up and watching.

Oliver: Yes, that was definitely too much. Full frontal on the boys and girls from different countries… Frankly, I was rather offended. And, what about the format? I mean *Country Cousin*. Where's that from? Do you know?

Christine: Yeah, well, yes, each person in the house, well, they arrive, and they have a cousin to come to visit in the house but, they've never met them. Then, they all live together for 2 months and try to figure out who is their real cousin though they've never met them. It must take some research on the programmer's part to get it all happening.

Oliver: Yeah, a bit of a waste of energy, if you ask me. And they can't ask direct questions, can they? Like to each other about family or something.

Christine: No, they can't. No direct questions are allowed.

Oliver: And they aren't allowed to talk in private, with no people around, are they?

Christine: No, they aren't.

Oliver: Also, they don't mention mutual relations or family members that could give it away, do they?

Christine: No, they don't, Oliver. They just have to live a normal life and work it all out.

Oliver: Look. To me, Christine, it just seems like a poor version of *Big Brother* where the audience watches people living, washing, walking around being bored and eating. Pretty boring.

Christine: Yeah, I see what you mean but, for me, the interesting thing is their personalities. The show is weak as far as format goes, but I do like getting to know the people.

Oliver: But what about the fact that they never do anything?

Christine: But isn't it really a question of doing what people normally do when they are not at work, is it? They <u>are</u> doing <u>something</u>. I mean they <u>are</u> talking and relating to one another.

Oliver: But surely, people don't want to waste their time on this rubbish?

Christine: Well, that's your value judgement, your opinion. I don't really think of it as rubbish, more, more like a window into a group of people who are forced to interact with one another. It's interesting in a sociological sort of way, I think.

Lecturer: Oh yeah, that's a … justification for watching it.

Christine: It's also quite funny at times. And you always find someone you like in the group and someone you just hate.

Oliver: Well, I, I hear what you're saying, but for my money, not that you have to spend it to watch this TV program, I'd rather wait for a good movie to come on another channel. Reality TV is not my cup of tea. Better yet, I'd hire out a DVD of any of Hayao Miyazaki films, thanks. Something like *My Neighbour Totoro* or *Spirited Away* would be a much better way to spend my time, as far as I'm concerned.

> **ANSWERS**
>
> 1. Which summary *best* describes Christine's opinions of the show?
>   **b.** *She thinks it is weak in places but that it's entertaining and funny at times.*
>
> 2. Which summary *best* describes Oliver's opinions of the show?
>   **b.** *He thinks it is a waste of time to watch reality television, including this program.*

Students listen a second time and act out the following tag questions.

LANGUAGE SPOTLIGHT 2: TAG QUESTIONS

Task A | Practise speaking ▶▶ SB P. 94

In pairs, students read the dialogue from the Listening in this Unit. It's between two reviewers and they are talking about a TV program called *The Country Cousin*. Make sure students try to make their voices go down when asking the tag. Students swap roles.

Oliver: Yeah, a bit of a waste of energy, if you ask me. And they can't ask direct questions, can they? Like to each other about family or something.

Christine: No, they can't. No direct questions are allowed.

Oliver: And they aren't allowed to talk in private, with no people around, are they?

Christine: No, they aren't.

Oliver: Also, they don't mention mutual relations or family members that could give it away, do they?

Christine: No, they don't, Oliver. They just have to live a normal life and work it all out.

Task B | Voice down tag questions ▶▶ SB P. 94

VOICE DOWN TAGS

Students work in pairs for this task. Tell them to drop their voices at the end of each question. The questioner is quite certain of the answer and is seeking agreement.

Students need to answer yes or no and change the verb form.

For example:

1. 'You're wearing that dress tonight, aren't you?'
   Yes, I am.

2. 'You were born in Los Angeles, California, weren't you?'
   Yes, I was.

The *yes* or *no* must agree with the verb as a positive or negative.

NEVER – ~~Yes, I won't; No, I am; Yes, I'm not~~.

> **ANSWERS**
>
> 1. and 2. as above.
> 3. *Yes, I am.*
> 4. *Yes, he is.*
> 5. *Yes, he did.*
> 6. *Yes, there is.*
> 7. *Yes, it is.*
> 8. *No, I won't* (this one is difficult, students will probably say *Yes, I will*).

Task C | Voice up tag questions ▶▶ SB P. 94

VOICE UP TAGS

Students work in pairs. They should raise their voice up at the end of each question.

The questioner is not as certain of the answer.
For example:

1. 'You're not wearing that dress tonight, are you?'
   Yes, I am. (going to wear the dress) OR *No, I'm not.* (going to wear the dress)

NEVER – ~~Yes, I'm not~~. **NOR** ~~No, I am~~.

The *yes* or *no* must agree with the verb as a positive or negative.

2. 'You can't afford *that* car, *can you*?'
   No, I can't or *Yes, I can.*

> **ANSWERS**
>
> 1. and 2. as above
> 3. *Yes, I do* or *No, I don't.*
> 4. and 5. *Yes, she did* or *No, she didn't.*
> 6. *Yes, I can* or *No, I can't.*
> 7. *Yes, I am* or *No, I'm not.*
> 8. *Yes, they are* or *No, they aren't.*
> 9. *Yes, we are* or *No, we aren't.*
> 10. *Yes, they will* or *No, they won't.*

WRITING: YOUR OWN REVIEW

Task A | Writing a review ▶▶ SB P. 95

Students work on this task independently. Ask them to choose a work of art that they admire and have them write a review using their prior knowledge and the model of review. You could use one work of art displayed at the front of the class if you prefer. This will allow you to create a model of a review that can be checked against rather than each student writing about a different artwork.

They are provided a short model of a review in paragraph form (below) to help observe tense and staging. You might want to photocopy it and show the answer that way.

> **ANSWER**
>
> Students should underline the verbs in the extract below and note how many verbs are present tense and present continuous tense. Students should then write their own review of the work of art.

100 | EAP Now! Preliminary English for Academic Purposes Teacher's Book

Movie review model paragraph

Name of movie: *Blood and Guts*

Description of movie or thing being reviewed: It <u>is</u> a very long movie and very violent. The acting <u>is</u> pretty good and the actors <u>seem</u> happy doing what <u>they're doing</u>. *(present, present continuous)*

Comparison to same thing: Like most horror movies, the characters <u>wander</u> into very dark rooms, <u>separate</u> from each other and <u>wait</u> to die. <u>It's</u> pretty sad. <u>There's</u> a lot of screaming and a fair bit of grunting that goes <u>on</u> when people <u>are being stabbed</u> to death. But, compared to something like *Chainsaw Massacre*, <u>it's</u> tame.

Opinion and recommendation: I like horror so it <u>amused</u> me but if you don't, then <u>don't go see it</u>. *(past, present, imperative)*

FURTHER PRACTICE: READING, FILMS AND FUN

READING

Flanigan, R. (2001) *Gould's Book of Fish*, N.Y.: Grove Press.

Shedd, Julia A. (1896) *Famous Painters and Paintings*, Boston: Haughton, Mifflin and Co.

FILMS & TV

The Movie Show, ABC television (Australia).

Frida, directed by Julie Taymor, starring Selma Hayek. A confronting movie about the wife of another famous artist in Spain. Frida suffered a horrific bus accident and was severely injured. She was a beautiful woman and painted in ways that reflected her own mutilation and suffering.

Camille Claudel, French with subtitles. About a young sculptor who was the lover of Auguste Rodin.

Sister Wendy's American Collection, DVD. A nun reviews and informs about art.

QUESTIONS

1. Write a report about the folk art of your own country.

2. Write a review about a movie you saw recently.

3. Discuss the question – *Is art a waste of time?*

9 ARCHITECTURE

'the evils we bring on ourselves are the hardest to bear'

BY THE END OF THIS UNIT, STUDENTS SHOULD:

- have improved their ability around comparisons in speaking and writing . . . . Speaking: Tasks A, B and C **104**
- be able to recognise and use new vocabulary related to architecture and function and form . . . . Speaking: Tasks A, B and C **104**
- have increased their general knowledge . . . . Speaking: Task A; Reading: Task A **104**
- have increased their understanding around ancient and classical world architecture . . . . Reading: Task A **104**
- be able to comprehend a complex reading and write short answers to questions . . . . Writing 1: Tasks A and B **107**
- have an initial introduction to nominalisation and understand early steps in moving writing towards the more academic forms . . . . Language Spotlight and Writing 2: Task A **107**
- be able to recognise differences within texts in terms of more spoken writing vs academic writing . . . . Listening: Task A **108**
- have the ability to discuss and write phrases for hypothesis and factual information and understand differences between the two . . . . Listening: Task B **108**
- be able to use critical thinking to examine an important issue . . . . Listening: Task C **110**

ARCHITECTURE n. [UNCOUNTABLE]: 1 the style and design of a building or buildings: [+of] *the architecture of Venice.* 2 the art and practice of planning and designing buildings: *He studied architecture at university.* 3 the structure of something: *the architecture of DNA.* 4 *technical* the structure of a computer system and the way it works.

ARCHITECT n., pl. ARCHITECTS [UNCOUNTABLE AND COUNTABLE]: 1 someone whose job is to design buildings.

SPEAKING: BUILDING THE FIELD

Task A | Compare and contrast ▶▶ SB P. 98

❶ Students use adjectives for comparing and contrasting in discussion about similarities and differences. They use the photographs as a stimulus for their discussion.

❷ Students explain their idea of a perfect city using their imagination and previous knowledge. They can base their discussion on the places they know from experience.

Task B | Function (What's it for?) ▶▶ SB P. 99

This task focuses students' thinking around function and form. It prepares them for the reading where architecture is explained further. The skill of moving from image to function should stimulate awareness of the 'bigger picture' of architecture. The reading that follows should expand vocabulary around the topic.

ANSWERS

a. Religious – *Picture 1 WAT, Thailand; Picture 9 Tokyo Cathedral*
b. Housing – *Picture 10 Architect housing*
c. Housing and commerce areas – *Picture 7 Nagoya housing and business*
d. Sport – *Picture 2 Notre Dame stadium*
e. Government – *Picture 6 Castle*
f. Theatre, entertainment – *Picture 3 Sydney Opera House; Picture 8 Stratford Shakespeare theatre*
g. Education – *Picture 4 University of Scotland*
h. Retail, business – *Picture 5 Jenners shopping building*
i. Student answers will vary. Some other uses for buildings are for child care, retirement homes, medical, storage.
j. Rectangle; oval; ovoid; octagon; dome; hexagon; square; circle

Task C | Comparisons ▶▶ SB P. 99

Students are provided with some adjectives and discourse signals / linking devices for making comparisons. You can add to these in class through elicitation, for example, *pretty, functional, desirable, useful, short, shorter*, etc. Students underline both the adjectives and discourse signals in the model paragraph, then attempt a paragraph of their own comparing two of the buildings from the pictures.

ANSWERS

1. Underline both the *adjectives* and *linking devices* in the paragraph below;

   The Eiffel Tower is an <u>interesting and tall</u> building *(adjective link adjective)* located in Paris. It is considered <u>beautiful</u>. *(adjective)* <u>However</u>, *(link)* there are other towers that I think are <u>far more interesting and far more beautiful</u>. *(adjective adjective)* For example, the one in Beijing; it is <u>taller than</u> *(adverb)* the Eiffel Tower. <u>Whereas</u> *(link)* the first one is meant for people, the other is meant as a landmark.

2. Students make comparisons based upon the different look and function of two different types of architecture – a place of worship and an office building. The answers should include description, and a statement using *whereas*.
   For example, *The place of worship (church, mosque, temple) is for people to practise their religion, <u>whereas</u> the office is where they work and do business.*

READING: BROADENING GENERAL KNOWLEDGE

Task A | Classical and ancient architecture around the world ▶▶ SB P. 100

❶ Students should read the text *Architecture around the world*, looking for content and learning new vocabulary. The reading should broaden general knowledge as it includes several different places around the world.

The second time students read the text is to examine language. Then (in the Language Spotlight section) they work to make the first three paragraphs move up from a spoken style to a more academic, written style. This is explained further in Language Spotlight for you but in the reading the rewritten 'model' paragraphs are in bold.

❷ Personal pronouns are <u>underlined</u> **only** in the first paragraph of the Students' Book. For this question, students are to underline all the other personal pronouns they find in paras 2, 3 and 4 of the reading. In the next section they remove the personals and try to rewrite those paragraphs.

Note:
- italicised words in the reading are defined for students in the margin around the text.
- the **bolded** paragraphs in the reading are the answers to Task A Question 2 in the Writing 1 & Language Spotlight sections. These rewritten 'model' paragraphs (and there are many variations possible) are for you to photocopy and distribute when you get to that section.

ARCHITECTURE AROUND THE WORLD

commerce – trade

designed – created or made to

examination of architecture – looking at many things about architecture

1
Architecture is something that exists in every country in the world. World architecture represents the past, the present and the future. Buildings that manage to survive from the past tell people in the present a great deal of information about the people who used them. They show how people lived, shopped, worshipped and carried out *commerce* with the rest of the world. Who built those buildings, and why they were built or *designed* the way they were, is another important part of architecture. Generally, there are two main approaches to the *examination of architecture* and history.

Architecture is something that exists in every country in the world. World architecture represents the past, the present and the future. Buildings that manage to survive from the past tell the present a great deal of information about how they were used. [This sentence could also read; Buildings that manage to survive give insights to the present about their use in the past.] They show how life was lived, and teach the present generations about shopping, worshipping and the possible *commerce* that was carried on with the rest of the world. Who built those buildings, and why they were built or designed the way they were, is another important part of architecture. Generally, there are two main approaches to the examination of architecture and history.

link – connection between two or more things

technical status – how advanced people were with technology

era – a period of time

[Note: This paragraph is now more academic. It is longer. It reads as less spoken. It uses the passive more and personal pronouns have been removed.]

2
The first approach is to *link* buildings to great men or women who designed them. So a history of buildings would be about the architects. A second approach is to link buildings to the *technical status* of the *era*. In other words, building design is really about what materials were at hand and what sort of workers you had to help carry out your plan.

The first approach is to link buildings to those who designed them. So a history of buildings would be about great architects. A second approach is to link buildings to the technical status of the era. In other words, building design is really about what materials were at hand and what sort of available workers could be utilised.

that considers – that thinks about

3
Architecture is a form of art. It is about the style and design of buildings. It is an art *that considers* practical things like providing shelter for humans. Sometimes, it seems the shelter they made could be for dead people as much as for living ones. The pyramids of Egypt are an amazing example of architecture yet they were designed only for the dead. This tells us something about the people of that time. Were they more concerned with the afterlife than the present one? 3000 to 1500 BC is a very long time ago.

4 India has excavations at Harappa and Mohenjo-Daro of large cities. They were from a grid system and had main boulevards running right

citadels – forts, a building meant for protection from outsiders

across the city. The shape of the cities was rectangular. There were many small buildings surrounding a court and they seemed similar to early Egyptian architecture in their function. These cities were *citadels*. Sadly, they lasted but 1500 years and evidence (in the form of skeletons) suggests they were invaded and their civilization ended.

5

octagonal rotunda – round shape building having eight angles and eight sides with a dome

In the lifetime of Mohammed (d. 632) there is an early major work of Moslem architecture. It is the Ka'ba at Mekka. However, it is the Dome of the Rock, located in Jerusalem which is probably of greatest importance to architecture. It was begun in 643 and it still exists. It is said to be the site from which Mohammed made his night journey to heaven. It has a golden dome set over an *octagonal rotunda*. It has a well with a small *domed cupola*. Fresh water is always part of Middle Eastern architecture.

domed cupola – a rounded tower-like structure on top of a roof

6

Buildings and other architecture have the ability to *reflect most things about a culture*. The Great Wall of China is an *architectural wonder*. It goes across Northern China for some 4,000 miles. It is said to be the largest man-made structure in the world and was started around 200 BC. It is not about housing, because the wall was built for protection from the *nomads*.

reflect most things about a culture – tell you about the people and their ways of living

architectural wonder – something beautiful and unusual built by people

enclosures – spaces closed to the outside

7

It is interesting to note that the word for 'city' and 'wall' was the same in early China: *ch'eng*. Most parts of a city were walled and any palace had many walled *enclosures*. A city wall made of *rammed earth* was found and dated as early as the eleventh century BC.

rammed earth – dirt pounded down hard and tight

nomads – people who move from place to place/ sometimes in the desert

ch'eng – city and wall

8

Pagoda – a sacred building, usually tall and shaped like a pyramid or tower

The oldest brick building in China is a *Pagoda*: The Pagoda of the Sung Yueh temple, Mt Sung, Honan. This shows religion was very important just as it was in other parts of the world.

9

In Japan, natural forces affected their early architecture. Japan has many natural forces to worry about. There are earthquakes and fierce storms coming in from the Pacific. As islands, these things affect them in a serious way. This fact means that they often chose to build from stone (for castles) and wood, timber and bamboo. Designs have been kept and certain buildings built over again exactly as they were before, for example, *Shinto shrines*. Japanese gardens are a beautiful, unusual and important part of their design.

Shinto shrines – Shinto (native religion of Japan) shrine (a place of religion where special objects or remains are kept)

temple of Olympian Zeus – Zeus was the main Greek god who ruled the heavens. Olympus is a mountain in north-eastern Greece. The Olympic Games are held in honour of Zeus and began in 776 BC.

10

In Greece, in their ancient and classical period, there is the *temple of Olympian Zeus*. It was begun in 174 BC. The kind of building was called Corinthian and we still call the supports or pillars you see right up to now as Corinthian. They are an example of 'classical' design in the West.

Medieval – a period of time that is the Middle Ages – 700 to 1500 AD.

Renaissance – a new birth – in history; new birth or revival of art and learning in Europe during the 14th, 15th and 16th centuries. Moved out of the Medieval period into the Renaissance.

Gothic – in architecture refers to a style started in France in the 12th century. Pointed arches, high buildings, rib vaulting inside.

11

In the West, architecture moves across major periods such as *Medieval*, *Gothic*, *Renaissance* and into the modern period. But that is another reading!

WRITING 1 — SHORT ANSWERS

Task A | Comprehension ▶▶ SB P. 102

Students are asked a number of questions about the texts. Students write a complete sentence in answer to each question. You may have to assist with locating the core or stem of each question for inclusion. The first one is done for them.

ANSWERS

1. The country that had the earliest found architecture was India.
2. The country that built a wall about 4,000 miles long was China.
3. The name of the long wall built across China is The Great Wall of China.
4. The name for classical supports or pillars of Western origin is Corinthian.
5. Some countries, like Japan, considered weather in their design right from the first. Earthquakes and storms meant they chose materials that could be obtained again and re-built to match whatever was destroyed.
6. The earliest work of Moslem architecture is the Ka'ba (at Mekka).
7. Two examples of religious buildings are Mosque/ pagoda/ temple.
8. One function of early cities was that they were designed to protect the people in them. They were like citadels or forts.
9. Cities protected themselves by being walled.
10. Modern people would think that the early Egyptians were very interested in the dead and the afterlife because of their architecture – the Pyramids.
11. Zeus was the main god of ancient Greeks. He ruled the heavens.
12. No. There are no countries that have no architecture.

Task B | Finding the main ideas ▶▶ SB P. 103

Students use the same reading *Architecture around the world* and examine paragraphs for main ideas.

ANSWERS

1. Each paragraph has a different country featured and they match the country to the paragraph that describes its architectural history.
   a. Jerusalem – para 5
   b. China – paras 6,7,8
   c. Greece – para 10
   d. Egypt – para 3
   e. India – para 4
   f. The West – para 11

2. Students write the type of architecture described in each country.
   a. Jerusalem – the Dome of the Rock
   b. China – The Great Wall of China; a city wall; The Pagoda of the Sung Yueh temple, Mt Sung, Honan.
   c. Greece – the temple of Olympian Zeus
   d. Egypt – the pyramids
   e. India – large cities at Harappa and Mohenjo-Daro (citadels)
   f. The West – periods of architecture such as Medieval, Gothic, Renaissance and modern.

LANGUAGE SPOTLIGHT / WRITING 2 — NOMINALS AND NOMINALISATION (NOUNS)

Task A | Writing – Refer to *Architecture around the world* ▶▶ SB P. 103

Students continue working towards using nominalisation in their writing and recognising it in reading texts. Nominalisation occurs when words are grouped into noun phrases that pack a lot of meaning into them. For example, if we say:

- *Egyptian afterlife* – it incorporates the country of Egypt and implies something about their belief in a life after death. To 'unpack' a small nominalisation such as that might read thus; *In Egypt, the Egyptian people believed there was life after death.*
- *Deforestation* – there are forests, people come in and cut them down. After that, there is not much left. The forest floor is bare. *The forest is gone.*

Nominalisations use 'tion', 'ian', 'al', ism and 'ment' as endings on nouns. Verbs and verb phrases are converted to noun phrases that 'pack' meaning into them. They are shortcuts that remove human involvement and human action from them.

The majority of texts in this book avoid using too many nominalisations, with their difficult meanings and interpretations. However, in academic writing nominalisations abound. There are some in the more difficult listenings when lectures occur. The initial process in advancing students from simple texts that follow spoken language is to get them to remove the personal pronouns from a text and then rewrite it. This could be difficult for them.

Students can also attempt higher lexis (using bigger words) if possible. They will see that word order often changes as well. The ends of sentences can move to the beginning to make meaning clearer. Sometimes, the personal pronoun can just be removed and the sentence continues without change.

Ask students to change the following words from verbs to nouns. Write them on the whiteboard and work together to make the changes.

- to educate = education
- to inform = information
- to elucidate (make clearer) = elucidation
- to negotiate = negotiation
- to govern = government
- to resolve (decide) = resolution
- to inform = information
- to involve = involvement
- to conform = conformism

ANSWERS

1. *he, us, people, them, ours, our, me*, etc … (Students should be able to think of many personal pronouns once you get started.)
2. The ideal rewritten paragraphs are highlighted in bold in the previous section's reading *Architecture around the world*. You could distribute copies of the 'model' paragraphs or use an OHT.

LISTENING: DIFFERENTIATING BETWEEN HYPOTHESIS AND FACT

Task A | Pre-listening ▶▶ SB P. 104

① Students examine the following two sets of phrases then try to explain the differences between the two sets:

SET A
I think that
It's quite possible that …
In the future, it may happen that
I do not (don't) think that
Probably
I predict that
To me …
Trends show that …
We could see

It may be that
Maybe

SET B
We cannot (can't) predict …
It will be (It'll be) …
It's going to be …
This is going to be…
That is (That's) going to be …
It's about …
It is not (It isn't) about …
In the not too distant future, we will see (we'll see) …
What will (What'll) happen is …

ANSWERS

1. The differences between the two sets of phrases are as follows:
   a. B
   b. B
   c. A
   d. A
   e. B
   f. A

2. Students' answers will vary. They have to select from the correct set – A or B – to indicate the amount of certainty, facts, speculation, hypothesizing or future trends from Question 1.
   a. It's going to be/ In the not too distant future, we will see …
   b. It's about/ That's going to be …
   c. Maybe/ We could see/ It may be that …
   d. I think that/ It's quite possible that …
   e. This is …
   f. Trends show that …/ Probably …/ We could see …
3. Students may select different phrases for some of the sentences that still work in this context and that are correct. If they differ, they can read them for you to check.
   a. *I think that* dogs make good companions.
   b. *Trends show* that the population is ageing in many countries.
   c. *It's going to be* a very cold night. (or – *I think* that it's a very cold night).
   d. *In the not too distant future, we will* see hotter weather and global warming. Some think we're seeing it now.
   e. If a train goes too fast for the tracks, *then what will happen is* it will fly right off them.
   f. *It's* true.
   g. We *cannot predict* the time of our own death.
   h. She'll *probably* come to our wedding.
   i. He'll *probably* come as well.
   j. It *may* rain, but then again, it *may* not.

Task B | Listening for *certainty* versus *speculation* ▶▶ SB P. 104   CD 1 (14)

Students could listen to the recording three times in order to complete all tasks. They are to learn the language that introduces more or less certainty. *I will* is more certain than *I think*. *It will* is more certain than *it may*. *It's going to* is more certain than *I predict that* … and so forth.

They also listen for the content of the message that takes place when the workman raises concerns to the boss (Mark). Although the worker calls Mark over the first time by saying 'Mate', the power relationship is established in the Listening when Mark tells him to 'get back to work'.

① Students listen and tick the phrases they hear. The introductory language of facts comes from Set B in Task A. There are not many facts. There is more speculation, prediction and hypothesising than fact. This is what you point out to students.

② Students listen a second time and try to write the facts they hear. Most of the facts are found in the weather report and not in the body text except for – *No, but I saw* what happened before.

ANSWERS

2. **a.** No, but <u>I saw</u> what happened before.
   b. <u>It's going to be</u> a nasty evening.
   c. The temperature is dropping rapidly. <u>It will be</u> minus 28 degrees by six pm.
   d. The airport <u>is closed</u>.

3. Are there more facts in the text or more speculation and prediction? *There is more speculation and prediction.*

Recording script

CD 1, track 14: Architecture, Unit 9
(4 minutes, 11 seconds)

Listening: The building – Workmen on a building site

Narrator: This listening begins with a construction worker talking to his boss about his concerns with the quality of the materials and work on the site. The worker thinks the foundations may not be good enough for the size of the building they are constructing.

A Mate, Come over here and have a look at this.

B Yeah, what is it?

A Well, Whatcha think of this?

B I'm not sure I know what you mean by … this.

A I mean the foundations here … the foundations we've started building.

B Well, what do you wanna know?

A Well, I want to know what you think of them.

B Yeah, you said that.

A Are they safe?

B Safe for what?

A Alright, let's not play games. I mean this. How big a building um ah weight and that do you think these foundations are meant to take?

B Well, look at the specifications.

A Yeah, Exactly. And it's not good enough. The foundations are not designed to take 26 stories, as far as I'm concerned.

B Well, you're not the architect, *are* you? Did you design it?

A No, but <u>I saw</u> what happened before. You know that if it's not right, <u>we'll see</u> something happen. <u>It'll be</u> a disaster, like the one in Toucanisky.

B You better get on with the concrete pour and stop <u>speculating on the future</u>. That's not your job. We're just the contractors, we're hired to build it. So just get on and build it.

A You're the boss. (*more quietly*) <u>But I think it's going to be</u> a disaster.

C (*New segue music.*) One month later.

(*Machine noise, building noise, bulldozers.*)

B Hold it! Wait a minute! Mark, can you come here?

A Yeah, what is it? Oh … *You* again! …

B Well, frankly, I'm worried about these steel girders. <u>I don't think that</u> they're big enough to do the job. <u>I predict that</u> they'll give way if it snows too heavily or if there's ground movement.

A Snow? Well, we don't make the weather, now, do we?

B No, but … last year, <u>we saw</u> snow drifts up to 8 feet high. That's a lot of weight on a building.

A Well, Like I say, <u>we can't predict</u> the weather.

B No, but what about earthquakes? This is a region famous for them. Where's the reinforcements?

A Look, it's good that you're concerned, but, you're not the architect and you're not paying for it. <u>In the future, it may happen</u> that you're right, mate, but what can *we* do? It isn't about us. It's about this building and <u>it's going to get built</u>, that's a fact. <u>It's going to be built</u> by us and <u>what'll happen</u> is out of our hands.

B I know what you're saying, <u>but, to me</u>, it , it seems like we should tell someone.

A Yeah, well, you've told me. And frankly, <u>I think</u> it's fine. It's not our problem anyway. (pause) Now get back to work!

Unit 9 Architecture | 109

C *(New segue music.) 10 months later.*

And now, the weather report

D …. and this extreme weather is continuing. More severe storms are predicted for this afternoon. You are advised to stay in your homes and secure your windows and doors. The temperature is dropping rapidly and soon <u>it will be</u> minus 18 degrees. More heavy snow is predicted and <u>it's possible that</u> all roads <u>will be</u> closed. The airport <u>is</u> already closed.

(Crashing sound of building collapsing, people screaming.)

Task C | Thinking about the listening; value judgment ▶▶ SB P. 105

Students could either speak about this in a class discussion or groups; or, in pairs, answer the questions in writing.

ANSWERS

1. Yes, he was.
2. Because we hear the building collapse in the end.
3. He didn't seem to care. He said it was not their problem.
4. Twice.
5. That they'll (they would) give way if it snows too heavily or there's ground movement.
6. *We don't make the weather, we can't predict the weather. What'll happen is out of our hands.*
7. He might have reported it to the contractor or another higher authority.
8. That it was going to be a nasty evening.
9. Severe storms.
10. All roads will be closed (would be).
11. The airport is closed (was closed).
12. The answer to this would come from class discussion. Perhaps the worker might have quit due to his conscience. It depends on the amount of certainty he felt about his theory that the building foundations were weak. Perhaps he could have organised others to consider the problem, once he knew the 'boss' didn't care and would proceed regardless. If there was a Union involved that represented the workers, perhaps he could have contacted them with his concerns.

FURTHER PRACTICE: READING, FILMS AND FUN

READING

Phaidon Atlas of Contemporary World Architecture, Phaidon Press. (824 pages. The *Atlas* includes entries on 1052 buildings built over the last six years by 656 architects in 75 countries. The text is accompanied by 62 maps and 7000 illustrations. The book comes in its own clear plastic carrying case, and is a foot and a half tall and weighs 18 pounds.)

architecture.about.com/cs/ greatbuildings/f/worldstallest.htm
en.wikipedia.org/wiki/History_of_architecture

FILMS

Spiderman 1 and *Spiderman 2:* Here we see action, adventure and architecture galore! Beautiful graphics are devised for the city scapes where Spiderman hurls himself from building to building saving the world from crime.

Howl's Moving Castle: Another wonderful film by Japanese artist and director Hayao Miyazaki of *Spirited Away* fame. Miyazaki makes his central themes work within an actual moving castle that looks a little like a junk heap with magical rooms inside.

QUESTIONS

❶ Students choose a famous architect for themselves or choose one from the following list. Then they do some research and write a report about both the architect and his or her work: Frank Lloyd Wright, Avlar Aalto, Gaudi, Vladimir Tatlin.

❷ Research the tallest buildings in the world and describe them. Compare and contrast them, discussing their similarities and differences.

❸ Students explain the function of their favourite building. What does it look like?

10 INDIGENOUS PEOPLE

'all blood is alike ancient'

BY THE END OF THIS UNIT, STUDENTS SHOULD:

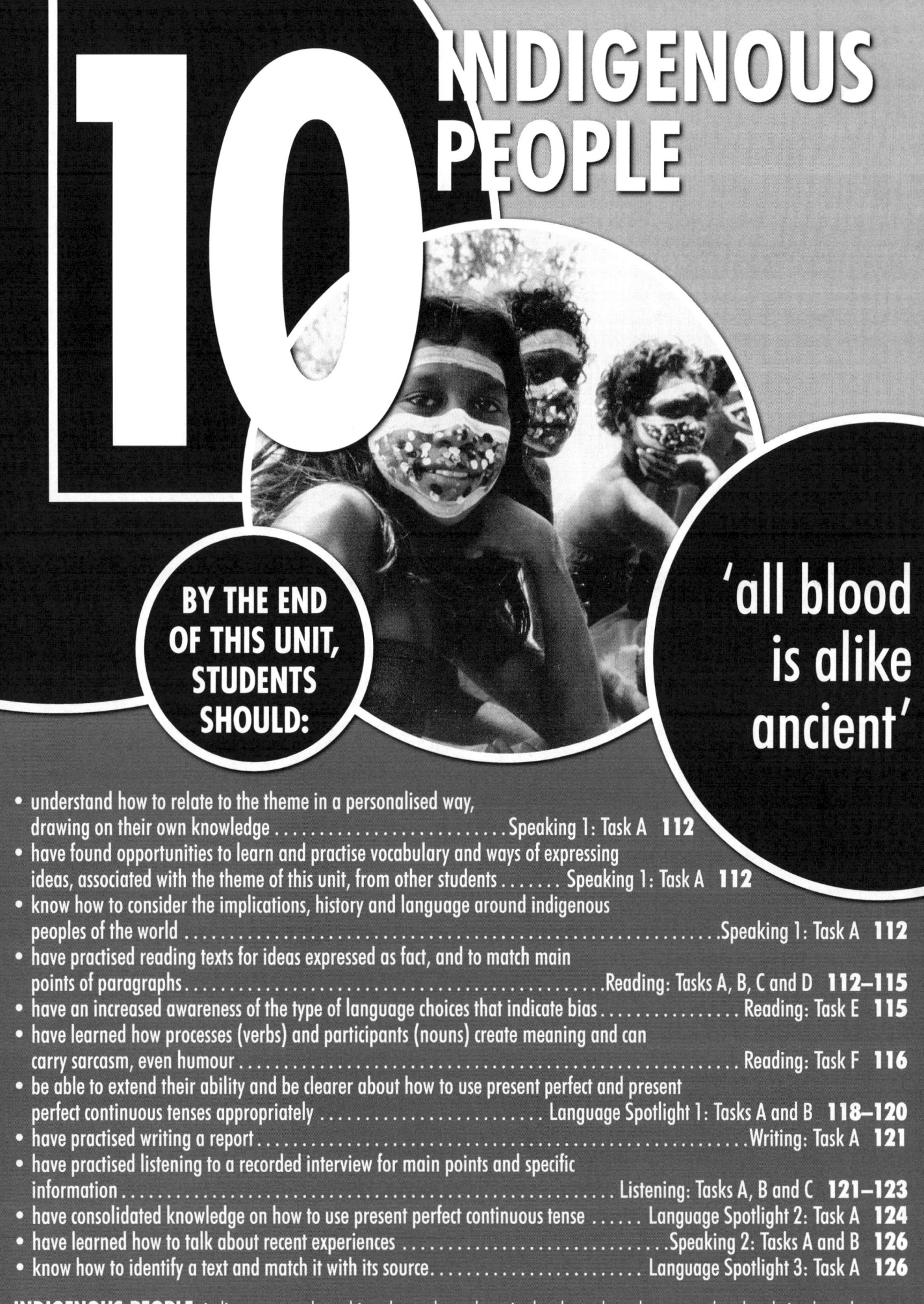

- understand how to relate to the theme in a personalised way, drawing on their own knowledge .... Speaking 1: Task A **112**
- have found opportunities to learn and practise vocabulary and ways of expressing ideas, associated with the theme of this unit, from other students .... Speaking 1: Task A **112**
- know how to consider the implications, history and language around indigenous peoples of the world .... Speaking 1: Task A **112**
- have practised reading texts for ideas expressed as fact, and to match main points of paragraphs .... Reading: Tasks A, B, C and D **112–115**
- have an increased awareness of the type of language choices that indicate bias .... Reading: Task E **115**
- have learned how processes (verbs) and participants (nouns) create meaning and can carry sarcasm, even humour .... Reading: Task F **116**
- be able to extend their ability and be clearer about how to use present perfect and present perfect continuous tenses appropriately .... Language Spotlight 1: Tasks A and B **118–120**
- have practised writing a report .... Writing: Task A **121**
- have practised listening to a recorded interview for main points and specific information .... Listening: Tasks A, B and C **121–123**
- have consolidated knowledge on how to use present perfect continuous tense ...... Language Spotlight 2: Task A **124**
- have learned how to talk about recent experiences .... Speaking 2: Tasks A and B **126**
- know how to identify a text and match it with its source........................ Language Spotlight 3: Task A **126**

INDIGENOUS PEOPLE: indigenous people or things have always been in the place where they are, rather than being brought there from somewhere else.

SPEAKING 1
BUILDING THE FIELD

Task A | Discussion – What do you know about Aboriginal people? ▶▶ SB P. 108

The purpose of this discussion is to orientate students to the field of this Unit, as much as possible by sharing their prior knowledge.

In small groups (mixed nationality if possible), students tell each other as much as they can in answer to the following questions. They can compete to say the most. Ask students to nominate a 'recorder' who writes down the various answers for their group. They can report back by changing recorders from one group to another.
1. Who were the first people to live in your country?
2. How long have they lived there?
3. Are they a minority or majority in your country now?
4. If they are a minority, in what ways is their culture different from the majority?
5. Look at the countries in the table below. From general knowledge, try to match the people in Column 1 with their country of origin from Column 2.

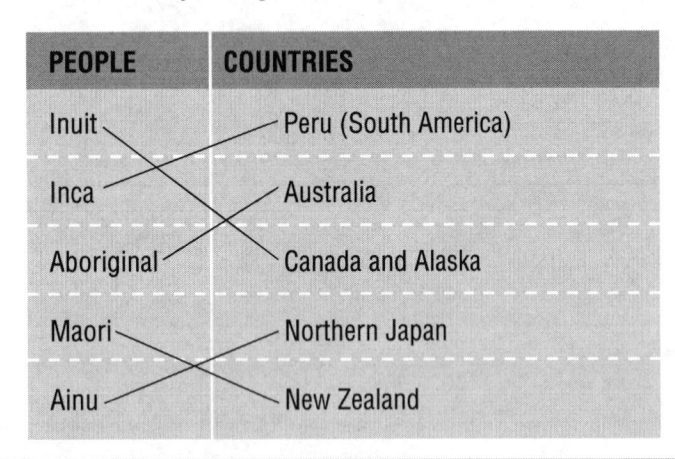

PEOPLE	COUNTRIES
Inuit	Peru (South America)
Inca	Australia
Aboriginal	Canada and Alaska
Maori	Northern Japan
Ainu	New Zealand

(Inuit → Canada and Alaska; Inca → Peru; Aboriginal → Australia; Maori → New Zealand; Ainu → Northern Japan)

READING
FACTUAL INFORMATION

Task A | The five questions for reading any text ▶▶ SB P. 108

① Students should read Text 2 in Task E of this section. They should use the five questions below to assist them to think critically about what they are reading.

ANSWERS

[a] **What is it?**
An article from a newspaper. The title is: 'Margin Call'.
[b] **What is the source?**
A newspaper called 'The Australian'.
[c] **Who is the writer?**
The writer is Michael West.
[d] **What purpose does the writer have for writing it?**
The purpose is to report the news about the court case being ruled in favour of the Aboriginal man, Mr Carriage. It also has the purpose to amuse, entertain and give a point of view.
[e] **Who is the intended audience?**
Readers of the newspaper.

Task B | Reading a report ▶▶ SB P. 108

The factual report below acquaints them with a neutral, bland way of writing about an issue. Students should recognise ideas expressed as facts and distinguish them from opinion. The report contains 22 paragraphs and has 1465 words. The primary theme of the report is the impact of modernisation on Aboriginal people since white settlement in Australia.

A report on a traditional group in Australian society showing the impact of modernisation on that group

1 • **Introduction**
General Statement
[1] A traditional group is a number of persons formed together due to their gender, nationality,
5 religion and traditions. In Australian society an example of a traditional group is Aboriginals.
A **tradition** is the passing down from generation to generation of ideas, customs, beliefs and stories. However, Aboriginals' traditions
10 have been changed due to colonisation and modernisation. **Colonisation** meant the taking over of the country by white people from the traditional owners, the Aboriginals. **Modernisation** can be best defined as the
15 process of social, cultural and technological change characterised by such things as large scale industrialisation, changes in political power, the emergence of new social classes, and higher literacy and improved education.
20 Modernisation is also accompanied by change. In the Aboriginals' case modernisation has caused change in traditions and beliefs, lifestyle, land ownership and population. This report will examine some of the changes as a result of
25 modernisation in relation to the preceding areas plus give some historical background.

• **Historical Background**
[2] When the first sailing ships of the Europeans arrived, the great white sails astonished the

Aborigines, as did the white people who looked so different to the confused Aborigines. Captain Cook and his party landed (29 April 1770) and the Aborigines ran off. When the Aborigines came close to Europeans, the whiteness of their skin particularly puzzled them. Aborigines investigated the explorers' with curiosity, astonishment and fear.

[3] Before the Aborigines realised that whites were merely people, they were afraid of them, believing them to be powerful spirits, and that they were Aborigines returned from the dead.

[4] As more white settlers came to Australia and came in contact with Aborigines, conflict increased. These early conflicts and contact led to hostility on both sides and set the stage for the destruction of Aboriginal culture by white settlement and colonisation. The problem was that most of the settlers were ignorant of the Aborigines' traditional society and culture. They did not understand what things were important to the Aborigines. Aborigines were not interested in possessions or working in a job for someone else. Some white people were so ignorant they thought the Aborigines had no religion.

[5] Many years later, the outbreak of World War II in 1939 pushed Aboriginal affairs into the background. However, the war also improved the position of Aborigines and helped to break down the cultural barrier of white prejudice. Due to white men at war, Aborigines were finally being benefited by colonisation; they were being called up to work for civil construction. War-time industrialisation created work opportunities and Aborigines began to move into cities.

[6] 1941 was the turning point in Aboriginal welfare, and the mark of the beginning of at least attempted equality of Aborigines and whites. The Commonwealth Government extended child endowments, and allowed Aborigines to claim old age pensions.

- **Traditions and Beliefs**

[7] Aborigines were the original inhabitants of Australia as opposed to the colonists. Unlike the colonists the Aborigines adapted to the harsh environment of Australia and developed a system and lifestyle of nomadic hunting and food gathering. Traditional Aboriginal systems of belief emphasised the Dreamtime and spiritual significance of the land.

[8] Aborigines obtained all their food by hunting, fishing and gathering and they were nomads. They moved from place to place in search of food. Most of their homes were temporary.

[9] Aborigines made weapons and tools from stone and wood. They were able to make axes, knives, chisels and scrapers from stone. They used spears, boomerangs and clubs for hunting. The effect of modernisation upon these traditional areas was to replace hunter-gatherer equipment with metal tools, weapons and even tin housing. Old traditions were practically completely wiped out with only some elders of tribes recalling old ways and remembering to pass them on in the oral tradition of storytelling that is part of Aboriginal culture.

- **Lifestyle**

[10] Aboriginals developed a way of life that was well suited to Australia. Although they lived simply and did not own many things, they were rarely hungry because they knew where to get food from around the land. Families and tribes helped them feel together and their religion linked them with the past.

[11] In the days before modernisation, there were over two hundred languages spoken by Aborigines around Australia. The grammar of the Aborigines' language was very complicated. Signs were also another form of communication between Aboriginal tribes.

- **Land Ownership**

[12] Importance of the land to the Aboriginal people developed an incredible complexity, which became part of society, as were relationships between people, and between people of their land. The landscape was connected to many beliefs and Dreamtime stories, and because Aborigines didn't have a written language, the landscape was a reminder. The landscape is therefore critical in maintaining the Aborigines' physical, mental and spiritual life. These landmarks or land are referred to as 'sacred sites'.

[13] Aborigines and the environment are considered as one. Aborigines believed that they were part of the living systems in nature because through their mythology they understood that their ancestors created the landscape and the life on it.

[14] Conflict started between the whites and Aborigines when the whites made permanent settlements. The whites killed their game, cattle trampled water holes and ate their plants. Whites forced the Aborigines off what Aboriginal people considered their own traditional land.

- **Population**

[15] Settlement and its ongoing modernisation have had a disastrous effect on Aboriginal population. White settlers died, however

140 Aborigines died in even greater numbers. Historians have estimated that the Aboriginal population declined from at least 300 000 in 1788 when white settlement began, to about 50 000 in the next 100 years.

145 [16] When the Commonwealth of Australia was formed in 1901, Aborigines were excluded. They were not citizens, and were not even counted in the census, so exact knowledge concerning Aboriginal population became more and more
150 difficult to obtain. It is known, however, that the figure declined dramatically under the impact of modernisation and settlement, which brought new disease, repressive and often brutal treatment, dispossession, and social and cultural
155 disruption. The Aboriginal population was still declining well into the twentieth century and continues to decline in the new millennium.

- **Aborigines Today**

[17] During the nineteenth century and the early
160 twentieth century there were various attempts to protect the Aborigines from white settlers. Both government and church missions set up reserves where they could live and be protected. In these reserves, however, the Aborigines were
165 generally unable to move away or take part in work without permission from the whites who ran the reserves. The laws prevented Aborigines from having human rights.

[18] The reserves brought problems for the
170 Aborigines. There were low levels of education facilities, unemployment, poor health, poor housing, breakdown in families, and loss of old traditions and beliefs. Luckily today Aborigines are slowly overcoming the past and acquiring
175 sacred land.

[19] The attitude of the government towards Aborigines has changed significantly due to modernisation. In 1937 the government encouraged **assimilation**, which means adopting
180 the way of life of the whites rather than keeping their own culture. In 1967 the policies began to change. An integration policy was introduced to recognise that Aborigines had their own way of life and culture.

185 [20] Colonisation brought diseases that the Aborigines hadn't encountered before, such as small pox and tuberculosis, and many of these health problems have remained into the twenty-first century. Colonisation also brought alcohol,
190 and this is another problem that modernisation has brought to the Aborigines.

[21] In most respects, Aboriginal society was, and is, the absolute opposite of modern European society, it is nomadic rather than settled and
195 self sufficient rather than dependent on others for food and materials. There was an absolute inevitability that Aboriginal society would pay a high price for modernisation due to the drastic differences between cultures. Rarely, if ever, has a
200 so-called 'modern' culture invaded a less modern one and learned from that culture. Modern societies always consider themselves superior and rarely acknowledge the sophisticated and well established patterns and knowledge that older
205 cultures often have. 50 000 years of knowledge about Australia's environment, and traditions and beliefs just as old, have been systematically destroyed and all but eliminated by, at times, partly well meaning white people.

210 [22] There may be an argument that Aboriginal people have had their lifestyle improved by modernisation in the sense of having access to white peoples' education systems, medical health systems and so forth. In some cases, this is true.
215 However, if the majority of people within the Aboriginal culture had had choice, it would seem they would have preferred to live in harmony with nature, as this had been their previous choice for more centuries than white people can
220 count as their own past history.

Task C | Recognising definitions in context ▶▶ SB P. 110
Task C tests the student's ability to locate ideas and vocabulary in context. Point out to students the language that signals that a definition of a word in context is about to happen. Sometimes, the words occur after, sometimes before. They are italicised and underlined in the four sentences in Answer 1.

❶ Students write definitions of words highlighted in bold in the text, eg tradition, colonisation, modernisation and assimilation.

ANSWERS

The first three definitions are found in the Introduction:
a. tradition – A tradition <u>is</u> the passing down from generation to generation of ideas, customs, beliefs and stories.

b. **colonisation** – *Colonisation meant* the taking over of the country by white people from the traditional owners, the Aboriginals.

c. **modernisation** – *can be best defined as* the process of social, cultural and technological change characterised by such things as large scale industrialisation, changes in political power, the emergence of new social classes, and higher literacy and improved education. Modernisation is also accompanied by change.

d. **assimilation** (para 19) – *...which means* adopting the way of life of the whites rather than keeping their own culture.

② Students now list which words signalled that the word was going to be defined. For answers see underlined words in text above.

Task D | Factual information in reports ▶▶ SB P. 111

① From the report, students select 10 concepts expressed as facts and write them in their notebooks. Within reports and all scientific, factual writing, forms of the verb to be are frequently used to state facts, ie the relationship between two sides of the sentence are equal: .... *is* ....

The introduction of dates or the use of the verb forms '*to have*', *has*, *had* implies factual information.
Answers will vary.

② Students match the following statements to the paragraph numbers listed below them. Advise them to look at the headings (in bold in the report) after they have read a statement, to see if it will guide them to the main idea and help them find the relevant paragraph. In the example, para 7 matches statement A.

For example:

A ⑦ *Aboriginals believe in the Dreamtime and spiritual significance of the land.* (*Para 7*: The heading is **Traditions and Beliefs**)

ANSWERS

A ⑦ See example above.

B ⑩ *Aborigines lived simply and did not own many things. They knew how to find food from the land.*

C ⑮ *Settlement and its ongoing modernisation have had a disastrous effect on Aboriginal population.*

D ③ *At first, when Aborigines saw white people, they were afraid of them. They believed they might be powerful spirits or returned from the dead.*

E ⑯ *When the Commonwealth of Australia was formed in 1901, Aborigines were excluded. They were not citizens, and were not even counted in the census.*

F ㉑ *Modern societies always consider themselves superior and rarely acknowledge the sophisticated and well established patterns and knowledge that older cultures often have.*

G ⑲ *Today, it is recognised that Aborigines have their own way of life and culture. This is because of an integration policy that was introduced in 1967 to recognise that Aborigines had their own way of life and culture.*

H ⑭ *The effect of modernisation in the sense of occupation was that, perhaps naturally, the Aborigines reacted with violence when they saw what was happening to their land.*

I ① *Modernisation can be best defined as the process of social, cultural and technological change characterised by such things as large scale industrialisation, changes in political power, the emergence of new social classes, and higher literacy and improved education.*

Task E | Comparing texts for bias ▶▶ SB P. 112

The two texts that follow are on the same topic and are based upon an extract from *The Australian* newspaper, 21 December 2004. They are written differently: Text 1 has been written in a neutral way; Text 2 is exactly as it appeared in the paper.

Students read and compare the texts first noting any differences they find. The work that follows will guide them as to where bias, sarcasm and point of view are found.

Stockland loses Sandon Point 2½ year court case

Property developer Stockland and its lawyers, Baker & McKenzie, lost a 2½ year court battle yesterday to Mr Carriage, an Aboriginal elder.

Mr Carriage had sued Stockland to try to stop the $7.6 billion developer from building hundreds of houses on Sandon Point, between Sydney and Wollongong. Sandon Point residents, plan to keep picketing into another year, their fourth, making this the world's longest-held picket. The battle has been hard fought.

Justice Pain of the Land and Environment Court awarded against Stockland with costs yesterday after finding the company unlawfully dumped thousands of tonnes of dirt on top of an ancient Aboriginal site at Sandon Point. Stockland pledged last night to keep suing Mr Carriage. The company had sought to bankrupt him over a $543 debt this year, spending tens of thousands of dollars in the process.

TEXT 1

Stockland has its nose rubbed in tonnes of Sandon dirt

STRUGGLING property developer Stockland and its lawyers, Baker & McKenzie, were shot down in a 2½ year court battle yesterday, succumbing to the lumbering might of 61-year-old Aboriginal elder Allan Carriage and his star chamber of legal eagles from the Voluntary Indigenous Advocacy Group.

Mr Carriage had sued Stockland to try to stop the $7.6 billion developer from building hundreds of houses on Sandon Point, between Sydney and Wollongong. Sandon Point residents, who clearly oppose progress and enlightened development, plan to keep picketing into another year, their fourth, making this the world's longest-held picket. The battle has been hard-fought.

Justice Pain of the Land and Environment Court awarded against the impoverished Stockland with costs yesterday after finding the company unlawfully dumped thousands of tonnes of fill on top of an ancient Aboriginal site at Sandon Point. However, justice may prevail for Stockland as it pledged last night to keep suing Mr Carriage, even though he doesn't have any money. The company had sought to bankrupt him over a $543 debt this year, spending tens of thousands of dollars in the process – just to make sure justice and truth carried the day.

Source: Michael West, 'Margin Call', The Australian, 21 December 2004.

TEXT 2

Task F | Locating language choices which create intention ▶▶ SB P. 112

SARCASM – How can you find it?

BIAS – How can you find it?

POINT OF VIEW – How can you find it?

❶ Students again examine the Text 2 below. Single underlining represents the participants or nouns and noun groups, while double underlining represents the processes or verbs and verb groups. Dotted underlining shows discourse cues, ie transitions leading to sarcasm. Processes are the 'goings on' that are being described in the text. They can be material processes – those of action, activity, events and behaviour; they can be mental processes – processes of sensing, perception, cognition, reaction; or relational processes – those of being and having.

1. Stockland has its nose rubbed in tonnes of Sandon dirt

STRUGGLING property developer Stockland and its lawyers, Baker & McKenzie, were shot down in a 2½ year court battle yesterday, succumbing to the lumbering might of 61-year-old Aboriginal elder Allan Carriage and his star chamber of legal eagles from the Voluntary Indigenous Advocacy Group.

Mr Carriage had sued Stockland to try to stop the $7.6 billion developer from building hundreds of houses on Sandon Point, between Sydney and Wollongong. Sandon Point residents, who clearly oppose progress and enlightened development, plan to keep picketing into another year, their fourth, making this the world's longest-held picket. The battle has been hard-fought.

Justice Pain of the Land and Environment Court awarded against the impoverished Stockland with costs yesterday after finding the company unlawfully dumped thousands of tonnes of fill on top of an ancient Aboriginal site at Sandon Point. However, justice may prevail for Stockland as it pledged last night to keep suing Mr Carriage, even though he doesn't have any money. The company had sought to bankrupt him over a $543 debt this year, spending tens of thousands of dollars in the process – just to make sure justice and truth carried the day.

Source: Michael West, 'Margin Call', *The Australian*, 21 December 2004.

TEXT 2

ANSWERS

2. The following are definitions of the words in the table below.

Processes: **verbs and verb groups**
1. *has (its nose) rubbed* – to make a point stronger. It means that the company mentioned (Stockland) has lost in a big way.
2. *shot down* – to lose. To be beaten.
3. *succumbing to* – to yield to, to give way
4. *clearly oppose* – are against
5. *to keep picketing* – a protest that is continuing, people (in this case) stay in a tent 24 hours a day and give information out about the Save Sandon Point action
6. *awarded against* – when the court system decides one side wins against the other, to lose
7. *finding* – legal term for discovering, deciding
8. *unlawfully dumped* – without permission or legal sanction, dumped something
9. *may prevail* – could change back, could win
10. *pledged ... to keep suing* – said or promised they would continue taking legal action for money against the other person
11. *(just) to make sure* – be positive, certain
12. *carried* – (the day) – this is an idiom (*to carry the day*) – it means: to win or to become the most important thing

Participants: **nouns and noun groups**
1. *(in) tonnes of Sandon dirt* – refers to the nose rubbing that the company received. In other words, Stockland lost and was shamed by the court action. There is a 'play on words' here, because they were accused of dumping soil or land fill illegally (dirt) onto an Aboriginal site (also dirt with buried treasures underneath).

VOCABULARY CHOICES BY THE WRITER

PROCESSES (DOUBLE UNDERLINING)	NOUN GROUPS (SINGLE UNDERLINING)
has (its nose) rubbed	(in) tonnes of Sandon dirt
were shot down	(in) a 2½ year court battle
succumbing to	the lumbering might of 61-year-old Aboriginal elder Allan Carriage and his star group of legal eagles (from) the Voluntary Indigenous Advocacy Group.
(residents who) clearly oppose	progress and enlightened development
to keep picketing	into another year
awarded against	the impoverished Stockland
finding	the company
dumped	thousands of tonnes of fill
may prevail	
(Stockland) pledged ... to keep suing	Mr Carriage
(just) to make sure	justice and truth
carried	the day

2. *2½ year court battle* – a contest between parties which has lasted for 2½ years in court
3. *the lumbering might* – an image of someone coming towards you, powerful, strong, but walking a little unevenly
4. *of 61-year-old Aboriginal elder Allan Carriage* – this noun group provides a description and image of an older, important man who is Aboriginal (61-year-old Aboriginal elder Allan Carriage)
5. *and his star group of legal eagles* – a group of lawyers who are 'stars'. This means they are very good at their job; 'legal eagles' refers to lawyers/solicitors/barristers who are so good that nothing misses their eye.
6. *(from) the Voluntary Indigenous Advocacy Group* – the lawyers/solicitors/barristers work for free. That is what *Voluntary* means. *Advocacy* – to advocate – to speak up for someone else.

3. Students decide which text is without prejudice or bias to one party or the other and tick the appropriate box.

   A. Text 1 ✓

   B. Text 2 _____

Task G | Rewrite ▶▶ SB P. 114
Students rewrite the text and fill in the missing word choices from the list below.

ANSWER

In the Students' Book these phrases have been removed from Text 2 but are out of order. Here they are listed in the order they are taken from the original text.

- STRUGGLING
- were shot down in
- succumbing to the lumbering might of 61-year-old Aboriginal elder Allan Carriage and his star chamber of legal eagles from the Voluntary Indigenous Advocacy Group.
- who clearly oppose progress and enlightened development,
- the impoverished
- However, justice may prevail for Stockland as it
- , even though he doesn't have any money
- just to make sure justice and truth carried the day.

PRESENT PERFECT TENSE

Task A | When do we use present perfect tense? ▶▶ SB P. 115

① Students read again the text entitled *A report on a traditional group in Australian society showing the impact of modernisation on that group* (see Task B in the Speaking 1 section), and underline the following examples of present perfect tense and past simple tense in the text.

ANSWERS

Answers in bold below.

Examples
- 'Historians [a] **have estimated** that the Aboriginal population [b] **declined** from at least 300 000 in 1788 … to about 50 000 in the next 100 years.' (para 15)
- 'The attitude of the government towards Aborigines [c] **has changed** significantly due to modernisation.' (para 19)
- '… many of these health problems [d] **have remained** into the twenty-first century. Colonisation also [e] **brought** alcohol … this is another problem that modernisation [f] **has brought** to the Aborigines'. (para 20)

② Students think about the context of each verb group, and write one of the following descriptions in each gap after the numbered sentences, as appropriate:
- past only
- change from past to now
- past but relevant now
- continues from the past to now

The first has been done as an example, which is explained in the Student's Book, and the students are given a hint that they should start with [c] and [d] because they are the easiest. If necessary, it may help to draw time lines to illustrate this example.

This activity can be done in pairs, or individually, followed by checking and discussion with a partner.

> **ANSWERS**
>
> a. Historians **have estimated** ... — past, but relevant now
> b. the Aboriginal population **declined** ... in the next 100 years — past only
> c. The attitude of the government towards Aborigines **has changed** ... — change from the past to now
> d. many of these health problems **have remained** ... — continues from the past to now
> e. Colonisation also **brought** alcohol ... — change from the past to now
> f. another problem that modernisation **has brought** ... — change from the past to now

(3) Students compare and discuss their answers with a partner.

(4) This question looks beyond the sentence level and highlights the connection between staging in genres, and grammatical patterns. Students are asked to find the paragraphs in the text that have the most examples of the present perfect tense, provide this section's title and suggest reasons that present perfect is particularly prevalent in this section.

> **ANSWERS**
>
> (i) Aborigines Today.
> (ii) Other sections mostly describe past situations that are now well and truly finished, so past simple is used. However, this section focuses on the present situation, including changes from the past and situations which continue from the past until the present, all of which can be expressed with present perfect.

(5) This question is based on the extract in Question 1. Here the question focuses on the form of the present perfect – notice that context and usage are dealt with before form. If necessary, you can remind the students about how to phrase the statement, question and negative forms for all persons.

> **ANSWERS**
>
> (i) Students underline the helping (auxiliary) verb (if there is one) and circle the main verb:
> - 'Historians [a] **have** (estimated) that the Aboriginal population [b] (declined) from at least 300 000 in 1788 ... to about 50 000 in the next 100 years.' (para 15)
> - 'The attitude of the government towards Aborigines [c] **has** (changed) significantly due to modernisation.' (para 19)
> - '...many of these health problems [d] **have** (remained) into the twenty first century. Colonisation also [e] (brought) alcohol ... this is another problem that modernisation [f] **has** (brought) to the Aborigines' (para 20).
> (ii) Which helping verb does present perfect tense use? **have/has**
> (iii) What is the form of the main verb in present perfect tense? **past participle**.

(6) The final step is to work on pronunciation. Read aloud the examples above with natural intonation. Drop your voice and emphasis where required. Each word, according to its context, will have a certain amount of emphasis. Ask students to listen carefully for the syllables that have less stress.

> **ANSWER**
>
> The helping verbs: *have* and *has*. *Have* is reduced to /həv/ and *has* is reduced to /həs/

Summary of present perfect (and past simple) tenses

As this is a complicated tense, a summary of its use, including typical contexts, has been included, and is reproduced below as it appears in the Students' Book:

Past simple tense is often used by accident instead of present perfect tense. In case you need it, here's a table to show some differences (students studied past simple tense in Unit 2).

PRESENT PERFECT TENSE	PAST SIMPLE TENSE
• events (eg changes) that started in the past and continue up to now	• time periods that are finished at the time of speaking/writing
• when something (a single event) is important now but happened in the past (example in Task A, Question 2)	• stories (real and not real) mostly use past simple
• events in time periods that aren't finished yet (eg at 11 am, you say *I've been very busy this morning*)	• events in time periods that are finished (eg at 2 pm, saying *I was very busy this morning*)
• often used with words like *yet, still, already, just* and *recently* (because these words link with the present)	• rarely used with *yet* and *still*
• often used with *for* and *since* when these words refer to a time period starting in the past and continuing to now	• never *used* with *since* • sometimes used with *for* but only when the period of time is completely in the past
• used to talk about lifetime experiences (eg if you say *I've been to Sydney three times*, it means that you've visited Sydney three times in your life, that is, a time period starting in the past and continuing to now). NB 'ever' is common in this usage, but only with questions.	• often an experience is introduced with the present perfect, but after that present simple is used to talk about the same event.
Typical contexts • quite common in casual conversation • quite common in narratives and newspaper articles • not so common in academic speaking or writing	*Typical contexts* • very common in most types of speaking and writing, academic and non-academic

Task B | Which tense? ▶▶ SB P. 117

This task gradually increases students' freedom to choose the correct tense. This progression culminates in the next task.

ANSWERS

1. In pairs, students work out the difference in meaning/context between the following sentences.
   a. (i) She lived in Adelaide for a few years: she doesn't live there now. *(All in the past.)*
      (ii) She's lived in Adelaide for a few years. *(She still lives in Adelaide; started in the past but relevant now.)*
   b. (i) He has had a great influence on Aboriginal art. *(The influence started in the past and hasn't finished; even now, the influence is still there.)*
      (ii) He had a great influence on Aboriginal art. *(The influence finished – perhaps he's dead now.)*
   c. (i) I've been to Disneyland. *(Sometime in my life, no time mentioned.)*
      (ii) I went to Disneyland. *(There must be something in the context that tells us when – maybe something mentioned before, or there's a time expression somewhere else in the sentence, or the whole conversation is about a specific time in the past.)*
   d. (i) I've been very busy recently. *(Still busy now.)*
      (ii) I was very busy recently. *(Not busy now.)*

2. Students circle the correct tenses in para 1 of the passage below, then compare their answers with a partner, discussing any differences.

3. In each gap in para 2, students write the best form of the verb in brackets (present perfect or past simple tense).

Paragraph 1
Aboriginal people [a] **lived/have lived** in Australia for tens of thousands of years. During these millennia, they grew to live in harmony with the land. They [b] **learnt/have learnt** to live in all the different ecosystems around the continent. Then, suddenly, just over 200 years ago, people from the far away country of Britain [c] **came/have come** to Australia, and soon they [d] **built/have built** towns and farms all over the country, and the way of life of the Aborigines [e] **changed/has changed** dramatically. Many of the traditions and ways of life of the past [f] **disappeared/have disappeared**, many of their languages [g] **died/have died**, and even whole cultural groups are no longer in existence. Fortunately, though, there are signs that this may [h] **started/have started** to change. In the last couple of decades, interest in Aboriginal issues [i] **increased/has increased**, and cultural activities are becoming better supported.

Paragraph 2
One example of this potential resurgence of Aboriginal culture is Aboriginal art, which [j] **has increased** in value dramatically over the last two decades or so, and is now being sold internationally. Further, projects [k] **have started** to revive languages and prevent them from dying. However, we must not get too comfortable about the situation that Aboriginals are in. For many, living standards [l] **have not changed** very much and [m] **have** certainly **not kept pace** with the rest of society. Life expectancy [n] **has remained** much lower than for the rest of Australia. Despite the signs of progress that [o] **have already occurred**, there is still a vast amount of progress that needs to be made, and changes seem to [p] **have slowed down**, or even reversed, since the mid-nineties.

Notes:
- [h] is not really present perfect, but the concepts used to obtain the answers, as well as the form, are very similar.
- Paragraph [1] provides a clear example of progression of tenses: present perfect to give the background information, followed by past simple to describe events, and present perfect to show changes between that time and now.

Task C | Personalised practice – Changes and experiences ▶▶ SB P. 118

(1) In pairs or small groups, students ask each other how the following things have changed, in their experience.

- their country (since their grandparents were children)
- their family (while they've known them)
- transport in their country (since the beginning of the 20th century)
- any other aspect of their country that they're interested in.

(2) a. Students mingle with others in the class, asking them about their most interesting or strangest experiences.
b. When they've finished, they decide which experiences they think are the most interesting.
c. They tell the class about the experiences they chose in Question 2 [b].

Note: Further personalised practice is provided in the Speaking 2 section, which follows on page 126.

WRITING — AN INFORMATION REPORT

Task A | Write a report ▶▶ SB P. 118
Students write an information report (example earlier in this Unit) about at least one of the following topics. If students need a reminder of the stages in an information report, the work in Unit 2 may help them. You may have to guide them through some research first. They should include changes between the past and now, events that happened only in the past, and events that occurred in the past but have an effect in the present.

Topic suggestions include the following. Add as appropriate to the contexts that your students can talk about, and which will be familiar to them.
- Their culture
- Their country, home town or region
- A famous person from their country.

LISTENING — INTERVIEW WITH AN AUSTRALIAN ABORIGINAL ARTIST

Task A | Introduction to Aboriginal art ▶▶ SB P. 118
In this task students practise listening for main points and for specific information in an interview based on the theme of the unit.

In groups, students discuss questions which appear in their books to orientate them to this topic. If your students have had limited experience on this topic, you may have to run this as an open class discussion and supply many of the answers yourself (there is plenty of information to be found on any of the websites listed at the end of this Unit). An alternative lead in to this section is to have your

Unit 10 Indigenous people | 121

students look at one of the websites to find the answers to some general questions about Aboriginal art. It may also be a good idea to show them some examples of Aboriginal art. The questions in the Students' Book are:

1 Have you ever seen Australian Aboriginal art? If so, where did you see it? Describe it.

2 Given what you have read in this Unit about the landscape, plants and animals of Australia, what tools do you think the Aboriginals used to create their art before white people came?

Task B | Listening for main points and details ▶▶ SB P. 118

1 Students read a list of points that appear on the recording, and then while listening to the recording, number them according to the order they hear them. Make sure they get a chance to read the headings before you begin to play the recording.

2 Students listen again, and in the blank lines below the headings, they write at least two points mentioned in relation to each heading. More than one answer is given below for some, but at this level, they wouldn't be expected to find all of them.

You may have to play this recording two or three times.

ANSWERS

1. Numbers next to the headings are the answers.
2. Bullet points are possible answers, though students are only expected to give two for each question.

[3] *Why people like the art*
- It comes from what is important to the author and his ancestors.
- It's pure
- It's from the heart

[1] *Traditional Aboriginal art*
- Involved pictures being drawn in the ground
- Occurred at ceremonies
- Was associated with dance and singing
- Celebrated the Dreamtime

[2] *Learning about Aboriginal art*
- They don't learn at school
- They learn from older people, eg uncles
- Everyone learns how to be an artist

[4] *The effect of commercial success*
- He will continue doing the same thing (ie commercial success doesn't change him)
- Art means more than just the money

Recording script

CD 2, track 1: Indigenous People, Unit 10
(7 minutes, 03 seconds)

Listening: Television interview with an Australian Aboriginal artist

Narrator: This listening takes place on television. It's an interview with an Australian indigenous or Aboriginal artist who is now famous in New York and other parts of the world. The program is a Sunday afternoon arts show.

(Open with didgeridoo.)

Interviewer: Hello viewers, and thank you for joining us this Sunday afternoon on the 'Life is Black' program. Today we're speaking with Aboriginal artist and traditional painter, Allan Cudgeemirra. Thanks for joining the program today, Allan.

Allan: That's OK, it's my pleasure.

Interviewer: So, you're now a very successful artist, but you haven't always been, have you?

Allan: Well, I started all those years ago, there were lots of artists. The men would draw pictures in the ground for the ceremonies, and dance and sing around them, and it was all part of the stories, to celebrate the dreamtime, to keep the memories alive and the stories to pass on to the younger fullas, and to help them understand how important the land is to us and the ancestors.

Interviewer: So, when did you start painting with paint, on canvas?

Allan: It was only a few years ago. You know, I'm over 60 now. I've been doing the pictures in the ground for a long time, learning from the elders, and one day I was in town and saw some of the mob I know painting. 'Cos I knew them, I asked them about it and they showed me what they were doing. And before long, I was selling them to the same shop. And the tourists liked them, and the big city fullas liked them, and they spent their big bucks. I've been painting for a long time now.

Interviewer: What, then, was your training? Which university did you go to?

Allan: Well, I never went to art school, nothing like that. In fact I didn't really go to to school much when I was a kid. I just learnt the tribal way, same as the people before me and the people before them. We just learnt from the older fullas. In the traditional way, everyone does the pictures, everyone learns the old ways. I just get my brush, add the colour and put it on the canvas, and it tells the old, old stories through the pictures, just like my people have been doing for thousands of years.

Interviewer: Who's influenced you … which famous artists have you borrowed ideas from?

Allan: All my ancestors. My father, his cousins, his father, his father before him and so on. My grandfather was a leader amongst our people, and everyone respected him, and the other elders said he was a good artist, but it wasn't from him I learned – I was too young to know the Dreamtime stories. It was my uncles that taught me everything I know now.

Interviewer: So, is there someone famous amongst them? Someone we all know?

Allan: Some were famous in our tribe and the neighbouring tribe. But they were never on television or anything like that, and in those days none of the white fellas wanted to know about our art.

Interviewer: And you're now very successful. I hear one of your paintings recently sold for the equivalent of 120,000 US dollars in Tokyo. What do you think the secret is for your success?

Allan: Well, well, I just do what I do. I just do what matters to me, what's important to me, and what the ancestors did, and it's pure, it's all from the heart. And, people like that, that's why they buy it. I've been doing it like that all the time, and it's the only way I know. It's what people like.

Interviewer: And, do you think your commercial success affected your art?

Allan: I just do what I do, just like my grandfather did, do it like that. And then, I think about the dreamtime, and paint the stories I want. If people want to pay money for it, that's good. And if people don't want to pay money, that's OK. I'll just carry on with what I do. For us, the stories mean so much more than the money.

Interviewer: Now, what do the symbols in your paintings mean? Or, should I say, what do the totems in your paintings mean? Do they have any connection with Western art?

Allan: No, they're all from Dreamtime stories. I draw lots of dots in different colours and different shapes, and they all mean many different things, and each one has a deeper and deeper meaning, and I can't tell you exactly the real meaning, that's only for the old fullas in the tribe. But, for example, we can say to anyone that a kind of u-shaped stick, that is a woman. And a straight stick is a man. If it's smaller, it's a child. A small circle can also be a child. The pictures are all in plan view – that's like looking at them from the air – so arrows are footprints of birds, showing where they travel in the story, and a single wavy line shows where a river flows, and parallel wavy lines symbolise a path. Circles mean there was a campsite or a meeting place there, and dots show rain and ants. My father and his father before him used the same totems to tell the stories.

Interviewer: Again, Allan, I can't thank you enough for coming along today. Let's give our viewers a look at some of these wonderful paintings now.

(Music.)

References: *Information from Cooinda Gallery (2004), Pwerte Marnte Marnte Aboriginal Corporation (2004) and Stevens (2003) was used in the preparation of this script. We thank Gerald Brown, the narrator of this script, for his assistance in adding authenticity to the wording.*

Task C | Listening for specific points – Shapes and forms ▶▶ SB P. 119

❶ The shapes in the diagram in the Students' Book will help in explaining the meaning of the words describing shapes or forms, such as *parallel, wavy, straight* and *plan view*. Pre-teach the words like *totem*. Ensure that students are sufficiently familiar with the pronunciation of these words that they can recognise them when spoken.

CD 2

Students then listen again to Allan's last turn, and write in the gaps in the diagrams the things that the shapes symbolise.

Students can gain further familiarity with this vocabulary at Question 2 where pairs compete with each other to list things with the same shape or form as those in the diagram.

ANSWERS

1. A single wavy line shows where a ***river flows***
2. Parallel wavy lines symbolise a ***path***
3. A kind of u-shaped stick represents a ***woman***
4. A straight stick is a ***man***
5. If it's smaller, it's a ***child***
6. ***Arrows*** are the footprints of birds
7. Concentric circles mean there was a ***campsite*** or ***meeting place***
8. Dots show ***rain*** and ***ants***.

❷ Students make a list of other things that are the same shape as the items in Figure 10.1. Answers will vary.

Unit 10 Indigenous people | 123

LANGUAGE SPOTLIGHT 2: PRESENT PERFECT CONTINUOUS TENSE

Task A | When do we use present perfect continuous tense? ▶▶ SB P. 120

Students listen to the interview with the Aboriginal artist again. As they listen, they tick the following examples of present perfect continuous and present perfect (sometimes called present perfect simple) in the extract below as they hear them (Question 1). This is to consolidate their understanding, draw their attention to the examples and ensure that they have heard them in context.

Next, following Question 2, students go into pairs, compare answers and discuss any differences. Then, (Question 3), for each of the numbered verb groups, they underline the helping verb(s) and circle the main verb, and answer questions about the form of present perfect continuous.

CD 2

> **ANSWERS**
>
> 1. Examples of present perfect continuous tense are in bold in the extract below. Students need to tick these examples.

2. Students check their answers with a partner and discuss any differences.

Examples from the recording
- '[1] I'**ve been** (painting) for a long time now' (*just before third question*)
- 'just like my people [2] **have been** (doing) for thousands of years' (*just before fourth question*)
- '… which famous artists [3] **have** you (borrowed) ideas from?' (*fourth question*)
- '[4] I'**ve been** (doing) it like that all the time' (*answer to sixth question*)

3. Students underline the helping (auxiliary) verb(s) and circle the main verb. Answers in the extract above.
   a. Which helping verbs do present perfect continuous use? **have/has been**
   b. Which form is the main verb in present perfect continuous? **past participle**

4. **Pronunciation:** Students listen again to the examples on the recording, and decide which words were pronounced weakly, and focus on the sound of the weak forms.
   have, *has* and *been* are pronounced weakly, to sound like /həv/, /həs/ and /bɪn/.

Summary of present perfect continuous tense and present perfect simple tense

This has been reproduced below as it appears in the Students' Book.

Present perfect simple tense and present perfect continuous tense are often mixed up. Here's a table to show the difference (you studied present perfect simple earlier in this unit).

PRESENT PERFECT CONTINUOUS TENSE	PRESENT PERFECT SIMPLE TENSE
• things started in the past and continuing through the present into the future	• things starting in the past, and continuing up to now
(almost the same, just a small difference in emphasis. Both are often used with *since* and *for*)	
• explaining a present situation (eg A: *You look very tired!* B: *Yes, I've been playing soccer*)	• n/a
• isn't used for: lifetime experiences, past events relevant now, saying how many times something happened, or with *yet* and *still*.	• is often used for: lifetime experiences, past events relevant now, saying how many times something happened, and with *yet* and *still*.
Typical contexts • used mainly in casual conversation • usually not used in academic speaking or writing	*Typical contexts* • more common than present perfect continuous (except the usage in the top row of this table)

Note:
- Similar to other continuous tenses, present perfect continuous has a sense of the action continuing through the present into the future.
- Again, as with other continuous tenses, present perfect continuous can show that something is temporary.
- Choosing present perfect continuous connects the action with the present more than present perfect simple.
  For example:
  I've been playing soccer = until now
  I've played soccer = not clear when in your life this happened: could be any time (lifetime experience).

Task B | Which tense? ▶▶ SB P. 121

① Students circle the correct tense in Conversation A in their books. If both answers are OK, they should circle both.

ANSWERS

Conversation A: Two students are talking about their exams coming soon …

Yvonne: Hi Tim… you look tired! What [a] **(have you been doing)**/have you done?
Tim: Yeah, well, [b] **(I've been staying)**/**I've stayed** up late to study – 5 hours sleep a night just isn't enough! My exam is coming soon, and [c] **(I've been reading)**/**(I've read)** most of the material, but there are still a couple of books I should look at.
Yvonne: Really! How many of the books [d] have you been reading/**(have you read)** so far?
Tim: Hmm, about five
Yvonne: [e] **(I've been studying hard)**/**I've studied hard** as well – [f] **I've been having**/**(I've had)** three exams already, and I've got two more next week. How are you going with maths? I remember you saying you were finding it difficult.
Tim: Yeah … pretty difficult, though [g] **(it's been getting)**/**it's got** easier since I bought another book to help. [h] **(I've been buying)**/**(I've bought)** a lot of books recently – and they're so expensive – I've nearly run out of money!

Notes
a. *What have you done?* would be appropriate if the evidence (*you look tired*) indicated a single action, eg a broken dish may indicate someone had been clumsy and dropped it. However, tiredness, as in this example, is more likely to be the result of a repeated or continuous action, hence the choice of present perfect continuous here.
b. The present perfect simple may be possible if the conversation is taking place late at night – but present perfect continuous (ppc) is more realistic!
c. Depending on your class, it may be useful to discuss the different emphasis given by the different answers: ppc emphasises more strongly that the reading is still going on, ie still in progress.
d. Just possible if all five books are being read simultaneously – but unlikely!!
e. A similar point to [c] can be made. However, the context at this point suggests more strongly the choice of ppc.
f. It is a good example to demonstrate how ppc can't be used when a number of events is mentioned.

② Students write the correct tense in the gaps in Conversation B in their books, changing the verb in brackets into present perfect or present perfect continuous as appropriate. If both tenses are possible, choose present perfect continuous.

ANSWERS

Conversation B: Outside a nightclub. S is a security guard, Tim and Rick are students wanting to go in.

S: ID please
Tim: What do you mean?
S: Please show me your ID. Without proof of age, you can't come in.
Tim: Why is there suddenly a problem? [i] **I've been coming** here every week for the last two months, and no one's asked me for ID before!
S: Well, [j] **I've been working** here for six years, and [k] **I've always asked** people who look as young as you for ID. [l] **I haven't seen** your ID yet, and until I do, you can't come in, simple as that.
Tim: But no one [m] **'s ever asked** me for it before.
S: So, [n] you**'ve been** lucky. But, by law, you have to show us your proof of age before we can let you in.
Tim: Will my student card do?
S: Hmm, no, it has to be a driving licence, official proof of age card or passport.
Rick: I had no problem with my student card a few months ago.
S: Unfortunately we [o] **haven't accepted** them since last month – there [p] **has been** a change of policy.

Unit 10 Indigenous people | 125

Task C | Personalised practice ▶▶ SB P. 121

❶ In groups, students ask and answer the following questions:
- How long have you been studying English?
- How long have you been living in this country?
- How long have you been living at your present address?
- How long have you been coming to this school?
- How long have you been studying in the class?
- Do you have a job? If so, how long have you been doing it?

❷ Students, in pairs, then think of similar questions that are relevant to their lives and ask them to each other.

> **Note:** Further personalised practice is provided in the Speaking 2 section which follows.

SPEAKING 2 — CONTEXTS FOR PRESENT PERFECT TENSE AND PRESENT PERFECT CONTINUOUS TENSE

Task A | Talking about recent experiences ▶▶ SB P. 121
Students practise the spoken language developed in this Unit in a fun, motivating way.

In small groups or pairs, students choose from a list of recent experiences reproduced below. Because they are choosing, they can avoid ones that do not reflect their experiences.
- a book they've been reading
- a TV program they've been watching
- something they've been thinking about
- something they've been worrying about
- something else they've been doing a lot

After each person has spoken, depending on your class and the students' relationship with teach other, speakers can be asked to comment on how much they used the present perfect or present perfect continuous, and to think about how the speaker could have used these tenses more.

Task B | Guess what I've been doing? ▶▶ SB P. 122
In small groups, students take turns to do the following activity:

❶ Act out something that could be the present evidence of either an action expressed through the present perfect continuous, or the present perfect simple with 'just'.

❷ The other students guess what the student who's acting has been doing by asking them questions. For example:

Have you been running?   No, I haven't
Has someone been chasing you?   No, they haven't
Have you just climbed a lot of stairs?   Yes, that's right.

This is not very realistic language, but it does provide a fun interlude while at the same time practising the 'explaining a current situation' usage of the tenses. The activity could be extended such that students prepare and act out a more realistic conversation based on one of the situations in the guessing game.

Task C | Whom do you admire? ▶▶ SB P. 122
This is quite a big task. Students imagine that their school, college or university has decided to invite a famous person to be an honorary head. It may be helpful to explain the concept of an honorary university chancellor if students are not familiar with this. Students first choose a famous person (living or dead, from any walk of life), and prepare a short speech to give to the committee in which they advocate for this person. The speech should focus on the person's lifetime experiences and personal qualities, hence there is plenty of scope to use present perfect simple and perhaps even present prefect continuous.

After the preparation phase is concluded, students come together into groups ('selection committees') of around four or five people, taking turns to give their mini-speeches. Then the debate starts, with the aim of choosing a single person.

As a follow-up, the students could write a report about the selection process (eg with stages such as: introduction, the candidates, the choice (with, of course, reasons).

LANGUAGE SPOTLIGHT 3 — WHERE DID THIS COME FROM?

Task A | Matching texts to their sources ▶▶ SB P. 122
The purpose of this task is for students to:
- Match some vocabulary to texts
- Examine various language differences that create a text
- Increase their knowledge of the issues surrounding Aboriginal affairs
- Apply their knowledge of genre learned in previous units.

❶ Students read and then match the six texts in their books to the six lettered sources found below the texts.

ANSWERS

a. __2__ 'Art & Law', Newsletter of the Arts Law Centre of Australia, September 2004, Issue 13.
b. __4__ *The stolen children, their stories*, 1998, ed. Carmel Bird, Random House, Australia, pp. 27, 37, 85,109.
c. __5__ Reynolds, Henry, 2001, *An Indelible Stain, the question of genocide in Australia's history*, Penguin Books, Australia, pp.15,16.
d. __6__ Email letter from one person to another.
e. __3__ 'Voices from the village', McMahon, D., 2005, *The South Sydney Herald*, Vol 1, No 28, p. 1.
f. __1__ University essay concerned with Aboriginal people of a certain area.

FURTHER PRACTICE: READING, FILMS AND FUN

This section provides further resources that teachers can use as jumping-off points to extend the activities in the book, or students can use for out of class practice.

READING

Students can get more reading practice on the topic of this Unit by looking at the following websites. Remind students that when they read it's best to read quickly first, without a dictionary, and after that, only look up words when they feel they are important for understanding.

> **Note:** You will see the words 'Koori' or 'Cooree' a lot. These are words for the Aboriginal people of the east coast of Australia.

- Hidden Histories: **http://www.mov.vic.gov.au/hidden_histories/histories/** This gives stories by Aborigines about their lives. It also has stories of native American people.
- The Australian Museum has a large site at **http://www.dreamtime.net.au/index.cfm**. This includes dreamtime stories, and information about Aboriginal culture and history. You can also listen to the stories on this site.
- **http://www.medicineau.net.au/AbHealth/contents.html** gives some very interesting information about Aboriginal culture.
- At **http://www.roebourne.wa.edu.au/default2.htm** is a website of a school where most of the students are Aboriginal.
- The following sites give lots of links to other sites about Aboriginal culture. These may be more difficult to read than those above, but they are still very interesting:
  - **http://www.aboriginalartwork.com/culture.html**
  - **http://www.ciolek.com/WWWVL-Aboriginal.html#TOC**

FILMS

- *Rabbit Proof Fence*
- *Storm Boy*
- *Yolngu Boy*
- *The Tracker*

QUESTIONS

Students will have to do some research (ie on the Internet) to answer these questions.

FACTUAL ESSAYS (INFORMATION REPORTS, EXPLANATIONS)

1. Describe Aboriginal musical instruments.

2. What are some of the social issues that Aborigines in Australia face?

OPINION ESSAYS (ARGUMENTS, DISCUSSIONS)

1. In all countries, governments have done things that, nowadays, people are unhappy about. Should governments say 'sorry' for things done in the past, even fifty or a hundred years ago?

2. Should a country's schools teach children about the indigenous culture of the country?

11 LANDSCAPES

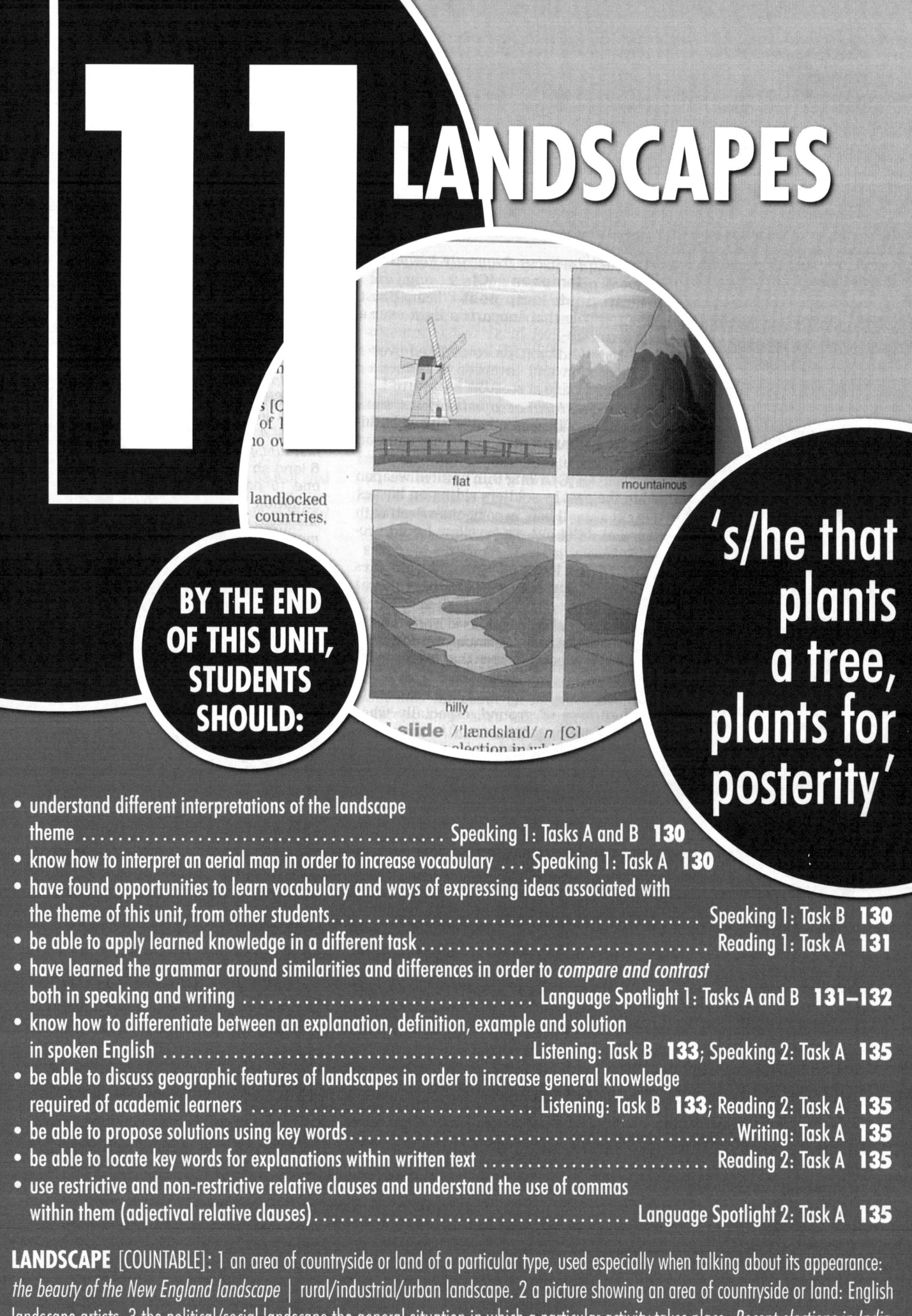

's/he that plants a tree, plants for posterity'

BY THE END OF THIS UNIT, STUDENTS SHOULD:

- understand different interpretations of the landscape theme .... Speaking 1: Tasks A and B **130**
- know how to interpret an aerial map in order to increase vocabulary ... Speaking 1: Task A **130**
- have found opportunities to learn vocabulary and ways of expressing ideas associated with the theme of this unit, from other students.. Speaking 1: Task B **130**
- be able to apply learned knowledge in a different task .... Reading 1: Task A **131**
- have learned the grammar around similarities and differences in order to *compare and contrast* both in speaking and writing .... Language Spotlight 1: Tasks A and B **131–132**
- know how to differentiate between an explanation, definition, example and solution in spoken English .... Listening: Task B **133**; Speaking 2: Task A **135**
- be able to discuss geographic features of landscapes in order to increase general knowledge required of academic learners .... Listening: Task B **133**; Reading 2: Task A **135**
- be able to propose solutions using key words...Writing: Task A **135**
- be able to locate key words for explanations within written text .... Reading 2: Task A **135**
- use restrictive and non-restrictive relative clauses and understand the use of commas within them (adjectival relative clauses)................................... Language Spotlight 2: Task A **135**

LANDSCAPE [COUNTABLE]: 1 an area of countryside or land of a particular type, used especially when talking about its appearance: *the beauty of the New England landscape* | rural/industrial/urban landscape. 2 a picture showing an area of countryside or land: English landscape artists. 3 the political/social landscape the general situation in which a particular activity takes place: *Recent elections in India have changed the political landscape.*

SPEAKING 1

BUILDING THE FIELD

Task A | Discussion ▶▶ SB P. 126

Ask students to nominate a 'recorder' who writes down the various answers in their group. They can report back by changing recorders from one group to another. If all your students are from one country, it doesn't matter because they can still discuss the geographic features from the questions.

❶ Introduction to Cumberland aerial map. Students must find and label the geographic features on the map: river, air strip, 2 dams, creek, bridge, cultivated river flats, 2 housing areas.

A River
B Air strip
C₁ Dam
C₂ Dam
D Creek
E Bridge
F Cultivated river flats
G₁ Housing areas
G₂ Housing areas

❷ In small groups (mixed nationality if possible), students examine the world map they have in their books (page 126) and tell each other as much as they can in answer to Questions I–VIII in the Students' Book. The questions are student based around geography and other features that their own locations may have. They can discuss, then write their individual answers.

Answers will vary. Monitor by walking around the room and listening to groups and providing assistance. The purpose is for students to activate their own knowledge concerning landscapes where they live.

Task B | Vocabulary ▶▶ SB P. 127

The vocabulary in this section is quite difficult. However, teachers have told the authors on many occasions that students lack enough general knowledge to succeed in academic settings. The work here should extend students' general knowledge to include the kinds of things expected of native speakers from a fairly early stage. This rationale also applies to Unit 8 Art, where students were challenged with higher lexis and a broad base of knowledge.

Students have the list of words below and they need to insert them correctly in the table next to the geographic term which they are closest to in meaning.

Pacific	mangrove	alpine
prairie	highlands	semi-arid &
outback	sand & Death	arid
marine	Valley	black earth
winding	Atlantic	elevated plateau,
corridors	Barchans	tropical and
habitat	(crescent	rain
mud flats	shaped	rich organic soil
sequoia & pine	dunes)	deposits
& oak	sea of grass	basins
islands	lowland or	waving grasses
alluvial deposits	coastal	& grassland

Students should be able to collocate some words (such as 'winding') with 'rivers' which is one of the geographic features from Column 1. Collocations are common in English, they comprise word combinations that we expect to hear and that are commonly associated with each other. For example *tall trees; mountain ranges; arid or semi arid deserts; tropical rain forests; Pacific Ocean; Atlantic Ocean; winding rivers; river basins; mountain steppes; and, in general, blue skies; job market; young woman/man; global warming; fossil fuels; boundless enthusiasm/ energy.*

In this task most of the words are nouns and are often associated with the land features. Note that when explaining answers, Column 1 words may be singular or plural.

> **Extension:** For extension, students may come up with additional words. They are given extra space for this in their books.

> **Note:** The table may be given to students as a vocabulary learning sheet.

130 | EAP Now! Preliminary English for Academic Purposes Teacher's Book

ANSWERS

GEOGRAPHIC FEATURES	DESCRIPTIONS			
mountains	highlands	elevated plateau	alpine	ranges
deserts	barchans (crescent shaped dunes)	sand & death valley	semi-arid & arid	outback
forests	sequoia & pine & oak	mangrove	tropical and rain	habitat
plains	waving grasses & grassland	alluvial	lowland or coastal	prairie
seas / oceans	islands	Pacific	Atlantic	marine
rivers	basins	mud flats	rich organic soil deposits	winding
steppes	black earth	rich grazing	mountains	

READING 1: COMPREHENSION

Task A | Applying knowledge ▶▶ SB P. 127

This task provides comprehension and diagnostic practice. It allows students to apply the vocabulary to factual statements rather than have the words floating. Students must read and understand each statement and match it to the geographic term/s from the vocabulary table they completed or studied with you in the previous section. This task should be individual work so each student can discover what they understand and what they don't.

ANSWERS

1. Students read the factual statements [a]–[h] below. They provide information while at the same time choosing vocabulary from the table above that fits the description. They apply knowledge of the definitions.
   a. To the east of the Tibetan plateau the ramparts of the Himalayas fall away in a series of mountain ranges which form the highlands of south-western China and northern Burma. _mountains, steppes, ranges_
   b. The rain forests of South America and Africa form a continuous block in their continent. _forests; rain; habitat_
   c. South America is a continent that is isolated (alone). It has a mountain spine, the mighty (big and powerful) Andes that reaches for thousands of miles from the northern hemisphere almost to Antarctica. _mountains_
   d. South America has the mighty Amazon River and the Galapagos islands. _river, islands, rain_
   e. There are many Pacific islands. _islands, Pacific ocean_
   f. The northern half of the African continent is almost wholly desert. It reaches from the Atlantic to the Red Sea and beyond…It is the largest desert on earth. _deserts, sand, dry, arid_
   g. The Indonesian Islands stretch for many kilometres North West of Australia. _islands, ocean_
   h. The Mediterranean Sea is surrounded by parts of Europe and North Africa. _sea, land_

2. Students write five factual statements using their own country of origin or the place they are now living. They should use the vocabulary they have learned and include locations as the statements above have done.

Answers will vary.

LANGUAGE SPOTLIGHT 1: MAKING COMPARISONS

Task A | Similar and different ▶▶ SB P. 128

The maps students studied earlier in this Unit showed very different countries and different landscapes. Their similarities and differences require the language of contrast in order to differentiate between them; for example, a rainforest is not the same as a prairie or a desert.

Students work in pairs.

① Students assign a list of words and phrases to the correct columns marked Similar or Different (see list below).

② Using words from the columns, they will talk about things that are the same as each other and that are different from each other.
   Students write the sentences first, then read them to a partner. If your students can speak using the phrases/words without writing the descriptions, move directly to that.

ANSWERS

Similar	Different
just like	more than
in the same way as / that	taller than
the same as	larger than
similar to the or a ...	different from
analogous to	not similar to the or a ...
like	not like or unlike the or a ...
something like	less than
	smaller than
	shorter than

Students should learn to use 'but' and 'although' rather than 'while'. 'While' is best used to express 'during the time that'.

Ellipses
Point out 'ellipses' to students. For example, in the sentence *In Australia, the Pacific Ocean is beautiful but dangerous* (the Pacific Ocean (is)). The second 'Pacific Ocean' is ellipsed or left out. Likewise in, *The Himalayan mountains of Tibet are breathtakingly beautiful but freezing cold.* (The second 'the Himalayan mountains' is ellipsed.) The reader in English supplies it mentally. Students need to do this in order to make the decision whether or not they are 'comparing or contrasting elements of the same thing'. If they are the sentence requires 'but' rather than 'while' or 'whereas'. Ellipses is used to avoid repetition.

Task B | Compare and contrast ▶▶ SB P. 129

  but   whereas   while

But, whereas and while can cause confusion. Students should study the examples in their books, then write out the exercises. A small oral test follows. You can give this test now (at the beginning of Task B for diagnostic purposes) or at the end to determine whether the differences are clear to students. The test is on page 130 of the Students' Book.

ANSWERS

1. Students write 10 sentences of their own using **but**. This should be pretty easy if they follow the rule that **but** is used to compare or contrast elements of the same thing – never two different things.
2. Students put the missing word – either **whereas** or **but** in sentences I to IX. The correct answers are underlined below.
   I. Winter is lovely in Russia <u>but</u> it's always cold.
   II. Summer is lovely in Hawaii <u>but</u> it's always hot.

ORAL TEST
Read aloud the following sentences and ask students to write either 'but', 'whereas' or 'while' in the pause/blank. Read each sentence twice.
1. In Australia, the Pacific Ocean is beautiful <u>blank</u> dangerous. (but)
2. I think in every country, the desert is beautiful <u>blank</u> dangerous. (but)
3. William smoked <u>blank</u> walking. (while)
4. Susan walked <u>blank</u> smoking. (while)
5. Dogs are faithful, loving and obedient <u>blank</u> cats are independent, affectionate and do their own thing. (but OR while)
6. <u>Blank</u> the sun is hot, it feels lovely on your shoulders. (while meaning 'although')
7. Parts of New Zealand, Wales, Ireland and Scotland all have very green grass <u>blank</u> parts of Australia, India, Dubai and Mongolia have brown grass or none at all. (whereas)
8. Wood comes from forests <u>blank</u> bricks can come from sand, mud or concrete. (whereas)
9. Reading takes some imagination <u>blank</u> watching TV. is a fairly passive activity. (whereas)
10. I invited her for a row in a boat on the river <u>blank</u> she declined. (but) (**Note**: *her* and *she* are one and the same.)

- III. Rivers are gorgeous when clean and fresh <u>whereas</u> mountains are always clean and fresh if you climb high enough.
- IV. Tall trees are pretty <u>but</u> if you live under them, they really are shady.
- V. Tall trees are pretty <u>whereas</u> tall shrubs look like weeds.
- VI. Deserts are landscapes to be respected because they are dangerous <u>whereas</u> parks are just there for pleasure.
- VII. Wooden houses can look quite original and have flexibility <u>but</u> they probably won't last as long as brick, stone or marble.
- VIII. The beach is marvellous in summer <u>but</u> in winter the waves are huge and threatening.
- IX. The Scottish Highlands are filled with castles and stunning remnants of the past <u>whereas</u> the New Zealand Highlands are filled with scenery and sheep.

3. Students tick the sentences that use 'while' correctly.

Here is an example that demonstrates the meaning 'during the time that' for 'while'.

during the time that

↕

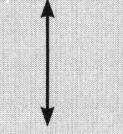

eg. Arnold cooked dinner <u>while</u> Susan bathed the children.

- I. ✓ While I studied, the birds outside made a huge racket.
- II. ✓ Nero fiddled while Rome burned.
- III. X While he's good looking, he's a pain in the neck.
- IV. X While I know what to do, I don't want to do it.
- V. ✓ How about you drive, while I concentrate on the map?
- VI. ✓ What say you walk faster, while I ride alongside of you on my bike?

4. Students should write a paragraph describing some landscape from their own country or the country in which they now live. They can do this task individually and apply contrast and comparison language learned earlier in this Unit. For more uniform answers you could place two different (contrasting) pictures of landscapes before the students and ask them to compare the landscapes. (Use pictures from this Unit if needed.) The primary purpose is to apply knowledge.

LISTENING: INTERVIEW WITH AN AUSTRALIAN FARMER

Task A | Pre-listening ▶▶ SB P. 131

This pre-listening task is an orientation to the topic.

Students listen once for gist. They listen a second time for key words which signal explanations, examples and solutions.

Before listening, ask students to consider the following questions together or alone:
1. What is a farm?
2. What is a farmer?
3. What is agriculture?
4. How does weather affect farming?
5. What do you know about dry land or drought?
6. What do you know about salination?
7. Students look up 'salination' in their dictionaries.
8. Where do we get our food from?
9. They examine the photographs and compare what they see.
10. Students mark up photographs.

Task B | Explanations, definitions, examples, solutions ▶▶ SB P. 131

The skills focus here is listening for key words and phrases that signal solutions, explanations or examples. Students tick the words when they hear them, then listen for what follows.

The listening focuses on explanations, definitions, examples and solutions and the terms that introduce those functions when speaking. These <u>explanations are sometimes definitions</u> as well.

The key words in this listening for **explanations** are: *it has; it happens because; it turns ...' ; that means.*
There is also an **example** signalled by: '*Let me give you an example*'.
Solutions are signalled with: '*One way* (in other words, one way to solve the problem) *would be to ...*'

1. Students listen to the interview with the Australian farmer and look for these key word phrases and for what follows them.
2. If they can listen for that specific purpose, they can learn to differentiate and locate *explanations, examples* and *solutions* when listening to a lecture or reading a text. In the listening the farmer offers some solutions, explanations and examples. Students number the boxes that match the language they hear.

ANSWER

Key words are underlined in the recording script. The signal they represent is in parenthesis.

Recording script

CD 2, track 2: Landscapes, Unit 11
(5 minutes, 21 seconds)

Listening: Radio interview with an Australian farmer about salination

Narrator: This listening takes place on the radio. It is like what you would hear on the Australian Broadcasting Corporation. It's an interview and the program is a country program. It is rural and concerns farms and farmers. But its subject concerns everyone.

(Open with radio farm program music.)

Interviewer: Good morning listeners, and welcome to the program. This morning, we are talking with Mr Ben Murray from Western Australia about the very important and worrisome problem of salination. Ben is an expert on the subject and I hope we can make, help make you experts as well.

Good morning, Ben and welcome to the program.

Farmer: Yeah, ah g'day, Leyland.

Interviewer: Let's begin by finding out what we mean when we're talking about salination. What is salination?

Farmer: Well, basically, it's … ah … (explanation) salt that lies on the ground. It has (explanation) come up from under the ground. It comes up from the soil or earth. It comes up and sits on the top of the ground.

Interviewer: So, why does it happen?

Farmer: Well, Mostly, in fact maybe only, because of clearing trees. It happens because (explanation) cutting the trees down means the soil becomes acidic and the wind blows it away.

Interviewer: So, salination means that the land has salt rising up from below the earth?

Farmer: Yes, exactly. It turns the ground white and (explanation) you can't grow crops. You can't grow grass for feeding animals. You can grow a little, you know, sea-barley grass but no real crops.

Interviewer: Does farming cause salination?

Farmer: It does, if (explanation) you farm too hard. That means (explanation / definition) if you clear all the land.

Interviewer: Is over farming the reason for salination, then?

Farmer: Well, no, not exactly. See, they haven't over farmed, they just cleared the land too much. We didn't know that we should leave trees and some plants on the land. We use European farming methods.

Interviewer: Is this a problem anywhere else in the world or in history?

Farmer: Oh yeah, for sure. Let me give you an example (example) from history. See, historians think that the whole civilization of ancient Sumer in Iraq was destroyed by salt in the land. They grew wheat and barley back in 3500 BC. They used canals for irrigation and it took about 500 years, but records show that Sumer lost the land because their crops disappeared when salt came up.

Interviewer: Are there any solutions to this problem?

Farmer: Well, right now, yes, there is something that can be done. One way would be to (solution) plant more trees. Salt comes up from a rising water table beneath the earth. This happens because (explanation) there are no trees on the land. Trees and shrubs soak up water underground and keep the land safe from rising salt.

Interviewer: Isn't it expensive to plant millions of hectares?

Farmer: Ah. Of course it is. And you need to fence them off if you have animals because they will eat the little, yummy green saplings – the little trees that are planted.

Let me tell you a story … There's a good story about volunteers coming from the big city to plant trees on weekends. It's happening out in Western Australia now, and it started over ten years ago in 1995. A company asked if any of their employees wanted to work without pay in the weekend in the country. You know, They could take their families and everything would be paid for. They just had to plant trees.

Interviewer: What happened?

Farmer: Well, you wouldn't believe it. Everyone wanted to help. They ended up with about 600 volunteers planting trees and plenty more wanted to help! The name of that organisation is Western Power. Other organisations trying to help are Land Care and Project Safe. There are things that can be done. It's about (explanation) people seeing the problem and caring about the problem. Everyone just wants to blame farmers. Ah, We have to get together to fix this problem of salination, or in the future we won't have our own food any more, you know Leyland.

Interviewer: Do you really believe that?

Farmer: Oh yes, I do. I do really believe that. We have to work with organisations, government and people to solve one of the biggest problems farmers are facing right now … (voice pauses to offer the definition or explanation of 'the biggest problem') salination.

(Music fades.)

SPEAKING 2: SOLUTIONS

Task A | Discussion – Proposing solutions ▶▶ SB P. 132

This task is open ended. Students choose a problem to discuss from the following list.
1. Climate change (the world getting hotter)
2. Drug taking by young people
3. Teenage suicide
4. Deforestation (cutting down too many trees).

Encourage students to use the key words from Task B Listening in their discussion.

> **Extension:** You could set up role plays in groups where relevant positions are assumed. Students could research their issue and present to other groups. For example, Problem 1 Climate change could include a leading scientist who explains the problem, a government leader who does not believe it exists. Problem 4 Deforestation could include a logger who is interested in his job and the town and an environmentalist trying to protect trees. Together they must find a solution. Don't worry if students argue, for speaking practice will take place and that is the purpose of the activity.

WRITING: SOLUTIONS

Task A | Writing a solution ▶▶ SB P. 132

In the previous task, students discussed a solution to a problem of their or your choice. In this task, they all write two to three paragraphs on the same solution. Oral literacy around this task precedes writing so students should have some capability. As an open-ended task, students might peer assess the writing and use the Listening Task B language as a checklist. Students should include some of the Listening Task B language at the beginning of sentences so that their solution is sign-posted by the correct language.

READING 2: COMPREHENSION

Task A | Meaning in context and recognising facts ▶▶ SB P. 133

Students read the text *Our world, the earth* and answer the questions in the spaces provided in their books. Key words signal explanations and facts. Facts are signalled by equality on either side of the verb. (A mosquito is an insect); (A desert has sand).

ANSWERS

1. Asia
2. Four
3. 71%
4. 4,600 million years
5. rotation
6. circumference
7. 40,076
8. paragraph 1 (*What is meant when you say or hear that?*)
9. paragraph 4 (*Our world rotates, it spins around …*)
10. Nepal (& China)

LANGUAGE SPOTLIGHT 2: HOW TO ADD EXTRA INFORMATION

Task A | Adjectival relative clauses ▶▶ SB P. 134

Adjectival clauses may be either **restrictive** or **non-restrictive**.

If a relative clause is essential to identify (or restrict) the noun it modifies then it is restrictive:

The orchids that my grandmother grows are pretty.
(The clause *that my grandmother grows* identifies which orchids are pretty.)

If a relative clause is not essential to identify the noun it modifies then it is non-restrictive. The clause adds information about the noun but it is not essential to the meaning:

Orchids, which grow wild in the bush, are my favourite flowers.
(The clause *,which grow wild in the bush,* does not essentially change the meaning nor restrict it. Orchids are still '*my favourite flowers*'.)

> No matter what the introductory relative pronoun (*who/whom/that/which/*) is, non-restrictive clauses are **always** set off from the main clause by commas, and restrictive clauses are **never** set off by commas.
>
> - *that* is used ONLY to introduce restrictive clauses
> - *which/ who/ whom* may be used to introduce either type of clause.

Unit 11 Landscapes | 135

ANSWERS

1. Students label clauses either restrictive (R) or non-restrictive (NR).
   a. NR
   b. NR
   c. NR
   d. R
   e. NR
   f. R
   g. NR
   h. NR
   i. NR
   j. R

2. Students then identify relative clauses (adjectival) in the following paragraph by placing parenthesis ( ) around each clause.

   Denise: So, where have you been?
   Rosie: Well, I drifted around out west, (which is where the sun nearly kills you,) then headed for the coast.
   Denise: Which coast did you go to?
   Rosie: Sorry, I went up North and stayed with my cousin (who lives in Maroochydore).
   Denise: Really? Maroochydore? I've been up there too. It was there on the Sunshine Coast that I met Michael (whom I'm engaged to now.)
   Rosie: Michael? I don't remember meeting any Michael.
   Denise: Naw, you haven't met him yet, you've been away for six months, remember, but you'll see him on TV soon.
   Rosie: TV?
   Denise: Yep.
   Rosie: Why's that?
   Denise: He's in a band (that won a major music prize) (which includes a recording contract as well as television performance spots.)
   Rosie: Cool.

3. Students have had modelling and practice. They should now attempt to:
   a. Think up five sentences that have **restrictive relative clauses**
   b. Think up five sentences that have **non-restrictive relative clauses**.

   Student answers will vary.

Peer checking and/or walking around the room checking and/or reading some aloud will check comprehension. This could also be conducted as an oral task, but commas are a key and need to be reflected in voice pauses if not written.

FURTHER PRACTICE: READING, FILMS AND FUN

READING

The *Macquarie World Atlas* (or any good Atlas)

Dale Lightfoot's Cultural Landscapes from Around the World: This site includes popular culture as global culture/ folk customs from around the world and global cola wars.
http://www.geog.okstate.edu/users/lightfoot/lfoot.htm

Woophy: This site has pictures of our world, landscape, cityscapes, etc. It is interactive and you can share your pictures as well as view other people's pictures.
http://www.woophy.com/map/index.php

FILMS

Each of the following films portray interesting stories which have amazing landscapes that are central to the themes.

- *Himalaya*
- *Baraka, Samsara, Koyaanisqatsi*
- *Brokeback Mountain*
- *The Chronicles of Narnia*

QUESTIONS

1. Write a description of the most noteworthy geographic feature in your own region or country.

2. Research a river system which has been polluted and propose a solution (or solutions) for making it clean again.

12 WORLD

'all the world's a stage, and all the men and women merely players'

BY THE END OF THIS UNIT, STUDENTS SHOULD:

- be able to talk about various world topics more
  fluently . . . . Speaking 1: Task A **138**; Reading: Tasks A and E **138–139**
- have had more practice in skimming, scanning and note-taking from written texts and
  finding meaning from context . . . . Reading: Tasks B and D **138–139**
- have increased their confidence and skill in understanding nominalisations in
  formal writing (unpacking nominals) . . . . Language Spotlight 1: Task A **140**
- have reviewed the essay genres that they may have to write at college
  or university . . . . Writing: Tasks A and B **140–141**
- have seen connections between essay questions and the genre of the answer . . . . Writing: Task B **141**
- have practised writing an opinion essay using at least one essay genre . . . . Writing: Task C **142**
- know some of the learning and assessment tasks that they are likely to have in their
  college or university course, especially tutorials . . . . Listening: Tasks A and B **142–143**
- have practised listening for specific information . . . . Listening: Task B **143**
- be more accurate in choosing the right future tense . . . . Language Spotlight 2: Tasks A, B and C **145**
- have practised the speaking skills required in a tutorial . . . . Speaking 2: Task A **146**

WORLD n. [COUNTABLE]: the planet we live on, and all the people, cities, and countries on it.

SPEAKING 1

BUILDING THE FIELD

Task A | Quiz – Making guesses ▶▶ SB P. 138

Students should help each other in pairs or small groups to answer the questions in the quiz. They should circle their answers. The purpose is for students to develop confidence in giving and discussing hypotheses.

ANSWERS

1. Around the world, do most people live in cities and towns, or in the countryside?
   a. far more in the countryside
   b. far more in cities and towns
   c. **about fifty-fifty** ← the figure in 2005, expected to increase to 60% living in towns and cities by 2015
2. How many countries are there in the world, approximately?
   a. about 100
   b. **about 200** ← *correct*
   c. about 300
3. The world population was around 6 billion in 2004. What do you think will be the world population in the year 2100?
   a. about 6 billion
   b. **about 10 billion** ← *correct*
   c. about 20 billion
4. How big is the Sahara Desert?
   a. much smaller than the USA
   b. **slightly smaller than the USA** ← *correct*
   c. much bigger than the USA
5. Rainforest used to cover 14% of the Earth's surface. Now it covers:
   a. around 20%
   b. around 14%
   c. **around 6%** ← *correct*
6. Megacities are cities with over 10 million people. In 1985, there was only one of these in the world. How many were there in 2005?
   a. 5
   b. 10
   c. **25** ← *correct*

Sources for answers: Encyclopaedia of the Orient (2006), Moore Foundation (2005), United Nations (2003), United Nations (2004).

READING

SKIMMING, SCANNING AND NOTE-TAKING; FINDING MEANING FROM CONTEXT

Task A | Cities – Your experiences ▶▶ SB P. 138

In small groups, students ask and answer some wide-ranging questions around some of the topics mentioned in Task A as a lead-in to the next reading, *Megacities – a good or bad future?*

Task B | Skimming, scanning and note-taking ▶▶ SB P. 139

This section reviews skimming and scanning, introduced in Units 1 and 2 of this book and practised in several other units.

1 Students skim the article (*Megacities: a good or bad future?*) on page 140 of their books and write the main idea of each paragraph. It is in the style of a magazine section of a weekend newspaper, although rather shorter than normal.

ANSWERS

The answers the students provide don't have to be these exact words:

Paragraph 1: *More people live in cities*
Paragraph 2: *Cities are increasing in size and number (especially in developing countries)*
Paragraph 3: *Reasons for the growth of cities/Why people move to cities*
Paragraph 4: *Definition and growth of mega-cities*
Paragraph 5: *Some problems with mega-cities (resources, energy production and waste)*
Paragraph 6: *Problems with housing and poverty*
Paragraph 7: *Problems for governments*
Paragraph 8: *Conclusion/minimise problems*

2 Students have some questions in their books about the article and now scan the article to locate the answers. They may have to read in detail around the place they have located through scanning. As the purpose of this activity is to practise scanning, the order of the questions is random.

ANSWERS

a. A hundred years ago, what proportion of people lived in towns and cities? *One in ten, 10%, one-tenth (para 1)*
b. What proportion are expected to live in rural areas 10 years after the article was written? *four in ten, 40%, four-tenths (para 1) (though this answer does involve the assumption that all who don't live in cities, live in the countryside, ie there's nothing in between city and countryside.)*
c. Where are shanty towns being built? *on the edges of cities (para 6)*
d. In developing countries, where do people earn more money, the city or the countryside? *the city (para 3)*
e. How many megacities were there in 1985? *one (para 4)*
f. How many megacities were there in 2005? *25 (para 4)*

g. What proportion of the world's 10 largest cities were in industrialised countries in 1973? *one in two, 50%, a half (para 2)*
h. What are two problems of energy production nowadays? *global warming, pollution (para 5)*

❸ Students now take notes from the reading, in any way they feel comfortable with. For example, they could use the main ideas that they identified in Question 1 as headings, they could use the format illustrated in the Listening section of Unit 7, or they could use a bubble diagram.

Task C | The five questions for any text ▶▶ SB P. 141

As in other units of this book, students answer five questions about the text *Megacities: a good or bad future?*.

ANSWERS

[a] **What is it?**
A magazine article (the kind that appear in magazine supplements to weekend newspapers).
[b] **What is the source?**
A magazine.
[c] **Who is the writer?**
Magdalena Thornton, a freelance writer. (You may have to explain the meaning of freelance *to the students.)*
[d] **What purpose does the writer have for writing it?**
To create an interesting article that people will want to read so that they are more likely to pay attention to the surrounding advertisements; to convey information about the growth of megacities; to stimulate thought about whether megacities are good or bad.
[e] **Who is the intended audience?**
A general audience who is interested in what is happening in the world (we have no more specific information about this because we don't know which newspaper or the target audience of the newspaper).

Task D | Finding meaning from context ▶▶ SB P. 141

❶ Students scan for words in the article *Megacities: a good or bad future?* and underline them in the text.

- coping with (appears twice in the text)
- wealth
- booming
- flocking to
- lifestyles
- backward
- emergence
- resources
- dumps
- thriving economic powerhouses

❷ Students then look at the context of the words and match the words to their closest meanings in the table in their books.

ANSWERS

MEANINGS	WORDS
companies, places or countries that are very, very successful	thriving economic powerhouses
a large amount of money that someone has	wealth
when something appears, or when people start to know it	emergence
being very successful, increasing very quickly	booming
doing well with something difficult (maybe a task, or a problem)	coping with (appears twice)
big places to put waste	dumps
the way a person lives, especially in their free time	lifestyles
old-fashioned, or developing slowly	backward
go somewhere in large numbers (usually because the place is interesting or exciting)	flocking to …
things like food, water, energy, people, money	resources

Task E | Discussion ▶▶ SB P. 141

Students wrap up this Reading section by discussing four questions based around the topic. This gives them an opportunity to react to the text. Brainstorming ideas during this discussion could also help students prepare for the writing they will do later in the Writing section. The questions are:

a. What do you think are the advantages and disadvantages of megacities for the people who live there?
b. How can megacities be of benefit to countries? (Think, for example, about megacities you have heard of. What are they famous for? How does this benefit the country? Do smaller cities and rural areas provide the same benefits to the country?)
c. What problems can megacities cause? (Try to think of ideas beyond what the reading is about.)
d. Would you like to live in a megacity? Give as many reasons as you can for your answer.

LANGUAGE SPOTLIGHT 1: UNPACKING NOMINALS

Task A | Written style ▶▶ SB P. 142

Ask students to look at the two following sentences in their course books.
- Some countries try to control where people go.
- Some countries try to control the movement of people.

One (the second) is taken from the *Megacities* reading in the previous section, in paragraph 6, while the other is a more spoken-style paraphrase of it.

① Students are asked to identify which sentence sounds more spoken, and then further questions lead them to finding out why this is so.

They may remember the work on nominalisation from Unit 7 (see Students' Book page 77), and this task is provided here mainly for review and consolidation. They should do this in pairs – there is no need to write anything down.

② After this, ensure that students are familiar with the idea that expressions can be made to sound more formal by changing the lexis and shifting meaning, where possible, from verb to noun.

ANSWERS

1. Which sounds more spoken? Which sounds more written?
   The first sounds more spoken.

2. Look at the part of each sentence after the word 'control'. Which carries more meaning through nouns? Which has the more formal vocabulary?
   The second carries more meaning through nouns ('where ... go' in the first is replaced by the noun 'movement' in the second). As 'movement' is more formal than the more conversational 'where ... go', we can say the second also has the more formal vocabulary.

③ In the next question, they practise this by changing some formally written sentences (some would say pompous!) to less formal, more conversational expressions. If they find this difficult, the teacher could supply some words for them to use, or provide the beginnings of sentences. Essentially, this is an exercise in paraphrase, with some guidance as to the effect and context of the different expressions. Warn students that some of the expressions in the questions are overly academic and/or contain redundancy and shouldn't be used by students (even if some professional writers do use them!)

*The meanings of some of the words used are given in the Students' Book after the questions. For those teachers dipping into this Unit rather than working from beginning to end with their class, please note that **reduction**, which would otherwise appear in the 'To help you' section, appears frequently throughout this book and should be familiar to students by the time they reach this unit.*

ANSWERS

3. (Answers below are suggestions only. Anything that carries the right meaning and tone should be acceptable.)
   a. The result is the emergence of megacities.
      So, megacities have appeared.
      So, there are now more megacities.
   b. in the cities ... a greater need for fuel-burning trucks and trains.
      The cities need more trucks and trains, and they use fuel.
   c. rises in oil prices will mean a reduction in oil use.
      Oil prices will go up, so people will use less oil.
   d. methods of greenhouse gas reduction.
      Ways to stop making so much greenhouse gas.
   e. A large majority of people will count megacities as their place of residence in the future.
      Many people will live in megacities in the future.
   f. There is a reasonable possibility that there will be economic problems in rural areas in the future.
      Rural areas might get poorer.
   g. A point of significant importance is that there should be participation by all citizens in the reduction of energy use.
      It's important for everyone to use less energy. Everyone should use less energy – that's very important.

WRITING: REVIEW OF GENRES; MATCHING GENRES TO TASK

Task A | Review of genres ▶▶ SB P. 142

Ask students, in groups, to tell each other what they can remember about the genres covered in this textbook. They then fill in a table which summarises the purpose and stages of those genres they are most likely to have to produce at college or university (though this, of course, depends on their future courses). They can use this, or the more detailed checklist in Appendix 3, as a guide for future writing, and/or to self check that they have included all the stages. The table below and the appendix could also be used for peer checking activities in the remainder of their current EAP course, or the next level.

ANSWERS

GENRE	UNIT	PURPOSE	STAGES
Information report	2	To give facts (not opinions). To say what happened, or what exists.	– Introduction (general statement + optional justification) – Points (each has topic sentence + elaboration)
Explanation	3	To say how or why something happened or happens	– Introduction (general statement + preview/scope) – Explanation paragraphs (each has topic sentence + elaboration)
Argument	4	To put forward an opinion and give evidence to support the opinion	– Introduction (general statement + optional definition + preview/scope) – Body paragraphs (each has topic sentence + support/evidence) – Conclusion (summary + recommendation)
Discussion	6	To look at several opinions, with their evidence, and decide which has the stronger evidence	– Introduction (general statement + optional definition + position + preview/scope) – Body paragraphs for the position (each has: topic sentence + support/evidence) – Body paragraphs against the position (same format as body paragraphs for the position) – Conclusion (summary + recommendation)
Review	8	To inform others about something and to give an opinion or recommendation about it	– Description of thing being reviewed – Comparison to similar things – Opinion + recommendation

Task B | Matching genres to task ▶▶ SB P. 144

Now ask students to look at the questions in this task and choose which genre or genres best answers each. Thinking about whether the question asks for facts, opinions, or both, will help them. After working through this individually, they discuss their answers in pairs. You might want to give them the first answer if you think this task will be difficult for the class.

Some of these questions are unusual, but are included here to provide a set of questions on the same topic in order to make it easier to see the differences between each type of question.

ANSWERS

a. What is a megacity?
Information report: The word **what** is the biggest clue for students – information reports generally answer **what** questions.

b. Why have megacities developed?
Explanation: This genre answers questions such as **how** and **why**.

c. Megacities are good for society. To what extent do you agree with this point of view?
Discussion: This is most likely but the question could also be answered with argument, especially if the writer completely agrees or disagrees.

d. What are the factors in the development of megacities?
Explanation: Students should pick up that this is slightly more sophisticated way of phrasing [b].

e. Are megacities good for society? Give reasons for your answer.
Argument: In addition, discussion is possible as long as the essay takes a single position, consistent in both the introduction and conclusion.

f. What features are common to most megacities?
Information report: *As with [a], the word **what** should alert students.*

g. Describe a town or city where you have lived. What are the good and bad points of living there? What kinds of people would you recommend live there?
Review: *The key words (good or bad points, recommend) should make this quite clear to students.*

h. Some people say that megacities are good for society, while others say they are a negative development. Which opinion do you agree with?
Argument: *As with [e], though discussion is also possible as long as the author's view appears consistently.*

i. What are the advantages and disadvantages of megacities? Overall, are megacities beneficial or non-beneficial?
Discussion.

Note: It's difficult to give hard and fast rules about which question words are associated with each genre. For example, sometimes questions that appear to be asking for explanations may in fact require argument. The only way students can know this is from the context of their course. If course readings indicate that there is controversy over what has led to the emergence of megacities, for example, then with question [b] above, students may be expected to discuss and evaluate the different ideas, in which case it becomes discussion. Therefore, this task is to be considered a guide only.

Task C | Writing ▶▶ SB P. 145

In this task, students choose one of the essay questions from Task B that leads to an opinion essay (argument or discussion). The discussion activity at the end of the Reading section of this unit (Students' Book page 141) could substitute for the usual pre-writing discussion. Let students know how long the essay should be – if they are doing this in class and finishing for homework, that is, if there is no time limit, they should be able to write around 250 words or more. This activity may also be used with a time limit as exam preparation.

The Students' Book asks students to use the table in Task A to self-check their work after completing their first draft. This may be a good opportunity to remind them about the process of producing, revising and refining drafts of their written work.

The table in Task A and the checklist(s) in Appendix 3 could also be used for peer review work if appropriate for your class.

LISTENING — SPECIFIC INFORMATION – TUTORIAL

Task A | What do you do at college or university? ▶▶ SB P. 145

① Students use their own and/or each other's knowledge to help match vocabulary about college or university activities with descriptions of what they are. The purpose of this task is to ensure that all students have shared common knowledge about what tutorials and other academic tasks are.

ANSWERS

tutorial A small group activity focusing on a discussion about the week's lectures or lessons. Students are expected to prepare and take part in the tutorial discussion. It can take place in a classroom, the lecturer's office, or even outdoors!

lecture In this, students listen to someone talk. Often, there are many students – sometime over 100.

practical This is often used in science, engineering or vocational courses. Students actually do the activities of the job they are studying for. For example, it could be done in a kitchen or a laboratory.

work placement Students work in a real company, and write reports about this work.

exam Students sit in silence, writing answers to questions.

assignment Students write an essay or report over a period of a few weeks. They should use books, journals, etc from the library for their information.

group project Students do work with other students and write a report. Each person writes a section of the report. This is especially common in business subjects because teamwork is important in business.

role play Students act out a situation, eg dealing with a customer, and get marks for how well they deal with it. This is common on vocational courses.

presentation Students give a talk to the other students and the lecturer.

---

② Students now share experiences of the above. If none has yet experienced tertiary education, they can ask you the questions in their books, and any others they think of.
- Which of the above activities did they do?
- How many people were in each activity?
- How did they feel about each?
- Which one helped them to learn the most?

Task B | Listening for specific information ▶▶ SB P. 145

The Listening for this Unit is a tutorial discussion in which geography students hear about, then discuss, an assignment which involves them planning a new suburb. One purpose of the Listening is to give students, especially those heading to university, an understanding of what a tutorial involves and what they might expect of university assignments. This is only for familiarisation – the next book in the series, *EAP Now!*, gives further, more detailed, practice of tutorial participation skills more suitable for those students who are closer to being ready to proceed to university.

The tutorial discussion also brings together some of the topics of previous units, such as energy, demographics and landscapes. It is the intention that in dealing with this Listening, students will use and be exposed to some of the language learned in previous units.

Although the topic and the type of assignment will be more relevant to students heading to university, many of the concepts mentioned will also be very relevant to students heading for vocational study (such as assignment details being in the subject notes).

① Students try to predict the topic of the Listening from the pictures in their books.

② Students read the specific information questions, which mix a variety of question types to give a range of practice. They should try to predict potential answers. A couple of points (eg [g] … the _____ is flat) are intentionally easy to predict, in order to develop confidence in this strategy.

After predicting (and perhaps discussing predictions with another student), they listen to the CD and check whether their predictions are correct.

CD 2, track 3

Depending on your students, it may be a good idea to divide this Listening into two or more parts.

Note: Unless you want to run this as practice for an exam that excludes words not heard on the recording from being possible answers, anything students write with the same meaning as the answers is OK.

▶ ANSWERS

2. a. How did students first know about the assignment? *Subject notes/subject handbook*
   b. How many words should the students write? *(around) 3000*
   c. What two things will be covered in the tutorial? Go through what to *consider* in their plans, and *discuss* some ideas.
   d. The students' design should last for *200* years.
   e. Students should think about *social change* as well as environmental change.
   f. In the lecturer's opinion, is environmental change the easy part of the assignment? *yes*
   g. There might be floods because the *land* is flat and because of *sea level* change.
   h. The dike might stop *sea views* and access to the *beach*.
   i. The example mentioned of something with a temporary purpose is *a car park*.
   j. Empty nesters are people whose children have *left home* (logically, *grown up* cannot be accepted as it is not a complete answer in itself)
   k. Empty nesters often move into *apartments*
   l. Housing developments often have problems when there are no *schools*, *hospitals* or *railways*.
   m. The cost of services can come from *a tax* on every new house. *(also accept* levy*)*
   n. Students can get up to *10%* of their mark just for participating in the tutorials.
   o. The lecturer will pay special attention to students' *understanding* of the issues.

Recording script

Note: Braces are used to intended forms where conversational slips occur. For example, if the script says *They goes {go} to the party*, the correct form is *They go to the party*.

CD 2, track 3: World, Unit 12
(6 minutes, 47 seconds)

Tutorial about a project to plan a new suburb.

Narrator: Now you will hear a group of students, a tutorial group in fact, being prepared for their first assignments.

This is a part of a geography course at university, and involves town planning. As you will hear, they've done a little bit of work to prepare, but they will have to do a lot of thinking over the next few weeks …

Tutor: OK, how's it going, folks?

All students, simultaneously: Good, yeah, fine thanks …

Tutor: Well, today is the day, and we're going to talk about what you're all going to love – your assignment.

All: *(groans)*

Tutor: Oh, come on … as you've already seen from the subject notes you were all given at the beginning of the course, the assignment involves making an outline

Unit 12 World | 143

plan for a future suburb of a major city, and then writing up a 3000 word justification for what you decide. And, what we're going to do today is go through some of the things to consider in your plans and then, to give you a chance to discuss things, to bounce a few ideas around, you know, and get a bit of feedback. OK?

All: Yeah, OK, yeah

Tutor: Now, no doubt you've already seen the map of the area for which you have to plan, it's in the handbook for this subject. These show some of the geographical features of the area, and you should have immediately seen several environmental challenges that will have to be overcome. Now what I mean is, you should bear in mind at all times that you should future-proof your ideas as much as possible. Now what I mean by that is, you should design it to cope with technological, environmental and especially social changes predicted to happen over the next 200 years – because if past history is anything to go by, you can be practically certain that the suburb will still be there at that time.

Student 1: So, do we have to think about coal and oil running low and things like that?

Tutor: Oh, yeah, for sure. And don't forget to focus on social change as well as the environment. Sometimes you know, I think predicting the environmental effects are the easy bits of the assignment. People very often focus too much on these and not enough on the social side of things. Although coming up with good, efficient and politically acceptable solutions to the environmental problems is much more difficult.

Student 2: Yeah, the solutions will be tricky, I think. I noticed there's a large river estuary right by the area we're looking at, and the land is quite flat there – we'll have to make sure that sea level change won't cause the area to flood.

Tutor: Yes, and how do you propose to do that?

Student 2: Hmmm, how about building a big dike, like in Holland, to keep out the water.

Student 1: Yeah, but that would make it difficult to have sea views, or it may be hard to get to the beach.

Student 2: Yeah, that's a problem, but better than flooding!

Student 3: Instead of building dikes, would it be a good idea to kind of fill in the land, to make the ground higher?

Student 1: Yeah, well, sounds good in theory, but where would all the soil come from?

Tutor: Mmmm, well, sometimes the best solution is to build nothing in certain places, or something that only has a temporary purpose.

Student 3: So, a car park, perhaps.

Student 1, Student 2: *(Nervous laughter.)*

Student 1: Good thinking!

Tutor: OK, OK, OK, let's move on from the environment. How about changes to society? What did you come up with in your preparations?

Student 3: Well, demographics must be a major issue.

Tutor: Yeah, in what way?

Student 3: Well, with {the} ageing population, perhaps it could be that the need for new housing will be mainly with older people, empty nesters, perhaps.

Student 2: What are empty nesters?

Student 3: People whose children have grown up and left home. Often, they had a big house when they had their families with them, but when they're living just as a couple, the trouble and expense of looking after a big house are just not worth it. So they sell up, move into an apartment, often in a more central location, and enjoy the more convenient lifestyle.

Tutor: Yes, and what about in a 100 years time?

Student 3: Well, the main reason for the increase in life expense …, sorry, life expectan, life expectan …

Tutor: Expectancy …

Student 3: Expectancy, life expectancy, sorry, is medical technology … and this should get better and better, and therefore the demand for housing for the elderly will only increase.

Student 2: Yeah, umm as well, {as} the world population increases, the expectation is that more people will have to live in apartments, just because there won't be space for free-standing housing.

Tutor: Is there anyone who's looked at what problems have been caused by, say, poor planning in developments over the last 20 or 30 years or so.

Student 1: Well, I have. Things like lack of public services, um, things like schools, hospitals, railways?

Student 2: So we can just put these in our projects!

Student 3: Easier said than done. Where's the money going to come from?

Student 1: Yeah.

Student 2: I heard that some councils are placing a levy, like a tax, on each new house.

Student 3: Yep, I guess that'll help a lot to cover to cost.

Tutor: Now, OK, remember, er, there's a few more things as well that you'll have to think of by yourselves. And just to remind you, the overall mark for this assignment is 30% for the elegance, practicality and presentation of your solution to the problem, 60% is for the justification of the solution, and the remaining 10% is for your participation in these tutorials.

Now, remember, what we're looking for mostly is your understanding of the issues and their potential solutions. So, I don't expect really detailed, 100 page reports ready to go to council, because what's most important is the arguments in the justification. So next week we'll talk about some of the ideas that Waterdale published recently. So to prepare, make sure you read Waterdale, chapter 4, pages a hundred and ... *(fade out).*

LANGUAGE SPOTLIGHT 2 — REVIEW OF FUTURE TENSES

Task A | Intentions ▶▶ SB P. 146

CD 2 — 3

① Students listen again to the start of the tutorial, this time focusing on the intentions that are expressed by the lecturer/tutor, and the tense he uses for them (*going to* for intentions was introduced in Unit 6 (see page 68 of the Students' Book).

> **ANSWERS**
>
> 1. The tutor says:
>   - *we're going to talk about what you're all going to love – your assignment*
>   - *what we're going to do today is go through some of the things to consider in your plans ...*
>   and uses *going to* as the tense to express these intentions.
> 2. Students talk about their intentions for the rest of the day, the following week, the coming weekend, and after they finish their course, thus giving them opportunity to practice *going to* for intentions. (If they don't have any intentions, they should pretend that they do!)

Task B | Decisions, intentions and arrangements ▶▶ SB P. 146

The examples (conversation extracts) in the Students' Book are intended to clarify any lingering confusion students may have about the use of tense to express future actions (as opposed to predictions).

> **ANSWERS**
>
> **Situation 1:** *will* is used for a decision made at the time of speaking (introduced in Unit 5 (see Students' Book page 59)).
> **Situation 2:** *going to* is used here to express a decision already made; in other words, an intention, as in Task A.
> **Situation 3:** Nick has now made fixed arrangements for his trip. As his trip is now far more definite, he uses a different tense – present continuous for future meaning, which conveys better that feeling of definiteness.

Task C | Practice ▶▶ SB P. 146

Here, students practise choosing between the tenses covered in Task A.

The questions in their books suggest they talk to their partner about:

①
- Any fixed arrangements
- Any intentions they have, but which they haven't made arrangements for yet.

② Their plans, intentions or arrangements (or lack of them) to:
- See their parents
- Visit family members who live in another town
- Go to a party
- Meet friends
- Take a holiday
- Travel somewhere.

> **Extension:** Students could be encouraged to probe the meaning behind their partner's choice of tense by asking concept questions such as:
> - What arrangements have you made?
> - How long have you been planning to do that?
> - Did you only decide just now?

Students may have a tendency to fall back on the use of *will* to express all future meanings. If this happens, it could be pointed out to them that *will* can sound very strong, like a promise or an argument to disobey an instruction, if used for something the speaker has control over and it isn't a decision at the time of speaking.

Unit 12 World | 145

SPEAKING 2

PROJECT: ROLE-PLAY

Task A | Role-play ▶▶ SB P. 147
This task guides students through a mini version of the project explained in this Unit's Listening.

① Students form groups of three or four people, and draw a map. They can draw it any way they like, but it must include a river, some mountains and other features. There must also be sufficient space to build a suburb.

② Ask each group to swap maps with another group, and explain that they are going to plan a suburb on the new map. Then, give the students some quiet time to think individually about how they want to develop the area. Ask them to think especially about:
- The risk to areas close to the river from the river level rising (the river is close to the sea).
- What type of housing to have – eg big houses, high-rise apartments.
- Where the shopping area, schools, hospitals and other services will be.
- What form of transport to use – trains, motorways, trams, buses …
- Where you will get the money – eg levy on new buildings, special tax …?

③ Get students to explain their ideas to the rest of their group. Each group should then discuss the ideas and choose the best of them to make a single plan for the group.

④ Each group should then give a mini-presentation of their ideas to the whole class, giving the reasons they think their ideas will work.

⑤ After each presentation, the class discusses the ideas with the group who gave the presentation.

⑥ When all groups have finished, the class decides which group would get the highest marks based on the criteria given in the tutorial on the CD (30% for the elegance, practicality and presentation of the solution, and 60% for the justification/reasons for the solution – the tutor also mentioned 10% for contribution to tutorials, but this doesn't really apply here).

FURTHER PRACTICE: READING, FILMS AND FUN

As with every unit, these ideas are provided for further reading and listening, and some suggested questions for discussion and writing practice. They are reproduced below, as given in the Students' Book, for your convenience.

The last essay question refers to issues that students have come across earlier in the book, thus it can be used for review.

READING

Go to **http://about.com**, then click on Education ➔ Geography ➔ Lists: Countries Cities etc ➔ largest cities in history. You will find a short article about where the largest cities on earth were located over the last 4000 years.

http://www.cia.gov/cia/publications/factbook/geos/xx.html is an interesting place to find out about any country in the world.

More specifically, as you are learning English, it might be interesting to see what the future holds for the English language. Some interesting predictions are at: **http://www.english.co.uk/FoE/contents/cont.html**, the website of The English Company (UK).

FILMS

Around the world in 80 days, directed by Frank Coraci, starring Jackie Chan. A modern film based on the famous novel written by Jules Verne before the aeroplane was invented.

Waterworld, directed by Kevin Reynolds, starring Kevin Costner. Set on the Earth, but in a time when things are very different from now!

QUESTIONS

① How do you think your home town or city will change in the future? What are the factors behind your predictions?

② Some people say that if everyone used less energy, many world environmental problems could be solved. What can ordinary people do to use less energy?

③ Think of a problem that could cause big problems to countries in the future (eg childhood obesity, environmental issues, or demographic problems). What can countries do now to prevent these problems?

REFERENCES

Aitken, R (1992) *Teaching Tenses.* Surrey: Nelson.

Horn, A (ed) (2004) *Newsletter of the Arts Law Centre of Australia. Art + Law,* Issue 3, Sept., pp 1–3.

Belloli, A (1999) *Exploring World Art.* London: Francis Lincoln Limited.

Bird, C (1998) *The Stolen Children, their stories.* Australia: Random House.

Cooinda Gallery (2004) *Aboriginal Art.* http://www.cooinda-gallery.com.au/aboriginal_art.htm, accessed 2 April 2005.

Cox, S (1999) *Report on Aboriginals.* Wollongong, Australia: St Mary's College.

Cox, KK (1994) 'Tertiary Level Writing by Magic – Presto! Nominalisation'. *EA Journal* 12/1, Autumn 1994.

Cox, KK & Hill, D (2004) *EAP Now! English for Academic Purposes.* Sydney: Pearson Education Australia.

Coxhead, A (2000) 'A New Academic Word List', *TESOL Quarterly* 34/2: 213–38.

Encyclopaedia of the Orient (2006) *Sahara.* Accessed from http://lexicorient.com/e.o/sahara.htm, 20 August 2006.

Halliday, MAK & Matthiessen, CMIM (2004) *An Introduction to Functional Grammar* (3rd ed). London: Arnold.

Hartley, Stephen (2002) *The Trainer's Toolbox: Authentic Case Studies and Vignettes for Trainers, Educators, Consultants and Facilitators.* Sydney: Pearson Education Australia.

Heath, J (1997) 'Salination'. *Destinations.* May–June issue.

Hutton, D (ed) (1987) *Green Politics in Australia: Working towards a Peaceful & Achievable Future.* Australia: Angus & Robertson.

Internet Movie Database Inc (2006) *The Internet Movie Database.* http://www.imdb.com, accessed 2006.

Kennedy, G (2003) *Structure and meaning in English.* Harlow: Pearson.

Larsen-Freeman, D & Long, M (1991) *An Introduction to Second Language Acquisition Research.* New York: Longman.

Lewis, M (1993) *The Lexical Approach: The State of ELT and a Way Forward.* Hove: Language Teaching Publications.

Longman Dictionary of Contemporary English. England: Pearson Education.

McMahon, D (2005) 'Voices from the village', *The South Sydney Herald*, Vol 1, No 28, Feb, p 1.

Mehrabian, A (1971) *Silent messages.* Belmont, California: Wadsworth.

Moore Foundation (2005) *Andes-Amazon,* Moore Foundation. Accessed from http://www.moore.org/program_areas/environment/initiatives/amazon-andes/initiative_amazon-andes.asp, 20 August 2006.

Murphy, R (2004) *English Grammar in Use* (3rd ed). Cambridge: Cambridge University Press.

The Oracle Education Foundation (ND) *The Silk Road: Linking Europe and Asia by Trade.* Available: http://library.thinkquest.org/13406/sr/, accessed 30 May 2005.

Oxford University Press (2000) *Oxford Advanced Learner's Dictionary* (6th ed). Oxford: Oxford University Press.

Pwerte Marnte Marnte Aboriginal Corporation (2004) *Aboriginal Australia Art & Culture Centre: Iconography.* http://aboriginalart.com.au/gallery/iconography.html, accessed 2 April 2005.

Reynolds, H (2001) *An Indelible Stain? The Question of Genocide in Australia's History.* Australia: Penguin.

Stavrou, K (2004) Email, Milingimbi, Australia, 21 November.

Stavrou, K (2004) Photographs, Milingimbi children.

Stevens, K (2003) *Aboriginal Art of Australia: The symbols and their meanings.* Available at http://www.mainzdidgeridoos.com.au/art/artsymbols.html, accessed 2 April 2005.

Stevens, FS (ed) (1973) *Racism the Australian Experience, Vol. 2, Black versus White.* Redfern: Australia & New Zealand Book Company.

Timmons, C & Gibney, F (eds) (1980) *Britannica Book of English Usage.* USA: Library of Congress.

United Nations, Department of Economic and Social Affairs, Population Division (2003) *Urban Agglomerations Wallchart.* New York: United Nations.

United Nations, Department of Economic and Social Affairs, Population Division (2004) *World Population Trends Wallchart.* New York: United Nations.

Wikipedia contributors (2006) 'Nuclear and radiation accidents'. *Wikipedia, The Free Encyclopaedia.* Retrieved 08:15, 5 June 2006, from http://en.wikipedia.org/w/index.php?title=Nuclear_and_radiation_accidents&oldid=56035660.

APPENDIX 1

ACADEMIC WORD LIST AND PARTS OF SPEECH

The list in this appendix is intended to help students find the right part of speech, especially when writing. It is adapted from the list in Kennedy (2003) of words that appear in the academic word list produced by Coxhead (2000), as well as the British National Corpus list of the 2000 most common words in written and formal spoken British English. The Coxhead list was compiled from a corpus of 3.5 million words from 28 academic disciplines.

Empty boxes in the verb, noun and adjective columns show that the part of speech doesn't exist, or it is very unusual (some slightly less common forms of common words are included, but very rare forms have been left out). Columns are also left blank if a different form of the word exists but has a different meaning. For example *profess* could be said to be a verb form of the *professional* or *profession*, but its meaning is quite different. In the noun column [person] indicates the noun is only used for a person or a job.

Some tips have been included in the Students' Book for how students might use the lists, although there are many other ways. Although learning vocabulary from word lists is far from the most effective way, it is appreciated that many students insist on doing this, so the Students' Book gives some strategies to make this type of learning more effective.

VERB	NOUN	ADJECTIVE	IMPORTANT COLLOCATIONS
access	access	accessible	... have access to ...
achieve	achievement	achievable	... a (big) achievement ...
acquire	acquisition		
administrate	administration	administrative	
affect	effect		... have an effect on ... ... the effect of ...
aid	aid		
	alternative	alternative	... an alternative to ...
analyse	analysis	analytical	... an analysis of ...
		annual	
approach	approach		
	appropriateness	appropriate	... appropriate for ... ing ...
	area		
assemble	assembly		
	attitude		... have an attitude ...
author	author (person)		
authorise	authority	authoritarian	... have authority to ...
	availability	available	
	awareness	aware	... be aware of ... ... have an awareness of ...
benefit	benefit	beneficial	... be beneficial to ...
categorise	category		
challenge	challenge	challenging	... challenge someone to ... ... have a challenge ... ... give a challenge to ...
	circumstance	circumstantial	
civilise	civilisation	civil	
	colleague		
comment	comment		... make a comment about ...
communicate	communication	communicative	
	community		

Appendix 1 Academic word list and parts of speech | 149

VERB	NOUN	ADJECTIVE	IMPORTANT COLLOCATIONS
complicate	complexity	complex complicated	
concentrate	concentration		… concentration/concentrate on …
	concept	conceptual	
conclude	conclusion	conclusive	
confirm	confirmation		
conflict	conflict		… have a conflict with … … conflict with … … be in conflict with …
	consequence	consequent	… a consequence of …
consider	consideration		
consist			… consist of …
construct	construction		
consume	consumption		… consumption of …
contact	contact	contactable	… be in contact with …
contextualise	context	contextual	… in context …
contract	contract	contractual	… contract someone to …
contrast	contrast	contrasting	… in contrast to … … to contrast something with …
contribute	contribution	contributory	… to contribute to …
create	creation	creative	… a creative person…
credit	credit	creditable	… credit someone with something … … credit something to someone … … give credit to someone …
	decade		
debate	debate	debatable	… to debate something with someone …
decrease	decrease	decreasing	… a decrease in …
define	(a) definition	definable	… a definition of …
demonstrate	demonstration		
deny	denial		

VERB	NOUN	ADJECTIVE	IMPORTANT COLLOCATIONS
design	design	well designed, badly designed, etc	... a badly designed (building) ...
display	display		
distribute	distribution		
document	document	documented	
		domestic	
	economy	economic	
emphasise	emphasis	emphatic	... put/place/have an emphasis on ...
enable			... enable someone to do something ...
ensure			
	environment	environmental	
	event		
evidence	evidence	evident	... piece of evidence ... ... have evidence for/against ... ... it was evident that ...
exhibit	exhibition		... an exhibition of ...
	expert (person) expertise	expert	... be expert at ... ing ... ... be an expert at ... ing ... ... have expertise in ...
feature	feature		
finalise	final	final	
finance	finance	financial	
focus	focus	well focused, badly focused etc	... to focus on something ... ... it was a (clearly) focused lesson ...
function	function	functional	... function (smoothly) ...
fund	(a) fund funding	well funded, poorly funded etc	... find funding for ... ... a well funded (project) ...
	generation		
	goal		
identify	identification	identifying/identified	
illustrate	illustration	illustrated	
	income		

VERB	NOUN	ADJECTIVE	IMPORTANT COLLOCATIONS
increase	increase	increasing	… an increase in …
indicate	indication	indicative	
injure	injury	injured	… have a (head) injury … … have an injury to (his head) …
instruct	instruction	instructional instructive	… instruct someone to …
		internal	
interest	interest	interesting interested	… an interest in … … an interesting (film) … He was interested in (the film) …
investigate	investigation	investigative	… an investigation into …
involve	involvement		… involve someone in …
issue	issue		
	item		
labour	labour	laborious	
legalise	legality	legal	
link	link	linked	… a link to … … link something to something …
locate	location		
	majority		
manufacture	manufacture (process) factory (building)	manufacturing manufactured	
maximise	maximum	maximum	
	medicine	medical	
		medium	
mention	mention		
	military	military	
minimise	minimum	minimum	
	minority		
normalise	normality	normal	

152 | EAP Now! Preliminary English for Academic Purposes Teacher's Book

VERB	NOUN	ADJECTIVE	IMPORTANT COLLOCATIONS
object	objection		... make an objection to ... ... have an objection to ... ... object to ...
		obvious	
occur	occurrence		
opt	option	optional	... have an option to ... ... to opt for (the second choice) ...
output	output		
		overall	
	period	periodical	
	policy		
politicise	politics	political	
		positive	
		previous	
	prime	primary	
process	process	processed	
	profession	professional	
protest	protest		... protest against ...
range	range		(It) ranges from ... to ... ... has a large range ...
react	reaction		... react to ... ... a reaction to ...
reduce	reduction	reducible	... a reduction in ...
	region	regional	
regulate	regulation	regulatory	... make a regulation ...
reject	rejection	rejected	(He) felt rejected.
release	release	released	... release ... from ...
	relevance	relevant	... be relevant to ...
rely	reliance	reliable	... rely/reliance on ...
remove	removal	removable	
research	research		... a piece/an item of research ...

VERB	NOUN	ADJECTIVE	IMPORTANT COLLOCATIONS
retain	retention		
reveal	revelation		
	role		
	section		
secure	security	secure	… make something secure … … have security … … feel secure …
search	search	searchable	… search for … … carry out/conduct/do a search of …
select	selection	select	
	sign		
	significance	significant	… have significance …
	similarity	similar	… similar to …
specify		specific	
	structure	structural	
style	style	stylish	
suffice	sufficiency	sufficient	
survey	survey		
survive	survival survivor (person)		
target	target		
	technology technician (person)	technical	
	theme	thematic	
theorise	theory	theoretical	… a theory about/of …
	tradition	traditional	
transfer	transfer	transferable	… transfer something/someone to …
transport	transport transportation	transportable	… forms of transport/transportation …
vary	variation	varying	
	vehicle		
	version		

APPENDIX 2
SELF-CORRECTION MEMORY BANK

Here are some common mistakes made by students. Students should use the table to add their own mistakes from writing, as well as their corrected sentence and the grammar rule.

SENTENCE WITH MISTAKE	CORRECTED SENTENCE	GRAMMAR RULE
It sounds good, *isn't* it.	It sounds good, doesn't it.	verb choice/is/does
In regarding to my study …	Regarding my study … In regard to my study … With regard to my study … With regards to my study …	collocation
Her name is Jane, *who is* going to complete her studies in February.	Her name is Jane, and she is going to complete her studies in February. Jane, who is going to …	pronoun substitution dependent clause
I am writing to inform you that *I have to move the flat.*	I am writing to inform you that I have to move out of my flat. *or* … from my flat.	verb/object agreement sense requires a preposition (remember: the flat's too heavy to move!)
I am very *appreciate* it.	I appreciate it. I appreciate it very much. I am very appreciative of it.	verb/object agreement word order
I am taking my exam on next Monday.	I am taking my exam on Monday. I am taking my exam next Monday. Next Monday, I am taking my exam.	prepositional phrase (choice of preposition)

APPENDIX 3

SELF-CHECKING GUIDE – WRITING A PARAGRAPH

STRUCTURE: PARAGRAPH 1	YES	NO
First sentence – the topic sentence – what the paragraph is going to be about.		
Supporting sentences that <u>explain or give a reason</u> after the title sentence.		
A definition within the paragraph that links to the title and topic.		
One or more factual sentences that support the topic.		
A concluding sentence.		

STRUCTURE: PARAGRAPH 2		
First sentence – the topic sentence – what the paragraph is going to be about.		
Supporting sentences that <u>describe</u> the topic sentence.		
A definition within the paragraph that links to the title and topic.		
One or more factual sentences that support the topic.		
A concluding sentence.		

STRUCTURE: PARAGRAPH 3		
First sentence – the topic sentence – what the paragraph is going to be about.		
Supporting sentences that <u>evaluate</u> the topic sentence.		
A definition within the paragraph that links to the title and topic.		
One or more factual sentences that support the topic.		
A concluding sentence.		

STRUCTURE: PARAGRAPH 4		
First sentence – the topic sentence – what the paragraph is going to be about.		
Supporting sentences that <u>list details</u> of the topic sentence.		
A definition within the paragraph that links to the title and topic.		
One or more factual sentences that support the topic.		
A concluding sentence.		

STRUCTURE: PARAGRAPH 5	YES	NO
First sentence – the topic sentence – what the paragraph is going to be about.		
Supporting sentences that <u>contrast or compare</u> after the title sentence.		
A definition within the paragraph that links to the title and topic.		
One or more factual sentences that support the topic.		
A concluding sentence.		

STRUCTURE: PARAGRAPH 6		
First sentence – the topic sentence – what the paragraph is going to be about.		
Supporting sentences that <u>establish a cause</u> after the title sentence.		
A definition within the paragraph that links to the title and topic.		
One or more factual sentences that support the topic.		
A concluding sentence.		

INDEX

A
abbreviations 86
academic English 140
academic word list 148–154
accents 41
active voice 35–39
adjective 2
adjectival relative clauses 135–136
advice article
    stages in 83, 85
    writing 83, 85
agent (doer) 37
agreeing and disagreeing 70, 74–75
anaphoric referencing 81
appointment requests 63
Architecture around the world 105–106
argument
    conclusion 47–49, 51
    matching genres to task 141–142
    purpose and stages of 47, 141
    reading 47–49
    writing 49–51
arrangements, use of tense in 145
Art as technology 97
article, magazine 97
audience of text 4
auxiliary verb 73–74

B
bias, recognising 85, 115–118
body paragraphs 48, 50–51
'but' (uses of) 132–133

C
capitalisation 6–7
case study, rules for 18–19
cataphoric referencing 81
certainty *versus* speculation 108–109
changes and experiences 121
chronological order 7–8
circumstance 5
clarification expressions 43
clause structure 5–6, 42–43
Clean energy is possible 48
cohesion 5
collocations 130, 148
commas 25, 135–136
communication types 56
compare and contrast 104, 132–133
comparing texts for bias 115–116
comparisons, making 104, 131–132
complement 5
complex sentence 6
compound sentence 6

conclusion stage 47–49, 51
conditionals 65–66
conjunctions 6
Conversation between two students 12–13
coordinators 6
correspondence, writing 59–61
critical reading (five questions) 4–5, 22, 57, 80, 95, 97, 112, 139
critical thinking 70, 75
Cumberland aerial map 130

D
decisions, using tense for 65–66, 145
definitions
    construction of 33
    in context 46–47, 47–49, 114–115
    explanations as 133
demography and society 32
Dialogue between three friends 53
differences and similarities 104, 131–132
directions, writing down 64
discourse signals 46, 52–53, 83, 104
Discussing politics and religion 72–73
discussion essay
    features of individual paragraphs 70–71
    matching genre to task 141–142
    purpose and stages of 141
    reading 70–71
    schema or map of 71–72
drafts, writing 40, 142

E
Effective Communication! 58
elaboration 24–25, 39–40
ellipses 81, 132
emails and letter writing 59–61
Energy to burn 52
essays
    advice *see* advice article
    discussion *see* discussion essay
    example *see* example essay
    explanation *see* explanation essay
    information *see* information report
    introductory paragraphs in 33
    opinion *see* opinion essay
exam preparation 142
example essay 50–51
    body paragraphs 50
    conclusion 51
    introduction 50
experiences and changes 121
explanation essay
    generic features of 39–40
    matching genre to task 141–142
    purpose and stages of 141
    writing 39–40, 141

F

fact versus opinion 112, 141–142
facts, recognising 135
film making, stages in 90
finding meaning from context *see under* Reading
first conditionals (real conditionals) 65–66
formal and informal texts 80
formatting 50
function and form 104
future predictions 73–74
future tenses 65, 145

G

general questions 16
general statement 24, 39
generalisations 18–19
genre 7 *see also* text types (genres)
gerunds 51–52
'going to' (uses of) 73
Governments around the world need to spend money on ways to make the air cleaner 50
Graph of Radioactive Materials Release 47
graphs and tables 22–23
Greek and Latin into English! 70

H

headings in texts, uses 3
How to become a film star 84
How to make a film: a procedure 90
Human cost of occupation of war in Iraq 70
humour and irony, use of 80
hypotheses, giving and discussing 138
hypothesis and fact 108–110

I

IELTS (International English Language Testing System) 46, 50
imperatives 82–83
importance markers 75
infinitives 52
Information and summary report from a teacher 28
information report
    generic features of 24–25
    matching genre to task 141–142
    purpose and stages of 141
    reading 19–22
    writing 24–25, 121
instant decisions, tense in 65–66
instructions
    following 90–91
    giving 82–83
intentions, using tense for 145
Internet vocabulary 86
interrogative 'what' 52–53
intonation and stress 75, 77
    see also pronunciation
intonation in tag questions 100

introduction
    to an argument 47–49, 50
    to a discussion essay 72
    to an example essay 50
    to reading 2–5
    to text structure and purpose 3–4
introductory paragraphs, writing 33
issue, talking about 46–47

J

justification, stage in report 24

L

language of change 20, 40, 81
learning styles 16
Leaving a message 61–62
Lecture about media reports 88–89
lecture notes, taking 8, 85–86
Lecture on wedding customs for an education audience 9–10
letters and emails, writing 59–61
listening
    to compare 11–13
    to critically weigh up an issue 110
    differentiating between hypothesis and fact 108–110
    for discourse signals 52–53
    for expressions for phone calls 61–64
    to identify opinions 98–99
    identifying stages in instructions 90–91
    identifying stages in spoken explanations 27–28
    for interrogative 'what' 52
    for intonation and stress 75, 77
    for key words which signal explanations, examples and solutions 133
    to locate certainty 108–109
    for main ideas 8–10, 122
    for meaning and content 52
    note-taking 40–41, 75–77, 86–87
    for numbers 25–27
    in order to predict 8, 40–42
    for purpose and function 77
    for specific information 10–11, 61–64, 91, 122, 143
    to spoken information that links to visual information 123
Looking at art 95

M

making
    a film 90
    comparisons 104, 131–132
    generalisations 18–19
    requests 66
Market Segmentation 34
media bias 85
Megacities: a good or bad future? 138
Mini lecture on politics and government 75–77
modal auxiliary 73–74
modals, present and past 96

N

nominalisation 81–82, 107–108, 140
note-taking 40–41, 75–77
    formatting notes 86–87
    reading and 138–139
    suggested notes 87
noun
    nominalisation 81–82, 107–108, 140
    noun forms of verbs 23
    nouns/noun phrases as gerunds 52
    participants (nouns and noun groups) 117
    word stress and shifting stress 34–35
numbers, listening to 25–27

O

object of a sentence 5–6
offers 66
opinion essay 142
opinion versus fact 112, 141–142
opinions, identifying 98–99
opinions in the media 85
orientation booklet 4
Our world, the earth 135

P

paragraph writing (self-checking guide) 48, 50–51, 156–157
paragraphs in discussion essay 70–71
paraphrasing 82, 140
participant tracking 21–22
participants (nouns and noun groups) 117
participles 51–52
particles 14
parts of speech 23, 34–35, 148–154
passive voice 35–39
past perfect tense 28–29
past simple tense 28–29, 120
phrasal verbs 13–15
pictures in texts, using to predict 3
pluralisation 19
point of view 116–118
prediction 3, 8, 33, 40, 138
prefixes and suffixes 70
prepositional verbs 14
present continuous tense 42–43
present modals 19
present perfect continuous tense 124–125, 126
present perfect simple tense 117–120, 124, 126
present simple tense 19, 42–43, 74
preview/scope 39, 48
'probably' or 'possibly' (uses of) 73–74
procedural genre 83–85
processes (verbs and verb groups) 117
progression of ideas 7
pronouns
    personal 104
    relative 135
pronunciation 34–35, 41, 42, 119, 124

Property Auction 26–27
punctuation 6–7, 25, 135–136
purpose of texts 3–4

Q

question words 18
questions, specific and general 15–16

R

Radio interview with an Australian farmer about salination 134
reacting/instant decisions ('will') 65–66
reading *see also* critical reading
    ahead 86
    to apply knowledge 131
    for cohesion 81
    for detail 57–59
    different text types 80–81
    for factual information 112–118, 135
    finding meaning from context 20–21, 34, 135, 139
    historical information 104
    to identify style 80
    introduction to 2–5
    for language features 70–71
    locating language choices which create intention 116–118
    for main ideas 56–57
    making generalisations 18–19
    prediction 3, 33
    for purpose of texts 3–4
    to summarise 56–59
    tracking participants 21–22
    using inference 32–35
    vocabulary extension 130–131
real conditionals (first conditionals) 65–66
Reality TV show review 98–99
referencing and substitution 21
regular auxiliary 73–74
regular verbs 14
relative pronouns 135
repetition, avoiding 21
reports
    factual information in 115
    reading 112
    recognising definitions in context 114–115
Report on a traditional group in Australian society 112–114
reported speech 96–97
requests, making 66
restrictive and non-restrictive clauses 135–136
review
    matching genre to task 141–142
    model paragraph 101
    purpose and stages of 141
    reading 95–96
    writing 100–104
rheme 37
role play
    expressions for phone calls 64
    practising request structures 66

proposing solutions 135
tutorial project 146

S

salutations and endings 60
sarcasm 116–118
scanning 19–20, 57, 97, 138–139
self-correction memory bank 155
sentence
    complex 6
    simple 6
    structure 6–7
    topic 47
    transformation 23
signposting in talking about an issue 47
similar and different 131–132
skimming 3, 138–139
society and demography 32
source of text 4
speaking
    about Aboriginal art 121–122
    about communication 56
    about customs and traditions 2
    about demography and society 32
    about experience 121, 126
    about global trade 18
    about indigenous people 112
    about use of media 80
    agreeing and disagreeing 70, 74–75
    asking for clarification 43
    colloquialisms 29
    conducting a survey 91
    contexts for present perfect tenses 126
    expressing personal opinions 29
    for and against 46
    general knowledge quiz 138
    generally and specifically 2, 15–16
    making requests 66
    oral test 132
    in the passive voice 38
    practising conversations 29
    prediction 8
    proposing solutions 135
    recognising an issue 46
    signposting in talking about an issue 47
    tutorial project role-play 146
speculation *versus* certainty 108–109
spoken explanations 27–28
stages
    in an advice article 83, 85
    in an argument – outline, schema, map 47–49
    in argument writing 49–51, 141
    in a discussion essay 72–73, 141
    in an explanation essay 39, 141
    in an information report 24, 141
    in making a film 90
    in a review 141

    in a spoken explanation 27–28
    in texts 7
stress
    as emphasis 119
    listening for intonation and stress 75, 77
    in numbers 25
    sentence stress 29
    word stress and shifting stress 34–35
Students reports about their own countries' birth rates 41
subject notes 143
subject of a sentence 5–6
subordinators and coordinators 6
suffixes and prefixes 70
supporting statements 49
surveys, conducting 91

T

tag questions 100
Television interview with an Australian Aboriginal artist 122–123
tense
    choosing 120–121, 125
    passive voice construction 36
    past perfect tense 28–29
    past simple tense 28–29, 120
    present continuous tense 42–43
    present perfect continuous tense 124–125, 126
    present perfect simple tense 117–120, 124, 126
    present simple tense 19, 42–43, 74
    review of future tenses 145
    verb tense changes in reported speech 96–97
    zero conditional tense 42–43
text types (genres) *see also* argument; article; discussion essay; explanation essay; information report; review
    audience 4
    following a genre 7
    identifying 80
    matching genres to task 141–142
    matching texts and their sources 126–127
    procedural 83
    purpose of texts 3–4
    review of genres 140–141
    staging in texts 7
The call back 64
The Silk Road 19, 21
theme, identifying 24–25, 37, 39–40 *see also* topic sentence
time order 7–8
titles in texts 3
topic sentence 39, 47–49 *see also* theme
true and false statements 59
Tutorial: planning a new suburb 143–145
tutorials, knowledge of 142–143

U

'used to' (use of) 28–29

V

value judgments 110

verb
    auxiliary 73
    nominalisation 107–108
    processes (verbs and verb groups) 117
    regular and modal auxiliaries 73–74
    prepositional 14
verb forms and functions 51–52
verb group 5
verb tense changes in reported speech 96–97
vocabulary
    on architecture 104
    on art 94–95
    on communication 56, 57
    on customs 2
    on demography and society 32
    describing graphs and tables 22–23
    on energy 46, 49, 50
    on geographic features 130–131
    making generalisations 66
    on politics 70
    on romance and marriage 7–8
    on trade 18, 20–21
    on wedding customs 8
    on world issues 139

W

'whereas' (uses of) 132–133
'while' (uses of) 132–133
'will' (uses of) 65–66, 145
word stress and shifting stress 34–35
Workmen on building site 109–110
writer of text, identifying 4
writing
    to follow a genre 7
    introduction to text structure and purpose 3–4
    matching genres to task 141–142
    an opinion essay 142
    passive voice 35–39
    problems and solutions 135
    review of genres 140–141
    short answers 107
    staging in texts 7
    using nominalisation 107–108

Z

zero conditional tense 42–43